BUST OF GEORGE WYTHE
Library, William and Mary College

SERENE PATRIOT:
A LIFE OF GEORGE WYTHE

by
William Clarkin

Alan Publications
Albany, New York
1970

Lithographed in U.S.A. by

EDWARDS
BROTHERS
INCORPORATED

2500 SOUTH STATE STREET / ANN ARBOR, MICHIGAN 48104

To

Eleanor Sibley Riley

Foreword

George Wythe was one of the wonders of his age and country. He was the youngest Attorney General Colonial Virginia ever had. From his youth a lawyer, he became a member of the House of Burgesses under the aegis of the mighty Ben Waller. Then to the Clerkship of the House, the while training that splendid genius, Thomas Jefferson. Then to the Continental Congress, where he raised his star to its zenith while fighting for a declaration of independence from Britain. Then back to Virginia to become Speaker of the House. Eventually becoming sole Chancellor of Virginia, he at the same time acted as Professor of Law at William and Mary College, where he trained a whole generation of national and state politicians: John Marshall, John Breckenridge, William Branch Giles, and many others. A disciple of his own pupil, he helped keep Virginia loyal to Jefferson. A founder of the movement to free the slaves, he was far in advance of his times in his dealings with the Blacks. A great lawyer, a great Chancellor, Virginia and the nation owe him much.

Strangely, he has been almost forgotten. He lived in an age of giants, however—Washington, Adams, Jefferson, Marshall. And was overshadowed by them. It is the author's hope that this work will bring him once again to the memory of the American People.

Acknowledgments

I wish to give acknowledgment and thanks to the following:

William and Mary College for permission to quote extensively from Littleton Waller Tazewell's account of his childhood with George Wythe. Also for permission to use the photograph of the bust of Wythe which graces the College Library.

The Research Foundation of the State University of New York. A grant from the Foundation helped considerably towards the expenses of travel and reproduction of material.

The American Philosophical Society for permission to quote Wythe's letter to Benjamin Franklin of 23 June 1766.

Haverford College Library for permission to quote Wythe's letter to John Tabb of 22 September 1782. This letter is in the Charles Roberts Autograph Letter Collection.

Maine Historical Society for permission to quote Wythe's letter of 22 December 1773.

Mrs. Florence H. B. Shippen, William B. Shippen, and Edward Shippen of Old Greenwich, Connecticut, for permission to quote the letters of Thomas Lee Shippen now on deposit in the Library of Congress.

The American Historical Association for permission to quote from the "American Historical Review" the account by the French traveller of Patrick Henry's Stamp Act Speech in the House of Burgesses.

Harvard University Press for permission to quote from Helen Hill's work, *George Mason, Constitutionalist*.

Duke University Library for permission to quote Robert Carter's letter to George Wythe of 4 October 1772.

Colonial Williamsburg, Inc., for permission to quote the letters of Wythe to John Norton. These letters are contained in the John Norton and Sons Papers, Colonial Williamsburg, Inc., Williamsburg, Virginia.

Princeton University Press for permission to quote from the *Papers of Thomas Jefferson,* edited by Julian P. Boyd et al: Letters from Vol. 1, 1760–1776, (Copyright 1950 by Princeton University Press); from Vol. 6, 1781–1784, (Copyright 1952 by Princeton University Press); Vol. 11, 1787, (Copyright 1955 by Princeton University Press); Vol. 16, 1789–1790, (Copyright (©) 1961 by Princeton University Press), and Vol. 13, 1788, (Copyright (©) 1956 by Princeton University Press).

The Virginia Historical Society for permission to quote *The Diary* of Colonel Landon Carter of Sabine Hall 1752–1778, edited by Jack P. Greene (Charlottesville, 1965), and the Manuscript *History of Virginia* by Edmund Randolph.

The New York Public Library for permission to quote Wythe's letter to Samuel Adams of 1 August 1778, and Wythe's letter to Edmund Randolph of 16 June 1787.

The University of North Carolina Press for permission to quote from Chastellux *Travels in North America,* (Two Vols., Chapel Hill, 1963).

The Dietz Press, Inc., for permission to quote from Mary Haldane Coleman's work, *St. George Tucker, Citizen of No Mean City.*

Mrs. Robert H. Webb of Charlottesville, Virginia for permission to quote William Browne's letter to Joseph Prentis, Jr. of 24 September, 1804.

The New-York Historical Society for permission to quote Wythe's letter of 23 April 1785 to Duane, Jay, and Livingston.

The Carnegie Institution of Washington for permission to quote various excerpts from *Letters of Members of the Continental Congress,* edited by Edmund Cody Burnett, published by the Institution, Washington, 1921–36.

John Neverman of the Library, State University of New York at Albany, for many suggestions in regard to publication.

Table of Contents

CHAPTER I

The Early Life

Wythe came of a remarkable ancestry indeed. Among those with whom we are concerned in his family is his great grandfather, the redoubtable George Keith. This man, a Scotsman, was born in 1638 in Peterhead, Scotland, of Presbyterian parents. He became in the course of time a Quaker. And since in his day Quakers were persecuted, Keith was often jailed. The first jailing was in 1662, and on his being released, he went up and down Britain, being persecuted for his faith but always confessing it, and converting many. In 1648 Keith and his wife, his daughters Anne and Elizabeth sailed to the New World, to Perth Amboy where his first task was the settlement of a boundary line between East and West Jersey and Southern New York. He surveyed the land on which the town of Bergen was established, at the same time settling with people from Scotland the town of Freehold (which he owned). When not surveying and settling towns, Keith traveled about preaching, attempting to convert the world to the Quaker faith. Pennsylvania, East and West Jersey, Rhode Island, Massachusetts—these all saw his endeavors. He journeyed even to Boston and challenged the Puritans there to a debate. He was one of the first of the great anti-slavery leaders, it being in 1693 that he cautioned his followers against the buying and keeping of human being as slaves. In the coming centuries, his anti-slavery writings continued to inspire abolitionists and all those who believed in the freedom of man. For example, almost a century later the celebrated Benjamin Franklin quoted from Keith's writings. The great Doctor Franklin used his pamphlet, quoting his words that those Quakers who owned slaves ". . . should set their Negroes at liberty, after some reasonable time . . ."[1]

The year 1693 also saw Keith's return to England, while his daughter Anne remained in America. While he was gone, many of his followers apparently left the Quakers and became Baptists, while others became Anglicans. A few years later—in 1700, to be exact, Keith himself did just that, being ordained two years later as a minister of the Established Church by the Bishop of Worcester. Now as staunchly as he had once upheld Quakerism he attacked it. Laying about himself as vigorously as ever, he became a center of storm and heat. Shortly after Keith was ordained to the ministry, the Society for the Propagation of the Gospel—not unwilling to follow the counsel that Christians should be simple as doves and wise as serpents—sent Keith back to the Colonies as a missionary.

Again, in his labors, he traveled up and down the coast, from Maine to Virginia. In 1703, for example, Keith preached in Williamsburg before the convocation of the clergy in that very Bruton Parish Church of which his great grandson, George Wythe, would one day be a Vestryman. While in Virginia, Keith stayed with his daughter Anne who had met and married a Friend, George Walker, of Keckauton by the James River.[2] This Anne, alone of Keith's children, remained in the New World when the father, old and tired, returned to England and accepted the living of St. Andrew's Church in Sussex. It was there he died in 1716, some ten years before his celebrated great-grandson and namesake, George Wythe, came into the world.

It is impossible to discover how Anne Keith came to meet George Walker. Their marriage took place in 1697, when one assumes the father was in England. Walker was a pilot on the James River when the marriage took place. George Keith noted in his *Diary* that he had visited his daughter after her marriage, for he declared that she had

> ". . . fully come off from the Quakers and is a zealous member of the Church of England and brings up her children, so many of them as are capable through age, in the Christian religion; praise be to God for it."[3]

The daughter of the celebrated Anglican convert had indeed come off fully from the Quaker religion, for there exist records in which it is apparent that she tried to bring up her children as Anglicans rather than as Quakers—as her father had noted. The marriage was a turbulent one, for she made an appeal to the Council of State of Virginia declaring that her husband, George Walker, kept her and her children from going to church. The honorable members of the Council side-stepped the issue. A second time the lady attempted to get the Council to take a clear-cut position and again the Council prayed her that she should be loving to her husband. They did not want, apparently, to mix into anything quite as familial as this affair. This may have been because George Walker, while a Quaker, was quite important in the local government of that day. Strict Quakers were forbidden by their religion to take oaths or to go to war. Nonetheless, Walker became an officer of the government, being the searcher of vessels on the lower James River. Indeed, he was not only this, but in 1721 he gave bond as gunner and storekeeper of the Fort at Point Comfort.

He had to put up £100 lawful money of Great Britain that

">. . . George Walker shall well and truly execute that office during his continuance
therein . . . and shall safely keep and preserve all the stores of War which shall be delivered
to him, (ravage by storm and casualty excepted . . .) . . ."[4]

George and his wife must have made up their religious differences for in the
year 1728, it is reported by one Samuel Brown, a Quaker preacher, who visited
Hampton, the town in which Walker lived, that:

"George Walker was very kind, inviting us to stay at his house, his wife being more loving
that I expected. She was George Keith's daughter and in his younger days showed much
dissatisfaction with Freinds, [sic] but after her father's death the edge of that bitterness
abated and her husband was very loving and hearty to Friends, frequently having meetings
at his house."[5]

At this time George Wythe was about one year old. His home was at Chesterville, some distance from Hampton. It is important to note that Quakerism
remained a vital fact in the lives of the members of this family even into Wythe's
own lifetime. Although the religious quarrel abated somewhat, it is probable
that the wife had the final say in the matter, for as far as can be discovered no
one of the children (and there were several) was ever a Quaker. Wythe himself
was never a Friend, although it is most certain that this religious inheritance
influenced his life. He also acquired the strong tradition of intellectualism from
the Keith side of the family. Certainly George Keith would have trained his
daughter in the ancient languages and it was from his mother that Wythe
learned Greek and Latin. Many years later, a man who knew Wythe well
wrote:

"Mr. Wythe . . . I have often heard him say that he was entirely indebted to his mother
for his early education. She was an extraordinary woman . . . and having added to her other
acquirements a knowledge of the Latin language, she was the sole instructress of her son in
this also. He was very studious and industrious . . . he made himself one of the best Latin
scholars in America. Long after he had attained manhood and had engaged in the law . . .
teaching himself Greek . . . In a few years he made himself . . . the very best Greek scholar
I have ever seen . . . he afterwards in life . . . acquired the French language and became
deeply versed in Algebra, Mathematics and Natural Philosophy . . . ."[6]

This statement requires some acceptance, for it comes from Littleton Waller
Tazewell, a man who himself studied under Wythe and knew him better, perhaps, than anyone else. On this point of Wythe's early education, there is the
further evidence of Burnaby. This man was an English traveller who came to
America and stayed in Williamsburg, making the acquaintance, among others,
of Wythe:

"In Virginia, I have had the pleasure to know several gentlemen, adorned with many
virtues and accomplishments . . . Amongst others I cannot resist the inclination of mentioning George Wythe, Esquire, who to a perfect knowledge of the Greek language which was
taught him by his mother in the back woods . . . ."[7]

But if Wythe received the tradition of learning and a reverence for education from the Keith side of his family, he inherited his social position (and ultimately no little wealth) from his Wythe ancestry. The line of descent of the Wythe family (the name is pronounced *with*) must now be considered.

The first of the Wythes, Thomas the Immigrant, arrived in Virginia probably about 1680, bringing with him Thomas Wythe the Second, who may have been born some ten years earlier. The first Thomas, given the title in the documents of the day of 'Gent.', settled in Elizabeth City County on land near the Back River, an estate which was to be hereditary in the family for generations to come. The possession of this land automatically gave to the members of the Wythe family the status of aristocrats in Virginia. As a matter of fact, it placed the incumbent almost as a matter of course as a justice on the bench of the county court, for Elizabeth City County was to be known in the years to come as the "Wythe Magisterial District." At a time when his contemporary George Keith was still roaming around the colonies bent on converting the world, Thomas Wythe was well established in the colony of Virginia. When he died in 1694, he left his widow Anne and two children. There was Anne, who married William Mallory, the son of Captain Roger Mallory of New Kent or King and Queen County. And there was Thomas Wythe, Second, who enherited the Back River estate. He, in due course, married one Anne Shepard and died at the rather tender age of 24 years. From this marriage came Thomas Wythe, Third, the father of George. There is only slightly little more to be known of this Thomas (the Third) than of his father, the Second. Some few facts survive. It is known, for instance, that when he was only 19 years old he was a member of the local court of Elizabeth City County, to which he had apparently succeeded by virtue of family position. In a document of the day there is the following:

> ". . . for trying and taking up the 8 pirates, an account of the charges to the Judges, etc. . . . to Thomas Wythe, £ 1/15/0. Spotswood, Governor."[8]

We also know that he, together with William Dandridge, received a grant of a water-front in Hampton. Again, in approximately 1720, he was sheriff of Elizabeth City County, and was elected, between 1718–20, to the House of Burgesses. In the years 1723–26 he was again in the House. In 1719, he had married Anne Walker, the daughter of George and Anne Keith Walker. Of this union came three children: Thomas Wythe, Fourth, George Wythe, and Anne. George was perhaps born in the latter half of 1726 or the first part of 1727. It is typical that his birth date should be so uncertain, for we are likewise most uncertain of many other dates and facts of his early life. Although we must fall back to some degree on conjecture, we do know that in his infancy the children were left fatherless. For Thomas Wythe, Third, died intestate in the year 1729.

According to the law of primogeniture, the elder son, Thomas Wythe, Fourth, received the entire property of Chesterville, the estate on the Back River. This meant that as far as George could know, he would have to make his own way in the world. Although it was common for widows to remarry in those days—indeed, in some ways it was a necessity—there is no record that George's mother ever did so. And therefore the widow and her three children apparently lived on in the Chesterville home during George's childhood.

One supposes that the boy spent his days as the boys of that time and place normally passed their boyhoods—hunting, fishing, swimming in the creeks. Chesterville was about seven miles northwest of the town of Hampton, a village which had a population of about 1000 at the time of the Revolution. (In the 1730's, therefore, it must have been considerably smaller.) This means that there really weren't very many people in that part of the world—even though it was the area in which the first Europeans had originally settled.

A few miles to the west of Hampton on the road to Yorktown is "Kecought-an," which is to say, Cape Comfort. The Back River itself is actually merely a narrow creek and curls around the estate of Chesterville, forming the boundary line between Elizabeth City and York Counties. Only one mile away in this modern age is Langley Airfield. The house itself, a brick building, seems to have existed down until somewhat the beginning of this century—about 1907–08, when it burned, there being now on the place only a pile of bricks in an open meadow. The country thereabouts—since it is close to the sea—is flat and covered with pines and oak, hickory and brambles of honeysuckle. As a boy, George Wythe, hunted and fished on the property and in the adjacent woods and fields and marshes.

The school which Wythe may have attended is one which exists to this day—William and Mary College. The College was at this time divided into three parts: One was the Indian School, called the Brafferton, which attempted to educate Indians in the ways of the White Man. This attempt was a simple failure. The other two parts were the Grammar School (which it is quite possible and indeed probable that Wythe attended) and the actual College itself. In the Grammar School, the children continued their learning of Greek and Latin and their study of Mathematics, all of which Wythe in later years cultivated very carefully and lovingly. Although the records of the College have long since been burned to ashes in the numerous fires to which that school has been subjected, there does still exist one document which gives some reason for believing that Wythe did attend the school. There is scratched on the enduring walls of the Wren Building the following names and dates:

"John Marshall 1779, G. Wythe, R[ichard] Kennon 1729 R. G[est] 1789 . . . W. Tyler 1785, N. Burwell 1771"[9]

It is hardly likely that George Wythe, in his later association as an adult with the College—and a large part of his adult life was spent in one association or another with it—would have scratched his initials on the walls of the building. So if he did, then he must have done so as a child when perhaps he attended the school. And if he did go there, then he was a student there when he was very young—perhaps 14 or 15 years old. Lyon G. Tyler believes that it was so, that indeed he entered William and Mary in 1740, when he was 14 years old. He could have stayed only two years for he was perhaps 16 years of age when he began to study law under his uncle, Stephen Dewey, who had married his aunt, Elizabeth Walker.

There is reason to believe that Wythe was not happy with the legal education that Dewey gave him since we are told that his uncle treated him with "neglect." In fact, there are some who declare that it was Dewey who taught George Wythe how not to teach. Since in the history of Virginia, Wythe would be one of the greatest of teachers, this fact in itself is a matter of importance.

The Deweys lived on the south side of the James River some few miles (perhaps three or four) below Petersburg in Virginia. Dewey in addition to his other offices was one of the three officials who examined all who wished to be admitted to the bar. If Wythe was 15 when he went to Dewey's home, the year was 1742 or thereabouts. Wythe acted as a sort of clerk for Dewey, picking up such legal knowledge as might come his way during his apprenticeship, performing much of the drudgery of the legal offices of the time, copying out in longhand the dreary, involved legal documents, a task which occupied so much of the time of the apprentice of that day. There were many who complained (and very bitterly) about this sort of training for the law. Among them, for example, were John Jay and Thomas Jefferson, although the latter was never subjected to this sort of thing as far as can be discovered.

After perhaps three or four years of this training, Wythe felt himself at the age of about 20 to be ready to enter legal practice himself. He had first of all to pass an examination which was, of course, oral, and when successful in this he had to secure from some inferior court a certificate attesting to his moral standing and decency. A fee of some 20 shillings was likewise payable at this time and the candidate had also to take the oath. In 1745 a board of examiners in each county was set up to license beginners. The General Court of the Colony appointed these examiners and they consisted both of the judges on the Bench and the lawyers before the bar. In the records of Elizabeth City County there exists the statement that on the 18th of June, 1746, "George Wythe and John   , Gents. produced a commission to practice as attorneys, took the oath . . . to His Majesty's person and government, and subscribed to the Test and are admitted to plead in this court."[10] This is the first of the courts in which Wythe was a practicing attorney and it at least gives us a definite date. He thus lived and practiced for a short while in his native county. Now comes an inexplicable aspect of his life.

His elder brother, Thomas Wythe, Fourth, had inherited the estate and in addition was named a Justice of the Peace for the County on April 29, 1747.

"Ordered that a New Commission of the Peace issue for the County of Elizabeth City and that the following persons be added vizt Thomas Bingham Robert Armistead Cary Selden Thomas Wythe Charles King and Anthony Tucker."[11]

Thus the older Wythe was entrenched in the local seats of power. And it is quite probable that George did not wish to live on his brother's bounty. Surely with his family connections in Elizabeth City County he could have made for himself a decent living as a lawyer. However, he left his home county and went out to the frontier in the northern reaches of Virginia, to Spottsylvania County, being admitted to practice in the courts thereof in November 1746. There is a hint of the reason for Wythe's removal thereto in Landon Carter's *Diary:*

Carter, discussing a disputed election which shall concern us later on, declares that ". . . Waller . . . said he would not concern himself because Dewy was his father-in-law . . . ."[12] This was the famous Ben Waller and if he had married Dewey's daughter, then he must have been the husband of Wythe's cousin. This relationship may very well have been the tie which brought Wythe to try his fortunes in what was then the wild West, where the Wallers and *their* relatives, the Lewis family, lived. While in Spottsylvania (which is somewhat due south of the modern city of Washington), Wythe lived with a certain Zachary Lewis, who in 1726 had married Mary, the sister of Ben Waller. The Waller family was extremely influential—indeed, Governor Gooch's secretary was Ben's brother, William. Wythe thus in his subsequent days had not one but two friends at court in Williamsburg—William, who could prepare the way, and Benjamin, who was a power there in his own right. The names of Wythe and Ben Waller are inextricably entangled through the decades to come in the history of Virginia. The relationship between Wythe and Zachary Lewis also became extremely close, for Wythe married his friend's daughter on the day after Christmas, 1747.

During his stay in Spotsylvania, Wythe practiced against his father-in-law in many cases, as the Order Books of Orange County presently show. One supposes that Lewis was a tough and hard-bitten frontier lawyer, but apparently the rivalry which took place in the courtroom was not carried over in any way in their personal lives. On the 27th of August, 1747, for instance, a William Russell was the plaintiff against Thomas Dowd in a case of debt. Russell's attorney was George Wythe and Thomas Dowd's was Zachary Lewis. On the very same day there was the case of Keem Field against William Russell—the aforesaid William Russell apparently (it was a litigious age)—defendant in debt for retailing liquors without a license. Field's attorney was Zachary Lewis and Russell's was George Wythe. Also on the same day, Martin was the plaintiff against Micaijah Pickett for assault and battery. The plaintiff's attorney in this case was Zachary Lewis while Micaijah Pickett was defended by George Wythe.

The latter practiced in many different courts, for the Order Book of Augusta County has the entry for 21 May 1747: "Wythe's license . . . signed by Peyton Randolph, St. Lawrence Burford, Stephen Dewey and William Nimmo." He had previously been admitted to practice in Spottsylvania County in November 1746. Now that he was fully established in Spottsylvania there was even less reason for him to return to Elizabeth City County, for some time prior to this his mother had died. She lived at least until 15 August 1744 because on that day a citation from the Order Book of Elizabeth City County goes as follows:

> "An indenture between Margaret Wythe on the one part and Charles Sweny and Ann his wife on the other part was acknowledged in court by the said Margaret and ordered to be recorded. George McKenzie, James Wallace, John Brody, Wilson Cary, Merritt Sweeney gent., Justices."[13]

Another of the Counties for which Wythe qualified as an attorney was Caroline County, Thomas Buckner, Thomas Johnson and so on, being the justices present on 13 February, 1746.

Although Wythe was one of the most civilized men of his age, it is quite probable that he enjoyed the rough life of what must have been at that time the back woods of Virginia. It was by no means really the frontier. Only a short distance away was the home of George Washington and it should be remembered that Washington was 16 years of age before he ever saw an Indian. Life in Spottsylvania, whether upon the frontier or not, was nevertheless a matter of some crudeness. In riding around various law circuits of the Virginia of that time, the lawyers could stay at the ordinaries, that is, the taverns which might or indeed might not exist in any particular place. And accomodations therein were by no means luxurious. In the back woods, amusement was sometimes hard to come by and when court days came around the entire free population of the county descended upon the courthouse to listen to the oratory of the lawyers, to argue among themselves the various pros and contras of the cases, to stand with their friends or against their foes, to get drunk, to fight wildly among themselves, to court the women, to race horses, to pit game cocks against each other. And therefore court days took on all the appearances of a ragtag and bobtail fair. In their travels, Wythe and Lewis had naturally to go on horseback. The roads were terrible—mere sand tracks through the forest. There were few bridges and those that did exist were not well maintained. Oftimes there were only ferries, and sometimes not even these. As late as the Revolution the best road in all the state was that which went from Williamsburg, the old Capital, to Richmond, the new. The total distance was only some 63 miles, but it took two days to make the trip. In such a country everyone had to own horses. The only ones who walked were the negroes. Coaches did not come until much later since the roads were simply not good enough for wheeled vehicles. It is true that in Williamsburg some years later people had these but in Spottsylvania and Augusta Counties there were no roads to accommodate any such thing.

Wythe worked mostly in Orange County which had been created in 1734. This borders directly upon the Blue Ridge Mountains and therefore is just over the mountains from the Valley of Virginia—that beautiful valley Governor Spottswood had some years earlier (perhaps in the company of Wythe's father) discovered. It is interesting to note that this period of Wythe's life is perhaps the

only time when he lived in mountainous or even hilly country. The Williamsburg area is, of course, flat to the point of monotony. Only years later when he
went to the Continental Congress in Philadelphia would Wythe again see any
rolling countryside. Orange County, or certain parts of it, was on the frontier. It
should not be thought, however, that the frontier followed a straight line, but
rather it curved along the western edge of the settlements of Virginia and went
in and out as the whim of the settlers prevailed. To the south was Albemarle
County, erected in 1744. And of course in Charlottesville, there was the family
of Peter Jefferson. Perhaps it was here that Wythe first met the father of his
future pupil.

As we have seen, Wythe married Zachary Lewis' daughter, Anne, the day
after Christmas in 1747. Ann Lewis, like so many of the figures in Wythe's life,
is shadowy, vague, quickly disappearing. We know neither the girl's age or the
cause of her death. If the marriage was typical, then she must have been, by our
standards, young for early marriages were common. The marriage, however,
lasted only a year. This may be the reason why he, having at the early age of
twenty tasted some of the cruelty life has to offer, left Spottsylvania and returned
to Williamsburg to enter on one of the most energetic and productive periods of
his life. Anne Lewis Wythe died 8 August 1748, and, as Hemphill notes, after
September of that year, the Order Books of Orange County mention the young
widower no more. It is thus probable that Wythe left Northern Virginia immediately after his wife's death (or as soon as he could wind up his affairs). As far
as we know, he did not return to Fredericksburg until the Revolution.

Apparently his revulsion against slavery, which was to be so prominent in his
later life, had not yet come to dominate his mind, for he sold a negro slave girl at
this time to a certain Wray, a relative of his. Not until much later did he begin
his "sacred cause" of anti-slavery.

Back in Williamsburg, he was taken into the closed circle of those controlling
the government, being given at least a foothold on the bottom rung of the political ladder. His friendship with Ben Waller, who was a prominent Burgess in
the House at this time, and who was also and would continue to be one of Virginia's greatest legal minds, accounts for Wythe's entrance into Virginian politics.
Indeed, it was Waller who made Wythe the great lawyer he ultimately became,
that training his uncle Stephen Dewey had given him having been so poor. The
further experience he received in actual practice in the courts of the western
counties (in Caroline where he came up against such a lawyer as Pendleton)
was valuable for practical experience, but it did not give him the deep legal
training he acquired under Waller's instruction, since the latter now took him
on as a pupil.

It was Lyon G. Tyler who furthered the rumor that Wythe continued on in
Spottsylvania for "some eight years after his wife's death . . . ."[14] This sim-
ply isn't true. One year after Ann Lewis Wythe's death, on the 28th day of
October 1748, we find that Wythe is made clerk of two of the House of Bur-

gesses committees in Williamsburg. This appointment could hardly have been given him if he had remained in Spottsylvania—a far distance away. A further rumor is that Wythe led at this very time a life of dissipation and idle amusement. Here again Tyler, as well as others, has given this as a fact. It could not possibly be true, however, for we know that Wythe not only served as a clerk in the House committees, but very soon himself became a member of the Burgesses. He worked in the House and worked very hard. He could hardly be so busy and still follow a life of idleness. What is more, he continued at this time to practice law—as he did right down until the American Revolution closed the courts and he went on to greater things than law practice. It was at this time also that he deepened his knowledge of classical learning—a familiarity with Latin and Greek—which gave him the repute of being one of the finest scholars of his times. One can hardly study Greek while roistering about in the taverns and coffee houses.

The two committees of which Wythe became clerk were that of Privileges and Elections and that of Propositions and Grievances. These were standing (not *ad hoc*) committees and were extremely important, the first concerning itself with disputed elections and the second considering the many and varied petitions which rained upon the House from the citizenry. An indication of the Burgesses' idea of Wythe's ability (or of Waller's ability to get him a start) is to be seen in the fact that of the other three standing committees of the House, each had its own clerk, while Wythe clerked for two. His job was primarily to keep the minutes when the committees met after morning prayers (which the Chaplain read before the House). The committeemen were in meeting, all forty members, from 9 o'clock until 11 o'clock, when the whole House met in full session.

At the time Wythe's political career began, the political situation had split itself into two factions, roughly divided on the one hand into a group dominated by the Lee family with their control of the Ohio Company (which wished to seize the Ohio and Kentucky territories for itself) and on the other hand, the Loyal Company of Virginia (which likewise wanted to get its hands on vast areas of the Western Lands.) The Loyal Company was pretty much dominated by John Robinson, Thomas Nelson, Edmund Pendleton, Dr. Thomas Walker, John Lewis and Peter Jefferson. It must be noted that the various cliques never stayed stable for any great length of time. As in most familial infighting, members of either group changed sides as avarice, opportunities or just plain orneryness dictated. Although the rivalry within the aristocratic group was sometimes bitter in the extreme and always intense, it was not generally brought out into the open. Only in the private diaries and the supposedly private letters of the day do we get a glimpse of the vigorous factionalism which divided the cousinship. However much these men might fight among themselves, they conducted their manipulations in secrecy, dividing the spoils as they wished and as by bargaining they could manage.

The membership of the Committee of Privileges and Elections consisted of

Ludwell as Chairman, Carter, Lomax, Ben Waller, Beverly, Mr. Attorney (by which we mean Peyton Randolph, Wythe's old school friend), Fry, Reddick, Whiting, Burwell, Braxton, Mr. Secretary, i.e., Carter, Mr. Bland and Mr. William Waller. Wythe's other committee had the following prominent names: Carter, Digges, Braxton, Chiswell (of whom we shall hear later), Baylor, Moore, Merriwether, again Mr. Secretary Carter, Mr. Fry, Bolling, Spottswood, Fairfax (of the great Fairfax family), Fitzhugh, Burwell, Washington, Wormley, Ludwell, Lomax again and again Ben Waller, Grymes, again Mr. Attorney, Cary and Lee. Thus the roster of the really powerful men in the House of Burgesses. These committees held the power and to be on them was to share that power.

Consider for a moment some of the names mentioned. From the standpoint of nepotism and cousinship, all of these people were in some degree interrelated. Archibald Cary of Ampthill, one of Wythe's old schoolfellows from William and Mary College, was the son of Henry Cary, Jr. quondam High Sheriff of Henrico County. He had married Mary Randolph, the daughter of Richard Randolph of Curles, who had been a member of the House and also Treasurer of Virginia. His wife was a cousin of Peyton Randolph. The Randolph themselves formed a family complex which reached through all Virginia. While Benjamin Harrison was not on these committees, he was a member of the House and it is through Harrison (and by other relationships as well) that Peyton Randolph, the Attorney General, was connected with the Carters. For Peyton was Harrison's brother-in-law, having married Elizabeth Harrison. The vitriolic Landon Carter was Harrison's uncle and Richard Henry Lee was his cousin. The two Wallers were brothers, and of course, Mr. Secretary Carter was of the same family as Landon. Chiswell was *the* Colonel John Chiswell, the father-in-law of Speaker John Robinson. In the House membership, Wythe was also a member of the family complex. Stephen Dewey was a member and, as we have seen, was Wythe's uncle by marriage. Another member was John Norton, who had married Courtney Tucker, Wythe's cousin. The member from Caroline, John Baylor, had married another of Wythe's cousins, Frances Tucker.

It would be wrong to assume that relationship alone could bring a man to the front rank in Virginia. On the contrary, in this case one can cite the career of Richard Henry Lee. He, buttressed with all the strength of the Lee family and driven incessantly by a strong power urge, failed again and again in his attempts to enter the top power structure. But certainly membership in the family complex helped one at least to enter the House. And once there, a solid ability at sinuous intrigue, plus a further willingness to go along with the system would insure a career of some splendor.

We do not know where Wythe lived during the few years that he was clerk of these Burgesses' committees. One assumes that since he practiced law a while in the neighboring counties of York and Warwick he must have made his home in the town of Williamsburg. One can also assume that he often visited the old homestead on the Back River, only a few hours' ride away. The relationship between Wythe and Waller must have deepened greatly at this time, for we know from John Blair's Diary that Ben Waller buried his son now.[15] While Waller had other children, certainly one daughter, it can be assumed that the young lawyer would take the place of a son to the older man, and he may even have lived in the latter's home. Hospitality in this time was inherent (it had to be) in the Virginian society of Williamsburg. And if Wythe did live in Waller's home, this would have been the occasion when Waller trained Wythe so deeply in the legal science that the latter from this time on became one of Virginia's very great lawyers.

In his work not only in the law courts, but also in the clerkship of the House Committees, Wythe was able to further his law career. An instance of this took place shortly after his appointment. There were laws against procuring one's election by means of bribery and in 1752 such a case came before the House and therefore before the Committee. The case in point is one of the year 1752. On Wednesday, March 4,

> ". . . a certain Francis Eppes and others, Freeholders of the County of Prince George complaining of an undo election and return of Mr. Stephen Dewey to serve as the Burgess in this present General Assembly."

An investigation was begun on Thursday, March 5. (They lost no time.) In the boredom and loneliness of rural Virginia, election days held—as did court days—great fascination for the citizenry. Although very few of the people could vote, everybody, voting or not, attended. Each of the opposing candidates made speeches on his own behalf, his friends seconding him. The freeholders who came around were buttonholed by the candidate who solicited their votes. The candidates followed the unvarying rule of being present at the polling. This practice was very important, but the most clinching argument—an argument apparently even more decisive than personal persuasion and flattery—was the supply of liquor. In the year 1758, George Washington, with all the fame of his military success in the French and Indian War behind him, still felt it necessary when running for the Burgesses to provide 160 gallons of various liquors to the some 391 voters of Frederick County and the rag-tag and bob-tail onlookers who came to enjoy the sport of an election. There were some 28 gallons of rum, 50 gallons of rum punch, 46 gallons of beer, 34 gallons of wine, and of cider royal some two gallons. If the voters couldn't make up their minds with all that to drink, nothing could persuade them. Such were the election customs of the day.

Wythe was allowed to exercise his legal talents on behalf of the parties of the Eppes-Dewey contested election.[16] In other words, he fought the case for his client (his uncle) before the committee of which he was clerk. (One wonders, did he take the minutes of the case as well?) Eppes had accused Dewey of undue and corrupt practices, as those were defined by the law of 1745. Dewey and Eppes were rivals for election in Prince George County in 1752. It was March and therefore the snows of late winter lay on the ground. Travel was difficult and those who came from afar had to be accommodated somehow and so Dewey entertained those who had come from any distance (some as much as thirty miles). At any rate, a total of eighty voters came to Dewey's home (such was Virginian hospitality!). It must have been quite a party for these seemingly were given something to eat and the inevitable rum to drink. They were also provided with a place to sleep. (One wonders where! To accommodate eighty Virginians with beds would tax even the most hospitable candidate.) Mrs. Dewey herself testified that these accommodations had been supplied.

The night could not have been spent entirely in sleeping, however, for the testimony goes on to state that some of the voters were drunk when the morning's cold light showed them the world once again made new. It was stated, it must be admitted, that Dewey had not invited these people to come, nor had anyone else done so in his name. Nor had he (so goes the testimony) solicited votes from them. Indeed there were those who attended the affair who declared that they would have voted for him anyway.

Election day having arrived, Mrs. Dewey got a neighbor and some friend or other to bring a barrel or hogshead of punch to the court house itself. Lest any over-scrupulous protest, the barrel was placed a hundred yards from the court house door. Presumably, the voters could stagger that distance without too much trouble—either going or coming. The barrel was arranged (it was necessary to insert a spigot, to taste it, etc.). The helpers disposed all this and then went themselves into the court house to enjoy the fun, the punch barrel presumably being left unguarded. But it was not left alone. For some of Dewey's servants, hospitality itself, invited the voters to drink. In fact, they told the assembled Freeholders that those who would vote for Dewey could drink as much as they pleased. Nor were Dewey's servants the only ones who did so: Mrs. Dewey had been married before and had had by her first husband, a certain Mr. Hall, a son, William. This boy, who lived with the Deweys, likewise invited people to warm themselves from the barrel. However this may be, Stephen Dewey stoutly maintained that he had nothing to do with all this, that it had been done without his knowledge by the boy and the servants—who were presumably irresponsible. Indeed, Dewey maintained that he had refused to treat the voters as long as the polls were open, and that when his (Dewey's) friends discovered what was going on, they had closed up the punch barrel, pulling out the spigot.

All of this testimony was taken before the Committee of Privileges and Elections. None of these gentlemen could have been strangers to the matter, for presumably each of them had been elected to the Burgesses by means and methods entirely similar to those described here. The only question was: had the Deweys gone too far in these methods? But Wythe evidently defended his uncle successfully for on March 30, when all the evidence was in, the House ordered that the Committee of Claims was to regulate the costs of Mr. Dewey which the

Eppes petition had occasioned him, Francis Eppes having to pay them.[17]

Nor was this the only case in which the Clerk of the Committee argued on behalf of a client before the very committee he was serving. For previous to this he had received, on 3 March, the permission of the House to appear as counsel for Mr. Richard Booker who complained of the undue election of a certain Wood Jones. This dispute coincided with that of the Eppes-Dewey dispute, so Wythe must have been busy indeed. But his client lost, for on April 1, the House ordered that the petitioner was to pay the costs of Wood Jones occasioned by Booker's complaint. Wythe, by an order of 11 March, now had blanket permission to act as counsel in these cases, and his services were often sought after in the coming years.

There arrived now in Virginia the new Royal Governor, Robert Dinwiddie, who disembarked in Yorktown on November 21st, 1751, with his wife, his two daughters, Elizabeth and Rebecca, and his secretary, Nathaniel Walthoe. Dinwiddie had previously been a surveyor of customs in Virginia as early as 1741. And he had been, according to Edmund Randolph, ". . . the master of a little vessel trading in the river." The Randolphs had long memories and there had sprung up an enmity between the Randolph family and Dinwiddie. Edmund Randolph, writing in his Manuscript History of Virginia many years later characterized Dinwiddie as one ". . . who possessed neither science nor just ambition." The Earl of Albemarle was the titular Governor of Virginia, but he had as it were leased out the office to Dinwiddie, who shared the pay with him. The salary was the noble sum of £6660 a year. Half of this was to go to the English lord who, sitting in England, did absolutely nothing to earn it, and the other half would go to Dinwiddie. Even this was no small sum for those days, but there is no doubt that the brave and pugnacious if somewhat miserly Dinwiddie was determined to acquire a fortune if he could.

The opening act of the drama was the summoning by the new Governor of his first assembly, Friday, 17 January, 1752. It did not adjourn until April, and at the end of it, the Burgesses gave him a good will gift of £500. The English government frowned on this sort of thing, but Dinwiddie pocketed the money anyway. Despite their generosity, the Governor had a rather unpleasant surprise in store for the land-hungry magnates of Virginia. In order that a land grant might be legally issued by the government, it was necessary that what was called a patent should be taken out, duly signed by the Governor. Although he piously declared that the thought of money didn't enter into his mind, Dinwiddie now demanded the payment of one pistole for each patent so signed. The pistole was a tiny Spanish gold coin, and was by no means insignificant in purchasing power, for it would buy a ". . . good cow and calf and other things in like proportion."

Dinwiddie had already taken up this matter with his Council, so it is probable that the Burgesses had heard of his intention. The Council had agreed that this was a reasonable charge, and so it cannot be argued that the Governor stood alone. He also had the approval of the home government. Before telling the Burgesses what he was up to, he let them give him the £500. He also adjourned the Assembly. When the Burgesses discovered what their Governor planned to do, they were furious for there were—when Dinwiddie took office—more than 1000 applications for the various land parcels which the planters coveted. These accounted for almost a million acres of Virginian land. In addition, the planters had, contrary to the law, been possessing themselves of land without entering it on the book for payment of quitrents. This means that the Royal Revenues were defrauded for years of the taxes which should have been paid on hundreds of thousands of acres.

Now in Virginia, whenever a land grab was either in the offing or was being stymied, the great magnates always tried to place their action on a firm constitutional basis. Although the attempt to patent lands without paying a pistole fee was a fraud, it had gone on for so long that the planters felt that this was now their constitutional right. And they placed their quarrel, not on a basis of personal aggrandisment or selfish interest, but rather on the constitutional question of "Does the government have a right to tax us without our consent?" The House of Burgesses members denied that it did, declaring that constitutionally they alone could tax Virginians. How often this cry would echo in the coming years! "The demand of a pistole . . . is . . . an infringement of the rights of the people." They further declared that the Council's advice could not alter this matter, and would Dinwiddie therefore please desist? The quarrel went on for many, many months.

The Governor in his first Assembly had waited most circumspectly to dissolve the House, so that the Burgesses as a formal legal body would be unable to present any protest. (This trick will be used again and again in coming Virginia history.) He undoubtedly figured that in the months before the next session, there would be plenty of time for tempers to cool. However, he sadly misjudged the Virginians. The pressing requirements of the French and Indian warfare, brought on by the claims of the French to the Ohio Valley, demanded that the Governor and the House work most closely together. Their quarrel prevented this. Having discovered for himself how angry were the colonists over the pistole fee, Dinwiddie prorogued and prorogued the Assembly, putting off the calling of it month after month. By 1753, he had already sent George Washington to warn the French to get out of the Ohio Valley. When Washington arrived back in Williamsburg on 16 January, 1754, the Governor realized that he would have to call the Burgesses back into session in order that the Government might meet the French threat. So he had now to call a special session on 14 February, 1754, a year which was truly one of incredible advancement on the political scene for George Wythe. Dinwiddie needed money to fight the French and the only way he could get it was to have the Burgesses vote it to him.

When Dinwiddie faced them on that St. Valentine's Day, there were no love tokens exchanged. Although the Governor was worried to the point of illness by the French encroachments, the Burgesses' main amusement was how best to harrass the Governor.[18] It is the vitriolic Landon Carter who, in his *Diary* gives us an insight into the actual workings of the now-embittered House. It had been Carter who had earlier fought the very idea of giving the Governor his gift of the £500. He had then noted in his *Diary* the stature of Wythe's patron: ". . . And the famous Mr. Waller declared himself for it . . . I do assert this is the most popular gent I know." Carter now notes that there were many declarations about defending themselves ". . . against the insults of the French . . ."

> "Yet when they came to a Committee of the Whole House to consider of the thing, the Speaker to whom it is a Compliment due of moving First Sat Still and so did Everyone else till observing something like a Party that were not for Levying anything I got up and moved that the Committee should resolve that the sum of £20,000 should be levy'd . . . as soon as this was seconded the Speaker very strongly supported mov'd that the question should be put upon £10,000 alledging that he did not imagine any sum we could raise would be sufficient and therefore as it would be but throwing money away he was for throwing away the least sum. . . . Waller alledged we had told the King when we gave £10,000 before that we were very poor and the levying £20,000 or any sum now would be telling a lye and much more of the like which is but a low Popular Argument . . . ."[19]

A bill for £20,000 was finally voted and if the Governor would play low political tricks, so could the House. And to this appropriation, they therefore tacked on the sum of £2,500—to send the Attorney General, Peyton Randolph, to England. In modern money this would amount to some $12,000. And it is quite probable that much of it would go for the ever-present bribery, so necessary in the politics of the home government. Again, this £2,500 was almost equal to the Governor's annual salary (a fact insulting in itself). Peyton Randolph, of course, was one of the most important members of the Virginian government. Dinwiddie, choleric with rage, prorogued the House. He nonetheless had to accept the proviso, since otherwise he would not get any money to fight the French.

One of the great powers-that-be in Virginia was the Speaker, Robinson himself. He combined the Speakership with the Office of Treasurer, having held both offices since 1738. He was Mr. Virginia himself in political life, for right down to his death in 1766 Robinson dominated the colony, ruling it ". . . with a thousand subtle flatteries." Treasurer Robinson was directed to pay Randolph the £2,500 ". . . without the concurrence of other branches of the legislature."[20] This means that the Council, which had approved Dinwiddie's Pistole Fee, would not be consulted. Dinwiddie, already angry, denounced this as ". . . an encroachment of the prerogative of the Crown." Virginia politics during this year boiled with even more than its accustomed fever.

Dinwiddie's enmity to Randolph even extended to his refusing the latter permission to leave Virginia. Constitutionally, *was* Randolph while out of the colony still Attorney General? The House itself had some qualms in the matter, but despite this, Randolph went anyway. Dinwiddie felt the office was vacated and should be filled. The angry Governor picked the young George Wythe to fill the office. Wythe would have to walk on eggshells, treading between the two parties—that of the Governor and that of the planters—with great finesse.

Considering the precarious nature of Wythe's position between the two quarrelling forces in Virginia, we consult the *MS History of Virginia* of Edmund Randolph to see how the young politician handled it:

> "The Governor was wounded to the soul, and personal revenge was his weapon. He superceded Peyton Randolph from the office of Attorney-General, and appointed George Wythe in his room, but as the habits of a seducing and of a not wholly unambitious profession never warped him [Wythe] from friendship or patriotism, he accepted the Commission with the customary professions of gratitude, not disclosing his secret and honorable determination that he should resign it to his predecessor on his return. It is possible, however, that it had been intimated to the Governor from England, that he [Peyton Randolph] was to be restored, without such an instruction even this obdurate ruler would not have dared to contemn the lofty tones of the people."[21]

Wythe was in a peculiar position. He was a very young man and a member of the aristocracy. Probably during Dinwiddie's long residence near Williamsburg before his assumption of the Governorship, the then Surveyor-General of Customs had met and made the acquaintance of, if not Wythe himself, then certainly Wythe's family. For Wythe's brother, Thomas Wythe IV was prominent in Elizabeth City County as a justice and the Wythe family had a large place in the affairs of Williamsburg and the adjoining counties. Wythe as the protege of Waller would have come to the attention of Dinwiddie anyway, for, as we have seen, it was Waller in the House who had moved the gift of £500 to the Governor over the angry opposition of Landon Carter.

Again, Wythe as a lawyer, practiced often in the courts of Warwick, York, James City, and Elizabeth City Counties. And this also would have brought him to the eye of the Governor. Again his position as a clerk of the House committees must have given him a certain *éclat*. Although a young man, he alone had the clerkship of two committees. And now Wythe was brought directly into the House as a member. For the incumbent of Williamsburg, Armistead Burwell, had died and in the session of 22 August, 1754, it was ordered that new writs of election for the City be issued. For this George Wythe was chosen. So he now took his seat in the House.

There are some unkind enough to say that Wythe may have been chosen for this seat by default. This rather uncomplimentary view is maintained by the fact that all the other men of prominence were already busily caught up in the affairs of the day. A brief glance at the chronological order of events will show that this assumption could not possibly be so. For Wythe was made Attorney General of Virginia on 21 January 1754 which was *before* he was elected to the House. (The Governor had prorogued the Assembly on 19 December, 1753 and called it again 14 February, 1754.) The next session was Thursday, 22 August 1754. It was at this session that writs for the Election to fill the place of the deceased

Burwell were issued. Exactly when Peyton Randolph left for England is not known, but assuming that he reported to the Board of Trade as soon as he got there, he must have sailed about the time Wythe took the oath of office as Attorney General. All during the coming year, during Randolph's absence, Dinwiddie continued the quarrel with the Burgesses over paying Randolph's salary. But this quarrel did not affect Wythe. He was on his way up. There are very few men who go from being a clerk of a House committee to being the third or fourth man in Virginia's government.

And so:

> "At a Court held for York on Monday the twenty first day of January Anno Domini 1754. And in the twenty seventh Year of the Reign of our Sovereign Lord King GEORGE the Second.
> Present
> Daniel Moore   John Goodwin
> Samuel Reade   John Norton
>   Robert Shield Gent., Justices.
> George Wythe Esqr. his Majesty's Attorney General and Judge of the Court of the Vice Admiralty in this Colony this day in Court took the Oaths of Allegiance & Supremacy and the Adjuration Oath and Subscribed the said Abjuration Oath and repeated and subscribed the Test."[22]

The Test Oath was a hang-over from the old No-Popery days of English history. It went as follows:

> "We do declare that there is not any transubstantiation of ye Lord's supper, or in ye elements of bread and wine, at or after ye consecration thereof by any person whatsoever."[23]

This excursion into theology was apparently necessary before Wythe could possibly get on with the business of prosecuting criminals. About the time Wythe was swearing to the above theology (about which he probably knew little or nothing), Peyton Randolph was sailing over the ocean to England, there to face a sour welcome from Dinwiddie's friends on the Board of Trade.[24] Despite a cold reception, the Burgesses' agent won a partial victory. So did Dinwiddie, for at the end of 1754, the Privy Council had sustained the Royal Governor in the matter of the Pistole Fee. To the Burgesses' joy, however, the Government in England put definite bounds to the extent to which the Governor was allowed to impose the tax. And to this was added the injunction that Randolph be taken back as Attorney General.

Of Wythe's activities as Attorney General, we know very little. But much can be inferred from the fact that he was also *ex officio* Judge of the Court of Vice Admiralty. Another cause for anger by the Royal Governor had been the fact that even while the war against the French was going on, many Virginian traders did not scruple to sell to the enemy.

In his letter to the Lords of Trade and Plantations of 17 March 1755, Dinwiddie put an embargo on Virginian exports. Too many colonists were sending their goods to the French colonies of Guadaloupe and Martinique. Some were even brazenly sailing directly to Cape Breton and Quebec. It is to be expected that, smuggling being what it was all during the colonial time, there were some traders caught. And the task of prosecuting them fell to George Wythe.

It is not known how long young George Wythe remained Attorney General, nor do we know quite when Peyton Randolph returned from England. Nowhere in the House of Burgesses' Journals is it even mentioned that Randolph, while abroad, was superseded by Wythe. The Burgesses' sessions were as follows: 19 December, 1754, when Randolph was named to go to England; 14–23 February 1755 when Dinwiddie got his £10,000 to fight the French War. It very probably was at this session that the bill and its rider were accepted, however reluctantly, by the Governor. Surely then Randolph would not go to England before this time of 23 February 1754. At the next session, 22 August 1754, Burwell having died, Wythe was elected to the House in his own right. We continue all through this session to have mention in the Journals of "Mr. Attorney" but whoever he is, he is not named. But in the Journals for Thursday 1 May 1755, is the following:

> "Ordered, That an Address be made to the Governor, to order a new Writ to issue, for the electing a Burgess to serve in this present Assembly for the College of William and Mary, in the Room of Peyton Randolph, Esq.; who since his Election hath accepted of the Office of His Majesty's Attorney-General of this Colony . . . ."[25]

This means that by 1 May, 1755, Randolph had returned from England and had got back his coveted office. Wythe had become by 2 May 1755, Friday, just another member of the House, for on that date he was put on the Committees of which he had before been clerk—being the last-named on that of Privileges and Elections. His positions thereon were of some importance, as well as his standing—for the House members were extremely jealous of their rank on the various committees. Wythe's great rival, Pendleton, was also on two committees. Wythe was in addition a member of the Committee for the Court of Justice as was Peter Jefferson (Thomas' father).

Wythe did not, however, occupy all his time with politics in the House. For in this year of 1755, two very important things happened to him. First of all, his brother, Thomas Wythe, Fourth, died. Since his brother had no children, the estate of Chesterville went to George. This placed Wythe automatically in the company of the nobility, since he was now a landowner. With this went his almost automatic succession to the "Wythe Magisterial District," and so at the age of 28 he was appointed by the Governor as a Justice of the County Court of Elizabeth City County. To an almost full-time career in the House, he now added his duties as a Judge, listening to lawyers plead before the bench as he had himself so pleaded. Nor did he give up his private law practice. On the contrary, he worked as hard at it as ever. He was involved, for example, with Robert Carter Nicholas on cases concerning the Carroll family of Maryland. He likewise was retained by the immensely wealthy Robert Carter to fight his lawsuits. And ultimately George Washington also sought his services.

But he was active not only in his law work. He had, as we have seen, lost his young wife, Ann, in 1748. He must have been heartsick indeed at the loss, for he waited until this year 1755 to re-marry. When he did, however, he married a woman whose life is as shadowy and vague as that of her predecessor. Of Elizabeth Taliaferro we know almost nothing save that Wythe loved her very tenderly all their married life. The Taliaferros were a great and very rich family in Tidewater Virginia. The name, while Italianate in spelling, was English in pronunciation (Tolliver). The family's origin is confused, some accounts tracing it to medieval times, while others point out a post-Reformation descent. It would be Wythe's delight to trace his bride's family history but one cannot say that he succeeded. In the years to come, he would employ Thomas Jefferson—while that friend was Minister to France in the post-Revolutionary years—to inquire about in Italy as to the possible beginnings of the family. But a certain mystery always remained to it.

Elizabeth was the daughter of Richard Taliaferro, the man who designed the Governor's Palace and the rebuilt Capitol. He was the possessor of the splendid plantation of Powhatan on the James River a few miles from Williamsburg. With this marriage went (and probably—though it cannot be proved—at the very time of the marriage) the use of and later the possession of the beautiful town house which Richard built in Williamsburg. This mansion exists today in almost its original form. In this house, George and the new Mrs. Wythe set up housekeeping a delightful stone's throw away from, on the one hand, Bruton Church and, on the other, the Governor's Palace. He was close, therefore, to the powers of both Heaven and Earth. Wythe's situation must now have been delightful indeed for the house is one of the loveliest of the mansions of restored colonial Williamsburg—a town possessing many beautiful houses.

Like Thomas Jefferson and other colonial Virginians, Taliaferro made a gracious pleasure out of the practice of architecture, marrying dignity with utility in his buildings. The father-in-law did not die until the middle of the Revolution many years later, when he left life ownership to his daughter and son-in-law. The house itself is plain but elegant. It could not, of course, compare with the grandeur of the Governor's Palace, nor could it in any way equal the mansions the magnates of other colonies built to house themselves in such places as Newport, Annapolis, Philadelphia, or Charleston. Williamsburg was, after all, the little capital of a planters' society, and the houses the Virginia nobility built for themselves there were town houses only. The homes they really lived in were the spacious mansions of their home plantations. A house in Williamsburg was only for the times when the Burgesses were in session. It is true that the Wythe home was a permanent home, but Wythe's wife, of course, often visited the home plantation of Powhatan with her husband, and they also spent much time at Chesterville. The tradesmen, carpenters, printers, tavern keepers, merchants, doctors of medicine were the only people who lived year around in Williamsburg.

The house was certainly ideal for Wythe's career. Close to his old College, to Bruton Parish Church, to the Capitol, to the Governor's Palace, to the Raleigh Tavern, it was the focus around which Wythe built his married life. He had thus a home equal in size and beauty, in elegance of furnishings and convenience of arrangements even to Benjamin Waller's house, which was on a near-by street but a short distance away. Robert Carter of Nomini Hall, whose legal business Wythe performed for many years, also lived only a little ways away, directly adjacent to the Governor's Palace. And somewhat neighbor also to Carter was the house of Peyton Randolph, who filled so large a part of Wythe's life.

But despite the joy of the young bridegroom in the possession of his new bride, and in the pleasure they both must have taken in the ownership of their new home, there was still a war on. And it was not going well for the Virginians. While Washington had to face the French and the Indians, Dinwiddie had to face the Burgesses. There was money to raise, and political problems to be solved. And again the Governor approached the reluctant House. And, despite the antagonism, the House was not behindhand, for by the time the War was over, the Government of Virginia had spent $750,000, an exceedingly great sum of money for that time. This inflation played havoc with the fiscal health of Virginia and was the seedbed out of which grew the angry opposition to the Stamp Act and to the Townshend Duties. Eventually the Revolution came therefrom.

Notes to Chapter I

1. Benjamin Franklin. *The Complete Works of*—. Compiled and Edited by John Bigelow. (New York, 1887–88), Vol. 10, p. 403.
2. William and Mary College Quarterly. First Series, Vol. 18, p. 290.
3. George Keith. *A Journal of Travels from New Hampshire to Caratuck, on the Continent of North America.* (London, 1706), p. 11.
4. Virginia Magazine of History and Biography. Vol. 16, p. 157–8.
5. Lyon G. Tyler. *History of Hampton & Elizabeth City County.* (Published by the Board of Supervisors of Elizabeth City County, 1922), p. 32.
6. Littleton Waller Tazewell. *An Account and History of the Tazewell Family.* Typescript in the possession of William and Mary College, Williamsburg, Virginia, p. 154.
7. Andrew Burnaby. *Travels Through the Middle Settlements in North America*—. 3d ed., (London, T. Payne, 1798), p. 53.
8. Virginia. *Calendar of Virginia State Papers and Other Manuscripts Preserved in the Capitol at Richmond.* Ed. by W. P. Palmer. (Richmond, 1875–93), Vol. 1, p. 141.
9. William and Mary—. First Series, Vol. 10, p. 142.
10. Lyon G. Tyler. "George Wythe, 1726–1806" in, *Great American Lawyers, the Lives and Influence of Judges and Lawyers*—. Edited by William D. Lewis. (Philadelphia, Winston, 1907), p. 55.
11. Virginia (Colony). Council. *Executive Journals, Council of Colonial Virginia.* Edited by H. R. McIlwaine. (Richmond, D. Bottom, 1925), Vol. 5, p. 233.

12. Landon Carter. "Journals of the House of Burgesses" in, *Diary*, Vol. 1, p. 89. University Press of Virginia, 1965.
13. Elizabeth City County. *Order Book, 1731, 1747.*
14. Leon M. Bazile. Manuscript Account in the Virginia Historical Society Library, entitled "Discourse Refuting Statements Made That George Wythe At One Time Led A Life of Dissipation." In this work, Bazile declares that this calumny first appeared in 1825 in a work by Lempriere, entitled *Biographical Dictionary.* From there, Daniel Call abstracted it for it appears in his short account of Wythe's life. Next, Grigsby in his *Discourse on the Virginia Convention of 1776* carries on the rumour. B. B. Minor in 1825 repeated it. It is also in Henry Howe's *Historical Collections of Virginia* (1860). It is even in Lyon G. Tyler's account of Wythe in *Great American Lawyers,* edited by Lewis. Even N. M. Coleman in *The Constitution and Its Framers* repeats it. Curiously, there is great variance on when this dissipation occurred, what its nature was, and how long it lasted. Bazile's point is well taken—Wythe was simply too busy to dissipate, since that activity, like so much else, is allowed only to the idle.
15. The son's death took place in September, 1751. William and Mary,—. First Series, Vol. 1, p. 137.
16. Burgesses. Journals, 1752, p. 29. et sequor.
17. *Ibidem,* p. 63.
18. Louis K. Koontz. *Robert Dinwiddie, His Career in American Colonial Government and Westward Expansion.* (Glendale, California, Arthur H. Clark Co., 1941, p. 256.
19. Landon Carter. "Journal—" in *Diary*, Vol. 1, p. 111.
20. Burgesses. *Journals, 1752-55,* p. 203, et sequor.
21. Edmund Randolph. *Manuscript History of Virginia.* Virginia Historical Society, Richmond, p. 101.
22. York County. *Judgements and Orders Book, 1752-54,* p. 368.
23. Lyon G. Tyler, ed. *Letters and Times of the Tylers.* (Richmond, Whittet & Shepperson, 1884-96), Vol. 1, p. 44.
24. Board of Trade. *Minutes* (photostats). Historical Society of Pennsylvania, Philadelphia.
25. Burgesses. *Journals, 1752-55,* p. 233.

CHAPTER II

Wythe as a Virginian Legislator

But before anything like this could happen, the money had first to be voted. And on the 25th of March, 1756, that session of the Assembly passed an Act for raising the sum of some £25,000 for

". . . the Protection of the Inhabitants on the Frontier of this Colony and other Purposes
. . . ."

The Act itself named in precise detail those who were to implement it:

"And be it further enacted by the Authority foresaid that John Robinson, Peyton Randolph, Charles Carter, Esquires, Carter Burwell, Benjamin Waller, John Chiswell, Richard Bland, John Page, John Norton, William Harwood, George Wythe, Landon Carter, Edmund Pendleton, and Robert Carter Nicholas, Gentlemen, or any seven of them shall from time to time with the consent and approbation of the Governor . . . direct and appoint how the said money shall be applied . . . ."[1]

So the Burgesses did *not* leave to the Governor the spending of the money they voted. And Wythe was among those deputed to oversee the spending. The names on this committee were those of the most important men of Virginia, and even though Dinwiddie did not like it, he found these men looking over his shoulder as he spent the money. Or in some instances, they themselves supervised in minute detail how the money was spent. Wythe must have worked very hard and very closely on what was an exceedingly onerous and careful duty. For we find that George Washington in submitting his accounts to the committee at its meetings held on 14, 17, and 18 August 1756 named the most paltry and minute sums:

"At a Committee . . . Colonel Washingtons Accounts were examined.

The Article of £50 stolen from Cap. Peachy referred to the Assembly.
£3/19 due from G. Hedgeman to be got from him.
/6/10 paid to Jenkins to be got back.
11/18/8 due from Francis Triplett to be stop'd out of his pay . . .
/6/15 due from George Gordon to be stop'd out of his pay . . .
The Surgeon's pay to be augmented to 10 shillings per day. . . ."[2]

Many years later during the Revolution, Wythe and Washington were again to have exactly the same positions. Washington was to fight desperately in the field against the enemy. And Wythe was to supervise getting him supplies, men and money. In this the War against the French was a prelude to the later War against the English.

Now we see an instance of how closely the politics of Virginia were regulated. Wythe had heretofore represented Williamsburg in the Burgesses, but now he stood for election from Elizabeth City County and a most strange election this was indeed. How it happened that George Wythe at this time lost his Williamsburg seat does not appear. It must be assumed that Wythe was still in the good graces of the powerful. He had hitherto proved a most useful, hard-working, self-effacing, cooperative member of the House, and it is probable that the powers-that-be were loath to lose him. However that may be, his race in his home county was a disaster, despite the power of the Wythe family there. In this election there were three names figuring prominently. John Tabb, William Wager (a Captain in the militia) and George Wythe. We know something (not much) of the particulars of this election because on 30 March 1756, John Tabb complained to the House of Burgesses of unfair practices by the opposition, namely Mr. Wager.

Tabb maintained that Wager's election was invalid—that some had voted for Wager who had no right to vote at all. Tabb complained that the witnesses who could substantiate his testimony were too old to journey to Williamsburg. Would therefore the House sent a committee to Elizabeth City County to interview these old people, and to ascertain the facts? The House, agreeable to this, declared:

> "*Resolved*, that the persons who voted in the said election, whose freeholds are questioned . . . who are aged, infirm, and unable to attend the Committee of Privileges and Elections be examined upon oath before George Wythe, Jacob Walker, Robert Armistead, Booth Armistead, and Charles Jennings Gent. . . . or any three of them."[3]

This was certainly a strange development. For the defeated party to a contested election (Wythe) was now sitting in judgement on that very election. It is true that the inquiry was not about *his* (unsuccessful) candidacy, but much of the evidence which was to come out did bear directly on how his supporters had campaigned for him. (One assumes that Wythe was, at this time, since he had not been re-elected, a lame-duck member of the Burgesses, or was one of a commission of Elizabeth City County justices chosen for this duty.)

On the 8th of April following, the witnesses were examined and according to the Journals testified that:

> ". . . upon his invitation, several Freeholders went to Mr. Wager and were there kindly entertained, with Victuals and Drink, but no Solicitations or Threats were then used by Mr. Wager, touching the Election . . . And the said Craghead, declared, . . . that Mr. Wager had assisted him in his distress, and therefore he did treat the Freeholders at that Time, and would as often as Mr. Wager and Mr. Wythe should be candidates for that County. That Mr. Wager for many years past hath kept an hospitable House, and freely entertained all Persons that came there, as well Strangers as Freeholders. . . .
>
> It also appeared to your committee, That at a Meeting of sundry Freeholders . . . between the Test of the Writ and Day of Election, procured by Mr. Wythe who was the Candidate or his Friends, That some of Mr. Wythe's Friends declared, he would serve as Burgess for the said County for nothing, and that they would give Bond to repay any Thing that should be levied on the County for him, and Mr. Wager being at a Distance, and hearing of this Declaration, came up and said, he would serve on the same Terms, . . . upon which one Cary declared, now we have got two men that will serve us for nothing, which he was glad of, as he found it very difficult to pay his Taxes. . . ."[4]

This evidently was a time when a complaint was justified. For John Tabb was declared elected from Elizabeth City County. And now occurs an equally interesting and strange aspect of this affair: Wythe had not been re-elected. Nonetheless, on 25 March 1757, there is stated by Hening that the same committee for supervising the expenditures of money was set up. There were, it is true, some different names: John Power, for example. Also William Digges, Dudley Digges, and John Page. But almost all the earlier members of the Committee were named again. Including George Wythe![5] How he could be on this House Committee if he hadn't been re-elected surpasses understanding. However, he was there. Could it be possible that, being a Williamsburg resident, and therefore ever-available, it was so convenient to have him on a supervisory committee that he was put on it anyway, even though not a member of the House? Wythe at any rate in this election of 1756 had received fewer votes than any of the other candidates. So he was definitely out of the House for the time being.

On 11 July 1758 Wythe again stood for election, and again for Elizabeth City County. His fellow candidates and the results were as follows:

Colonel John Tabb—76 votes
Captain William Wager—95 votes
Captain Cary Selden—37 votes
Captain Richard Sweeney—13 votes
Robert Brough—2 votes
George Wythe—8 votes
William Armistead—11 votes[6]

Two interesting aspects of this election stand out: First, in Elizabeth City County George Wythe was certainly not tremendously popular with his fellow Freeholders. There is no apparent explanation for his unpopularity, for one cannot believe that it was occasioned by his displacing Randolph from the Attorney-Generalship. Neither can one believe that it was occasioned by his friendship for Dinwiddie. Secondly, judging by the military titles, this was a campaign by soldiers. Wythe was not a soldier, had not served on the frontier, had not done any fighting. This may explain his failure.

Having then twice failed in his home county, the ruling group found a seat for him in the House from his old College, William and Mary. If ever there was a safe seat, this would be it. In standing for election here, Wythe would have no malcontent Freeholders to court or treat. By the Royal Charter of 1693, the College was granted the "Full and absolute power, liberty, and authority, to nominate, elect and constitute one discreet and able person . . . to . . . the House of Burgesses of . . . our Colony of Virginia . . . ." This man was to represent the College, and the College, not the Board of Visitors or even the Alumni, was to elect him. In other words, this member of the House was chosen by the faculty—the "President and Masters." Thus fewer than a dozen persons would elect a burgess. With the backing of the powers-that-be in Virginia, how could Wythe lose? Peyton Randolph had been the College representative but had given up his seat in order to stand for election from Williamsburg. There can be only one reason: Randolph did so in order that Wythe might continue in the House. Randolph was simply too strong a man to have been defeated in the Williamsburg constituency and therefore took no risk. And so for the coming few years, William and Mary was Wythe's constituency.

Immediately upon his return to the House, Wythe was put to work on the various committees, both standing and the *ad hoc*. On 16 September 1758, he rejoined his old Committee of Privileges and Elections, along with Landon Carter, Randolph, Harrison, Ben Waller, etc. While this Committee was concerned with the honesty of elections, it also jealously watched over the prerogatives of the members of the House. They could not, for example, be arrested while the House was in session. Nor could they be slandered. And just about this time, a very serious accusation was made against Dr. Thomas Walker, member from Louisa. He had been Commissary General of the army during the past few years. Now he was declared to have cheated on his accounts. This was a serious accusation, for he stood well with the oligarchy, being as he was a member of it. This affected Wythe also, since he had—with several others—been on the committee which watched over wartime financial spending.

From the Journals of the House, Tuesday, 3rd of April 1759 is the following account:

> "It appears . . . that Mr. Johnson, at his own House, in the Evening of Louisa Court Day, in the Month of November last, introduced a Discourse concerning Mr. Walker's Conduct as a Contractor for Provisions, . . . in which discourse . . . he said, "That Mr. Walker had cheated the Country out of eleven hundred Pounds; and being asked how it was possible for Mr. Walker to impose upon so many Gentlemen as the House of Burgesses consisted of, and yet not only continue in Office, but be courted to do so; answered, "You know

little of the Plots, Schemes and Contrivances that are carried on there; in short, one holds the Lamb while the other skins; many of the members are in Places of Trust and Profit, and others want to get in, and they are willing to assist one another in passing their Accounts; and it would surprise any Man to see how the Country's Money is Squandered away, which he had used his endeavours to prevent, and could never succeed but once, and that to a trifling Amount. . . .'

Resolved, That the Aforementioned words, spoken by Mr. Johnson are false, scandalous and malicious, and reflect highly on the Honor of the House. . . . the Question being put . . . the House divided,, . . . Yeas, 37, Noes, 32 . . . Ordered . . . Mr. Johnson, was accordingly called in, and Mr. Speaker from the Chair, did reprimand him, in his Place. . . ."[7]

The margin of victory was so narrow that they did not dare to fine him. So, as a member of the House, he was merely reprimanded. Johnson would remember this incident and treasure hostility in his heart. Later, in the matter of the Stamp Act, he would be one of Henry's strongest supporters and thus a leader of the insurgents.

For Wythe, this was a period of intense work in the House. Again and again, he was named as a member of various committees. Perhaps the most important, and one which redounded with least credit to all concerned, and even to Wythe himself, was the committee entrusted with supervising the printing and disposal of paper money. As Virginia had been put to great expense in the late war, and as hard money of whatever kind (Spanish, French and English—and even Portuguese—circulated in the Colonies) invariably flowed from the colony to the Mother Country to pay for the many goods the colonists bought, it was necessary to provide a substitute. And this the colonial government found in paper money. The colonists apparently were well aware of Gresham's Law, as they were careful not to print too much of the paper money and to destroy it when it had served its purpose. Also, the English merchants hated this paper money and, if too much were printed, they might get the English government to disallow it. There was a running fight over the matter for the next few years.

In the Assembly of 14 September 1758 to 4 March 1760, there was enacted the following:

"An Act for granting the sum of £20,000 for the further security . . . that the paper bills of credit or Treasury notes, are properly sunk . . . ."

A committee was set up for this purpose and the task (and an important one it was) was assigned to Peyton Randolph, Robert Carter Nicholas, Ben Waller, Lewis Burwell, and George Wythe. At least twice a year they were to examine and burn all bills of credit redeemable on the 1st day of March 1765 as had been paid into the Treasury. It must be admitted that the committee did an abominable job, and out of their failure came a scandal which shook Virginia's social structure to its depths. For at Robinson's death it was to be discovered that he had, instead of destroying the notes, quietly helped his friends in their financial troubles—with Treasury notes. One of the amazing things about Virginian politics is that although Wythe was on this committee and was thus certainly responsible, after the scandal of the defalcation, Wythe was continued in his overseeing of the Treasury notes! This same committee was set up again in November 1761, with the same end in view as before.

Wythe was likewise on the Committee of Propositions and Grievances, another of his old committees, and he was also appointed to that of the Courts of Justice, along with Messrs. Tabb, Slaughter, Lewis (his old friend), Landon Carter, etc. In this same session of 27 February 1759, Wythe, together with Robert Carter Nicholas, Richard Bland and, again, Zachary Lewis, were put on a committee for bringing in a bill to enlarge the Town of Fredericksburg. This town, of course, was the old haunt of Wythe's younger days. It was to see him again during the Revolution, also. Again, part of Wythe's work in the House was to consider the cases of hardship from the war, and to Wythe, together with a colleague, Francis Lightfoot Lee, was given the task of inquiring into a petition of Adam Stephen, Esq., a Lieutenant Colonel and one of Washington's comrades-in-arms. The said petition declared that in the skirmishing

> ". . . before Fort DuQuesne, under the Command of Major Grant . . . the said Detachment being over-powered by the Enemy . . . obliged to retreat, with the loss of their Blankets and Shirts, and praying the consideration of the House . . . ."[8]

Wythe and Lee reported that the Virginia regiment ought to be allowed £175.

Potentially one of the most important but in the long run one of the least effectual of the committees on which Wythe worked was that setting up the "Act for encouraging Arts and Manufactures." In February 1759 this had been established to offer bounties and premiums to those who would aid in establishing industry in the country. For much of his life, Wythe had to do with this sort of thing, with silk worm cultivation, vineyards, and weaving mills in Williamsburg. A bounty not to exceed £20 was to be granted for useful inventions. That the House was really concerned with this (especially the production of wine—so much of Virginia's money was drained off abroad for this commodity) can be seen from the roster of the committee—it contained the name of every important politician of the time.

Since he was himself a plantation owner, Wythe was intensely interested in agriculture. He began to extend his holdings in the land adjacent to his Back River estate of Chesterville. At this time, 1760, he leased the entire acreage of the land belonging to the Syms Charity School. His payment to the school for this and for 11 head of cattle was the sum of £31/5 for a year, current money of Virginia. In addition to this payment, Wythe agreed to supply the school with four milk cows during the summer, to establish an orchard of 100 fruit trees, and to maintain such buildings as he should erect on the Syms property in good repair.

Nor was this the only instance in which Wythe extended his land holdings by lease or rent. For a decade later, in 1770, he advertised in the Williamsburg Gazette:

"One James Ransome of Gloucester, the 23d of November 1670 devised 50 acres of land, which is now in my possession, to Abraham Savey and Sarah his wife, for 99 years; and convenanted that he, or his heirs etc., at the expiration of that time, would make another lease, for the like term, to the leasees . . . they paying 100 pounds of tobacco. I long ago purchased the right of the leasees, and ever since the expiration of the former term have been, and now am, ready to take another lease, and pay the tobacco but I cannot discover who is the person entitled to the reversion. If he inclines to sell his reversion, I am willing to buy it for what it is worth. G. Wythe."[9]

Also, we should recall that Wythe, in addition to his work in the Burgesses, continued his private law practice. Not only this, but he sat the while as Justice on the Court of Elizabeth City County. So, what with managing his plantation of Chesterville, he was a very busy man.

It must not be imagined that with the departure of Dinwiddie from the Virginia scene, political life now quieted down. On the contrary, it became livelier than ever. There were few dull moments in Williamsburg, with accusations of cheating and of false elections. But one of the bitterest fights was just on the horizon. The position of the Anglican clergy—the ministers of the state church of Virginia—was an ambiguous one. They were servants of both the state and the church. It was, however, in effect the state which paid their salary—established by law at some 16,000 pounds of tobacco. This had been enacted in 1748 but in 1755, in the needs of the French War, the Assembly changed the Act, making the salaries payable not in tobacco but in the money value thereof, at the rate of 2d per pound of tobacco. The clergy appealed to Dinwiddie to veto the Act, but he refused. He gave for a reply: "What can I do? If I refuse to approve it, I shall have the people on my back." He had not used this argument in the Pistole Fee controversy, but that was a matter of his own pocket.

The Act was renewed in 1758—without the assent from the King (time was too short for it to travel across the ocean and back again). Now the planters experienced a crop failure, the which made the value of tobacco high since it was scarce. Naturally they did not want to share such profits as there were with the clergy. However, in the lack of the King's assent, the clergy argued that the Act was unconstitutional. By 1758, Dinwiddie had left Virginia and his place was taken by Francis Fauquier. When the clergy appealed to him to veto the law, he replied that it was not up to him to decide whether a law ". . . just or unjust, contrary or not . . . to his instructions, but whether the people wanted it."[10] Now the clergy sent John Camm to England to talk to the Privy Council. He returned victorious in 1760 but Fauquier managed to take the joy out of the victory, for his subtle mind was able to convince itself that the Royal Decree disallowing the Two Penny Act was not retroactive. And therefore the ministers would not receive the arrears in their salary to which they might otherwise be entitled. The argument boiled merrily on, for the ministers sued in the law-courts. The most celebrated of the trials over the Parson's Cause was the one in which the backwoods lawyer, Patrick Henry, took part.

Henry, an indolent, affectionate and ambitious man, with a flair for oratory and an ability to penetrate into the recesses of the human heart, had failed in about everything he had tried. He tried storekeeping but found that he loved to hunt more than to wait on customers. He then tried the law. Too lazy to study much, he set himself to this for a month or so, reading Coke upon Littleton, that standard on English law. He then applied to the two Randolphs, Peyton and John, to Edmund Pendleton and to George Wythe to sign his license. Many years later, in 1824, in recalling Patrick Henry to his visitors, Thomas Jefferson who knew him well and disliked him heartily, declared as follows:

> ". . . there were four examiners, Wythe, Pendleton, Peyton Randolph and John Randolph. Wythe and Pendleton at once rejected his application; the two Randolphs were . . . prevailed upon to sign the license; and having obtained their signature, he again applied to Pendleton, and after much entreaty and many promises of future study, succeeded also in obtaining his. He then turned out for a practicing Lawyer."[11]

How much of this is true it is hard to say. Jefferson said he got his information from the examiners themselves. Certainly he could have heard about it from Wythe. However, many years had gone by, and Jefferson's memory may very well have failed him. He would die in two more years, an old man, and the memories of old man are not very reliable. For we know from the court records of Goochland County that George Wythe did sign Henry's license admitting him to the bar. And Henry was a most successful lawyer.

In 1763, the Reverend James Maury sued his Vestry for the salary which he believed was due him for the period of some ten months between Fauquier's signature of the Assembly Two Penny Act and the official disallowance of it from England as brought back by John Camm. When the case was heard, the courtroom was packed, with the famous Matthew Lyons helping to try the case. The judge clearly ruled in Maury's favor. But so greatly had Henry mesmerized the jury that it brought in damages for Maury of only one penny.

Although it is Maury's case in Hanover County that has been remembered by historians, there were other lawsuits over this Two Penny Act. One of these took place in Elizabeth City County, and here the case was decided on the basis of law rather than oratory. For presiding over this Court was George Wythe. Unlike the Court of Hanover, Wythe's court, in which he was assisted by George Walker, Cary Mitchell, Wilson Miles Cary, John Tabb, George Wray and others, found the law of 1758 to be valid. The Reverend Thomas Warrington had brought the suit, which began on 5 January 1763 and was carried over until Wednesday 2 March 1763. We know none of the arguments presented in the Court, but the Justices found that the Reverend Warrington had no case. They arrived at this verdict *before* Patrick Henry's fulminations in the Maury case took place, and also before the Reverend John Camm's case (he likewise was suing—in the General Court in Williamsburg) had been decided. The verdict was that Warrington was right if the law of 1758 was invalid. On the other hand, Jeggitts (the defendant) was right if the 1758 law was constitutional. This was the decision of the jury. The question was thus thrown back on the Justices and they decided that the 1758 law was quite valid. Thus Warrington lost his case against the Vestry.[12]

In this lawsuit, two aspects stand out. First of all, it is clearly a case of judicial review. That is, the declaring by a court of law as to the constitutionality of a law passed by a legislature. This will be one of the practices of American courts right down to our day—and thus this is a matter of great historical importance.

Secondly, the whole matter was manifestly unfair. For the very men who as legislators had passed the law were sitting in judgment upon it as County Justices. The names of Wythe, Armistead, Wray, Tabb, Cary, Walker were registered in the Burgesses as members. How unprejudiced could they be in this matter? Furthermore, these very justices, as planters who grew tobacco and paid taxes to the Church of England, were concerned financially in the outcome of the case. George Wythe owned Chesterville on the Back River and was, of course, interested in how high his taxes would be. Again, Wythe was—as we shall see—the particular and intimate friend of Governor Fauquier, who had often expressed his hostility to the Church and its ministers. At this time, Deism was a favorite form of theological protest on the part of the Virginian upper classes, and Fauquier was, it is believed, a Deist. It is not too much to say that Wythe was one likewise—at least, at this period in his life. Again one asks how unprejudiced were these judges?

The name of Fauquier was written large in Wythe's life. Fauquier was made Governor on 10 February 1758 and arrived in Virginia on 7 June following. The eldest son of Dr. John Francis Fauquier and his wife, Elizabeth Chamberlayne, he had been born in 1704, which means that he was considerably older than Wythe. He had become a Director of the South Sea Company—that colossal, that monumental disaster—in the year 1751. His interest in science and natural philosophy is indicated by the fact that on the 15th of February 1753, he was made a fellow of the Royal Society. He had married Catherine Dalton, and, although his wife and family accompanied him to the New World, after some two or three years they returned to England. The Governor then stayed on in the Palace in Williamsburg living the life of a quasi-bachelor.

That Fauquier was a staunch Deist we know from a certain William Robinson's letter to the Bishop of London:

> "The Governor I am very well informed has desired the Minister of the Parish . . . to omit the Athanasian Creed and on the Minister's refusal to comply . . . desired to be excused as to his own particular from paying any regard to that part of the Church service."[13]

"The Parish" was, of course, Bruton Church in Williamsburg, where the Governor, as representative of the English King, occupied a throne-like seat with a most elaborate canopy. The Governor had strong opinions in the matter of the Christian religion and as a Deist (i.e., one who does not accept the divinity of Christ) he could not properly be called a Christian. Benjamin Franklin,

Thomas Jefferson, Wythe himself, and many other colonials were accounted Deists.

It may be that Governor Fauquier's enjoyment of science made him the good companion of Wythe whose other great love (beside the law) was natural philosophy (what we today call physical science). Wythe loved science and worked at it, even when he was busy with his Burgesses committee work and his law practice. He wrote, for example, in the strenuous year of 1755, the following letter:

> ". . . an aeloldepyle [sic] a receiver and wood cup for shower of mercury to be had of—and Blunt Mr. Shermer will be so good as to procure for
> G. Wythe."[14]

This love of science and its practical application was known to the Burgesses, who often gave Wythe the task of overseeing matters of that nature. Such a one was the petition of

> ". . . Mr. Aaron Miller . . . setting forth that he had at great trouble and expense invented a new Compass and Protractor, by which an Angle may be measured both in surveying and plotting with greater Accuracy than any other instrument . . . and praying such a Bounty as the Legislature may think he deserves . . . Ordered, That the said petition be referred . . . Mr. R. Bland, Richard Henry Lee, Wythe, Cary, and Mr. Mercer . . . ."[15]

Fauquier was also interested in science, so much so that he kept a weather diary for the entire period of his governorship. The Royal Society published in its Philosophical Transactions a paper he had written on hailstones.

When Fauquier became Governor, George Wythe acted as his personal advisor on Virginian politics.[16] In the House of Burgesses, the young lawyer gave the Governor's views to the members and carried back to Fauquier their attitudes. He did not, however, act in any way to the detriment of the House. That is to say, he was not a spy. His liaison work was, of course, unofficial.

It may have been Wythe who introduced Dr. William Small to the Governor, as it surely was Wythe who brought Fauquier and Jefferson together. Jefferson in after days remembered with delight his friendship with Governor Fauquier and declared that the latter was ". . . the ablest man who had ever filled . . . the Governor's office." Time after time Jefferson and Small and Wythe dined with Fauquier at the Palace. This in itself gives us an indication of Fauquier's character, for he was a man at this time of some 56 years. Jefferson himself was some 17 years of age; Dr. William Small was perhaps about 45 and Wythe was 33. These certainly made an oddly assorted foursome. It is probably in some measure due to the fact that Fauquier was without his own family that he became so intimate with the young Jefferson. Had Fauquier had his family with him, his own son and namesake, Francis, would probably have had Jefferson's place in Fauquier's affections.

Jefferson phrased his remembrance of the foursome in the following way:

> "He [William Small] returned to Europe in 1762, having previously filled up the measure of his goodness by procuring for me from his most intimate friend, George Wythe, a

reception as a student of law under his direction, and introduced me to the acquaintance and familiar table of Governor Fauquier, the ablest man who had ever filled that office. With him and at his table, Dr. Small and Mr. Wythe, his *Amici omnium horarum,* and myself formed a *partie quarée,* and to the habitual conversations on these occasions, I owed much instruction. Mr. Wythe continued to be my friend through life. In 1767, he led me into the practice of law, at the bar of the General Court, at which I continued till the Revolution shut up the Courts of Justice."[17]

Throughout his student days in Williamsburg, Jefferson was admitted freely to the Palace. The Governor probably gave the young man much insight into his own philosophy but whether or not he was the cause of Jefferson's being a Deist, one cannot say. Nonetheless, Deism was in the air, and must often have been in the conversation of the foursome. Fauquier, the oldest of the four friends, failed to influence Jefferson in other ways too. For the Governor was a gambler, and an enthusiastic one. Jefferson never was. Jefferson likewise all through his life was very abstemious in the matter of food and drink. And the Governor was a man who loved rich food and enjoyed good wine.

It is probable that Jefferson's asceticism in the matter of food and drink came to him more from Wythe, who was a notorious ascetic—especially in later life—than from the Governor. (Both Wythe and Jefferson lived to a great old age.) We know that Wythe, at least later on in his life, abstained entirely from flesh food—a remarkable thing in the Virginia of his day. And Jefferson was almost entirely a vegetarian. In their relationship, it was perhaps not so much Wythe's influencing Jefferson, as it was the fact that they already had minds which were complimentary. "To the mating of true minds let no impediment impair." So said Shakespeare. And none impaired the interaction of these two in the similarity of their characters. Both of them were most abstemious, both hard workers, both lovers of detail, both anxious to produce only the best. It was Jefferson's boast, as it was Wythe's pride, that the end of a long life had never seen the sunrise catch him in bed in fifty years. Wythe too greeted the sunrise each day of his whole life long. In a day of hard drinking, both were notable for their abstinence. And, in reality, although both possessed the normal amount of sociability, both were solitaries. They were not gregarious, although they were companionable.

Two favorite pastimes all four friends truly enjoyed—the first was good conversation and the second was music. Jefferson all through his life loved music with a deep and abiding passion—and Fauquier likewise delighted in it, as did Wythe. Every week a concert was staged in the Governor's drawing room. So much in love with music was Jefferson that he signed an agreement with John Randolph that if the latter survived Jefferson, he was to receive £100 worth of books from the Jefferson's library. (Even in that day, Jefferson had begun his collecting of books. Like Wythe, he loved books with a passion.) If Jefferson, however, outlived Randolph, the former was to receive Randolph's violin and all the music composed for it. George Wythe and Patrick Henry were, on 11 April 1771, witnesses to this compact.

Of the four members of this colonial diner's club, we know the least of William Small. He was Mathematics Professor at the College, and this was itself a connection between Small and Wythe, for the latter all his life delighted in mathematics. We do know that Small was on some occasions George Washington's physician, prescribing for him in 1761. At the College, he also taught Moral Philosophy, Literature and Rhetoric. It is probable that he gave some courses also in what we would call applied science. Exactly what part of Jefferson's formal education Small contributed we do not know. In 1762, however, he and the College authorities became unfriendly and Small returned to England to the city of Birmingham. But even in England, the friendship continued. Jefferson and Wythe continued to remember their English friend.

The coming decade was a busy and tumultuous one for Wythe with many calls being made on his time. Although he was a Deist, he was nonetheless made a Vestryman and Churchwarden of Bruton Parish Church in Williamsburg in 1760.

> "Even Mr. Jefferson, and Wythe, who did not conceal their disbelief of Christianity, took their parts in the duties of vestrymen, the one in Williamsburgh, the other in Albemarle; for they wished to be men of influence." [18]

There were twelve vestrymen altogether, among them being John Blair, Ben Waller, Robert Carter Nicholas (a true believer) and Thomas Everard. While the various duties were primarily religious, they were not exclusively so. The Vestry was really a governmental body, and in the lack of newspapers, it filled a great need in Virginia. For it made known to the people by public pronouncements all the new laws and regulations of the government, dealing with slaves and servants; publishing notices concerning runaways and the breaking of entails, etc. There are even cases on record where the Vestry set up schools, authorized ferries, and ordered roads to be built. Indeed, the county and the vestry were the two units of the Virginian government that were the closest to the people, who were very much concerned in all that both did. Membership in the vestries was, by the middle of the 18th Century, almost hereditary, the aristocracy pre-empting the positions thereon. Since the vestry had power, naturally the nobility, even if not believers, wished to be as Meade declares ". . . men of influence." In all the many and varied duties of the vestry of Bruton, Wythe had a part. He had, of course, much to do with Commissary Dawson since the latter was rector of the Church. As Dawson was likewise President of the College, Wythe had even more to do with him since now Wythe was appointed a Visitor of William and Mary.

It has been stated that Wythe served on more committees of the House than any other of the Burgesses.[19] And when one examines the Journals of the House, one can see how true this is. All during the 1760's, Wythe's duties in the House increased rather than diminished, and this at a time when in his personal life he took on many added duties. Besides serving as a Visitor of the College, and Vestryman of Bruton Church, and Judge in Elizabeth City County, and in addition to his own law practice and running his plantation, he continued his service in the House as William and Mary's representative.

The sending by the Burgesses of Peyton Randolph to England in the Pistole Fee quarrel was the forerunner of the actual appointing of a permanent agent in England. A certain Montague was chosen and now the House had to set up a committee to correspond with him, to give him information which he could use in his lobbying on Virginia's behalf in the House of Commons and in the Royal Government of England. To this committee Wythe was appointed, together with others of the foremost politicians of the day. The Committee of Correspondence first met on 2 May 1759. Present were William Nelson as chairman, Thomas Nelson, Philip Grymes, Peter Randolph, John Robinson (the Speaker himself), Peyton Randolph, Robert Carter Nicholas, and George Wythe. The men chosen for this work had to fulfill certain qualifications.

First of all, there was a matter of residence. Living in Williamsburg was, as always, important since a resident of the Capital area was usually available. Secondly, they had to be men of broad education. They had to know England's rights and even more important, Virginia's rights. They must understand trade and economics, British and Virginian politics, and be forthright yet diplomatic. They had to be articulate, since the letters to the Agent must be written with care that Virginia should not be put in a bad light. Above all, they must be loyal to Virginia. It was no accident that Wythe was included.

Of this committee, all were notable men. They were above all *leaders*. When finally constituted, there were six Burgesses and six Councilors, so the united voice of Virginia's legislature was speaking to the English government. Of the Councilors, two had been acting Governors and three had been President of the Council. Of the Burgesses, Robinson had been both Speaker and Treasurer for twenty-eight years; one Burgess was to be Treasurer, another would be Attorney General and later President of Virginia's revolutionary Convention and, later yet, President of the Second Continental Congress. Three would be members of the Revolutionary Convention and two others would likewise be members of the Continental Congress and one was to be a Signer of the Declaration of Independence (Wythe). These men had given and would continue to give long years of service to their native country of Virginia.

The committee meetings were held at the Capitol in Williamsburg, where the members conferred on the writing of a letter to William Montague. There were several items which were called to his attention. He was to ". . . use his endeavours to get the King's assent 'to an Act for Settling the Titles and Bounds of Lands and for Preventing Unlawful Hunting and Ranging." In addition, he was to use his most strenuous endeavours to prevent any additional duty on Tobacco. The British Government had granted to Virginia as a war measure some £20,000 and Montague was to get the vouchers thereto. It is interesting to note—and this is part of the whole question of taxation by Britain of the colonies, that at least as a war measure, a good deal of money did flow the other way; that is, from England to Virginia. This same Committee met again on 7

November 1759 since apparently the aforesaid letter had not yet been sent 'home.' A sub-committee of five was set up to prepare the second letter. Certainly this was moving at a most leisurely pace indeed. One week later, 14 November, the Committee again met and the reason for the delay was now obvious. For the Reverend John Camm had begun his lawsuit in the General Court to recover the salary he believed due him in the Parson's Cause. The committee had to decide what should be done if Camm were to appeal from the General Court's decision, should that go against him. Who would bear the expenses of fighting the case in England? Camm's home parish vestry which was defending itself in this suit would soon find the costs beyond its ability to pay, and so the Committee decided to refer the matter to the House. The Committee sat again 17 November, and again on the 18th, but it was not until the next day, 20 November, that the letter was completed. Montague in this final version of the letter was informed that he was officially appointed as agent with the annual salary of £500. Not bad! He was to try to get the British government to fulfill its promise to repay the colony, as Pitt, the Prime Minister, in his letters of 1758 had promised for Virginia's war expenditures. The agent was told to support Virginia's cause in the matter of ". . . all executions for sterling money levied at 25%" against the British merchants. Much was said justifying this levy. Camm's lawsuit is mentioned, and the agent was told that he should uphold the colony's cause in this matter from imputations of "Arbytrayness and Disloyalty." The agent was further told to ". . . secure proper persons to defend the vestrys against any proceedings that may be carried to England, in a suit that is just brought by one Mr. Camm. . . ."[20] The Committee sent, as always, three copies of each letter it composed to England by different ships. If two ships were captured by the French, surely one would get through.

The major preoccupation of the Burgesses from now on was the question of the debt and the means of paying it off. In the Spring session of the Burgesses, 6 March 1760, Charles Carter, "Mr. Attorney," Nicholas, Waller, Richard Henry Lee, Wythe and others were put on a Committee to find ways of raising £20,000 by which the Virginian regiment could be paid until the next April. On March 6 of the previous year Wythe and his fellows had already provided for raising the sum of £20,000. They had imposed a tax of one shilling and three pence on every hundred acres of land in the years 1767 and 1768 and two shillings on every titheable person in the colony in the year 1768 should be levied. It is interesting to note the ideas of finance of the time: the colonists raised taxes in the future at a definite time and for a definite period of time. Our own way to accomplish the same thing is to sell bonds.

Wythe in the following year, 1761, gave up his seat from William and Mary and for the first time the freeholders of his home county chose him as their Burgess, his colleague being William Wager. Wythe continued to serve on the regular committees (on which he was now higher in seniority than ever before)

—in fact, in this session Wythe alone served on more than three of the five standing committees, no other Burgess being placed on so many. In addition, he was likewise ordered, together with Richard Henry Lee, to be a committee of two to bring in a "Bill to enhance and more effectually to secure the credit or the Paper currency of this Colony." Another *ad hoc* committee on which he was put was that which should discover ways of recompensing the officers of the Virginia regiment for their bravery and the hardships they had undergone.

On 7 November 1761, William Wager was in trouble over his election. This time James Wallace accused Wager of having been wrongly elected. And the matter had to be fought out at once in the House. His old opponent, John Tabb, was on the committee which investigated the freeholders' right to vote, along with Cary Selden, Charles Jennings, George Wray, James Balfour and Jacob Wray. One point of testimony from the Journals of the House concerns

> ". . . the Reverend Thomas Warrington, Rector of the Parish of Elizabeth City in the said County . . . having been in full possession of his Glebe . . . about 100 acres, with competent Buildings thereon . . . offered to vote for Mr. Wythe and the Petitioner James Wallace but refusing (dubious of his right to vote) . . . to take the oath prescribed by Law . . . he was not allowed to vote at the said Election . . . ."[21]

Further testimony deduced that the Sheriff closed the poll too soon:

> ". . . John Lowry was not more than a Mile and a half distant from the Court House at the same Time; where he was stopped by a Messenger sent to inform him that the Poll was closed, when he expressed his Uneasiness that he should return without being of Service to his Friends, naming Mr. George Wythe and the Petitioner."

After all was said and done, Wager and the Petitioner had an equal number of votes, so Wager was declared elected!

All during the early part of the 1760's, Wythe and his companions were busy with letters to their English agent. One such letter was composed on 29 March 1763. In it they gave reasons for the new laws which they had passed, reasons which he could use in his endeavours to defend them before the English government. These laws concerned the election of Burgesses, the relief of insolvent debtors, a stray law, a law for regulating the coin of the German Empire (recall that all sorts of foreign money circulated in the colonies!). But it was in the matter of the printed money that the greatest difficulty was experienced by the Burgesses. Francis Fauquier had written a treatise on economics in the matter of taxing. Did he perhaps get his experience in this from the South Sea bubble? At any rate, he considered himself an expert on finance. There were three parties to the quarrel: The Virginians themselves, who wished to emit paper money; the English merchants who hated it, and Fauquier who opposed it in principle. The Governor had behind him not only his own economic principles, but also (more important) the British government, to which the merchants had appealed.

Fauquier called the House to meet on May 19, 1763, and gave the Burgesses a pretty good idea of where he stood in the matter. In fact, he was downright hostile. The Board of Trade and Plantations had told him that he must call the Virginia planters to order in this paper money, for the merchants wanted better security for the debts. These debts should be paid in sterling money which the merchants could use in England, and not in Virginian currency which they would have to discount at 25%.

But if Fauquier could be hostile, so could the Burgesses. We know that Fauquier had argued privately with various members—probably, indeed, with Wythe—for the Governor later admitted: "I think I brought but four gentlemen over to my opinion, to consider this matter in the light in which I consider it . . . ".[22] Certainly, despite their friendship, Wythe was not one of these four, since he, together with Charles Carter and Edmund Pendleton, was deputed to answer the Governor with a formal address. Conciliatory in nature, it was a reasoned argument for the Colonists' position. One of its points will be of great interest to us in the future. Evidently some of the Governor's Council were concerned that the paper money which had matured was not being withdrawn from circulation—i.e. burned. Wythe, the Speaker-Treasurer himself, and the Randolphs had been, as we have seen, assigned the task of seeing to it that this was done. Therefore, it was particularly fitting that Wythe should be the one to reassure those worried about this.

Nor did the affair end there. For 16 June 1763, the Committee of Correspondence wrote a long letter to Montague defending the Virginians in the paper money quarrel. The English merchants were angry and had threatened the King's displeasure. Although Fauquier had been very outspoken, declaring that the law must be changed, the correspondents defended themselves ably. The country was, first of all, exhausted of specie.

> ". . . avaricious men, determined at all Events to enrich themselves by ye Misfortunes of their fellow Subjects to take ye most injurious & oppressive Advantage of their Debtors who had not ye power of procuring Specie to discharge their Debts . . . "

In answer to the charge that the King had lost money on the paper emission, they stated that

> ". . . ye Assembly may with Justice be exculpated as they have by all their Acts provided that Paper Money should be no legal Tender in Payment of Quit Rents."

Quit rents were taxes paid by the colonists to the King—the nearest modern equivalent would be land taxes on land held in fee simple. The Committee further declared that

> ". . . His Majesty's Requisition first introduced paper money into ye Colonies & had ye Objections been made to it then that now are, we would not only have escaped Censure, but saved a great part of ye Exchange we were loaded with during ye War."[23]

Thus Wythe and his fellows told off the British government. Almost one year later, the Committee had an even more serious matter on its hands. On 15 June,

1764, Blair, the two Nelsons, Robert Carter, Mr. Speaker, Mr. Attorney, Wythe, Nicholas and Burwell gather together to write again to Montague. What really alarmed them was the ". . . Attempt in parliament to lay a Duty . . . on Madeira Wine & the proposal for a Stamp Duty." Mr. Wythe and Mr. Nicholas were to prepare the formal wording of the letter. In it, Montague was told

> ". . . to oppose . . . with all his Influence . . . insist on the Injustice of laying any Duties on us & particularly taxing the internal Trade of the Colony without their consent."

Thus quietly began a struggle which would tear apart the British government and alienate the American colonists from the mother country.

Notes to Chapter II

1. Virginia (State). *The Statutes at Large, Being A Collection of All The Laws of Virginia from . . . 1619. . . .* William Hening, Compiler. (Richmond, Samuel Pleasants, 1809), Vol. 7, p. 13. (Hereafter cited as *Hening.*)
2. Stanislaus M. Hamilton, ed. *Letters to Washington, and Accompanying Papers.* (Boston, Houghton Mifflin, 1898–1902), vol. 1, p. 340.
3. *Ibidem,* p. 342.
4. *Ibidem,* p. 360.
5. *Hening.* Vol. 7, p. 77.
6. William and Mary—. First Series, Vol. 6, p. 11.
7. Burgesses. *Journals, 1758–61,* p. 114.
8. *Ibidem,* p. 97.
9. Virginia Gazette (Purdie & Dixon), 8 March 1770.
10. Lyon G. Tyler. *The College of William and Mary: Its History and Work, 1693–1907.* (Richmond, Whittet & Shepperson, 1907), p. 40.
11. William Wirt Henry. *Patrick Henry: Life, Correspondence and Speeches.* (New York, Chas. Scribner's Sons, 1891), Vol. 1, p. 22–3.
12. William and Mary—. First Series, Vol. 20, p. 172.
13. William S. Perry, ed. *Papers Relating to the History of the Church in Virginia, A.D., 1650–1776.* (Richmond, 1870) p. 493.
14. Manuscript Collection. Haverford College.
15. Burgesses. *Journals, 1761–65,* p. 283.
16. Douglas S. Freeman. *George Washington—.* (New York, Scribners, 1948), Vol. 3, p. 3–4.
17. Thomas Jefferson. *Memoir, Correspondence and Miscellanies from the Papers of—.* Edited by Thomas Jefferson Randolph. (Boston, Gray & Brown, 1830), Vol. 1, p. 2.
18. William Meade. *Old Churches, Ministers and Families of Virginia.* (Philadelphia, Lippincott, 1861), Vol. 1, p. 191.
19. Randolph Macon College. *John P. Branch Historical Papers.* (Richmond, 1901–18), Vol. 3, p. 289.
20. Virginia Magazine—. Vol. 9, p. 364; Vol. 10, p. 338.
21. Burgesses. *Journals, 1761–65,* p. 89.
22. *Ibidem.* p. xxxv.
23. Virginia Magazine—. Vol. 11, p. 345

CHAPTER III

Thomas Jefferson becomes His Pupil.

It is not often that a man has a chance to train a genius—which Jefferson was. Nor is it frequent that a student has a Wythe for a teacher.

It was in 1762 that Jefferson, having completed his studies at William and Mary, began a course in the study of law under Wythe—a course which lasted some five years. Jefferson was perhaps nineteen years old at this time and his mind must have been sufficiently plastic that Wythe was able to mould it to his own ideas. An instance of this influence is the egalitarianism which Wythe implanted in the young man's mind—a doctrine which extended even to such a thing as grammar. For the older man, becoming staunchingly democratic, regarded even the capitalization of nouns as aristocratic (the 18th Century people gave capitals to the first letters of all nouns, even when such words came in the middle of sentences). So far did Wythe push this that he even refused to use a capital for the first person singular. Thus his letters present a strange appearance, for whenever he refers to himself it is as "i." Jefferson, however, didn't follow him this far.

It was Wythe's belief that a man trained in the legal science should not know law only, but history and literature as well—indeed, he should likewise be as accomplished in the natural sciences as possible. No lesson plans or schedules prepared by Wythe for Jefferson have come down to us, so we have to use the next best thing to see what Wythe planned for his pupil. In the late 1760's, Jefferson set up a plan or regimen for a law student which may have been modeled on what he himself had followed under Wythe. The student was to rise early in the morning (Wythe himself rose from bed by the dawn's light all his life long. Even in his extreme old age he did so, giving himself a cold shower immediately upon rising.) After this, Jefferson prescribed that the student should read books dealing with Agriculture, Chemistry, Botany, Ethics, Natural Religion and Zoology. Jethro Tull and Arthur Young (the current authorities in England) were to be studied for Agriculture. Ethics could be gleaned from the writings of Locke, Stewart, Condorcet, Cicero and Seneca. Religion was the province of the Bible, Sterne's *Sermons,* and Priestley's *History of the Corruptions of Christianity.* (This, however, must have been a later addition. The *History* was not written until 1782.) Vattel was to be studied for Natural Law. After eight o'clock, the student was to peruse law. From noon until one o'clock Politics should be studied. John Locke, Sidney's *Discourses Concerning Government,* Hatsell's *Precedents of the House of Commons,* and the *Select Parliamentary Debates of the Parliaments of England and Ireland* were the works Jefferson cited for this. (Wythe wrote to England to his relative, John Norton, to secure these last for the House of Burgesses. Jefferson, naturally, had the use of them as Wythe's student.)

To a knowledge of Milton (Jefferson was already familiar with Shakespeare), he added Euripides—this apparently in the original Greek. For Wythe was now celebrated for his knowledge of both Greek and Latin, and his pupil was expert in these tongues too. (There were some ancient Greeks, however, that Jefferson never cared for—Plato and Aristotle.) He knew Vergil well, and was familiar with the work of Seneca, his *Maxims,* that is, and the *Letters* and *Orations* of Cicero. All this, of course, was splendid preparation for his eventual work not only in the court room but in the senate chamber.

Jefferson himself stated of Wythe's influence on him: "To his enlightened and affectionate guidance of my studies . . . I am indebted for everything." In Wythe's training of Jefferson, however, it is highly improbable that the young man was ever an apprentice of the older in the sense that Wythe had been an apprentice of Stephen Dewey. Certainly Jefferson had never to spend long onerous hours copying out dull legal documents in longhand. This is all the more probable since no record can be found of such an apprenticeship. This, again, is, of course, only the argument from absence, an argument notoriously untrustworthy. Again, we do not know why Jefferson went to Wythe for training rather than to his own relatives, Peyton or John Randolph, both of whom were excellent lawyers, Peyton being Attorney General. Whatever may be the reason, it was Wythe who, in the midst of his extremely busy life, gave Jefferson the sound legal training he ever after exhibited.

The young man studied hard at the law, not only because he was a perfectionist, and not only because he wished to please Wythe, but also because his beloved sister had just died and in seeking consolation he turned even more deeply to his books. We know that in later years he wrote to Dr. Thomas Cooper about his studies:

> ". . . When I was a student of the law . . . after getting through Coke, Littleton, whose matters cannot be abridged, I was in the habit of abridging and commonplacing what I read, merriting it and of sometimes fixing my own reflections on the subject . . . They were writ-

ten at a time of life when I was bold in the pursuit of knowledge, never fearing to follow truth and reason to whatever results they led and bearding every authority which stood in their way."[1]

If this is true, what a time Wythe must have had, for such a student can give an instructor a lively time. In this, however, Jefferson was merely mentioning that he had begun a "Commonplace Book," in which he jotted down his thoughts and ideas as they came to him from his reading and probably also as they were inspired by the words and teaching of Wythe. One who wishes to study the formation of the as yet immature mind of the young Jefferson could do no better than to turn to this Commonplace Book, for in it one will find the sources of this colonial law student's education.

In his actual readings under Wythe, we cannot place exactly the books that Jefferson read. But we do know that he studied the statutes of English law, the precedents of the common law, the famous Coke on Littleton, and the laws which had been enacted by the Burgesses of Virginia since 1619. Blackstone's *Commentaries* had not yet been published, the first volume appearing in 1765, with the last coming into print in 1769. They could not then have been used by Jefferson, being available to Virginian lawyers only in the coming decade. As far as Coke was concerned, we know that the student disliked that work extremely, saying—in a letter to John Page of December 1761: ". . . an old dull scoundrel." Nonetheless, when he came later to study Blackstone, he declared that he preferred by far Coke to the latter. It was Jefferson's opinion delivered many many years later on 17 February 1826, when he had but four months more to live, in a letter to James Madison that Blackstone would make even a good Whig 'slide into Toryism.' *Coke on Littleton* is in reality a melange extremely strange for any but the most serious student of the law, for it has within itself many old Latin expressions. Since these were medieval Latin, only a dedicated student such as Wythe could understand them.

We do know that Jefferson studied the following works (most of which concerned themselves not with law but rather with political science and philosophy): Harrington's *Oceana*, Sidney's *Discourses on Government*, Filmer's *Patriarcha*, Beccaria's *Crime and Punishment*. What an effect this last would have at the time of the Revolution, when Jefferson, Wythe and Pendleton collaborated to revise the entire corpus of Virginia's law!

In the first year of his law studies, his teacher had written out for Jefferson a course of study and reading to be followed at his home in Albemarle County. Returning there to the hilly country around Charlottesville for the winter of 1762–63, he worked in his extensive library at home. (Jefferson always possessed many books, as did Wythe. Indeed, they often exchanged books.) Jefferson apparently did not return to Williamsburg until the October of 1763 when the General Court was in session. Wythe at this time was deeply involved in the Justiceship of his home county of Elizabeth City. (For it will be recalled that it was in 1763 that the Warrington trial in the matter of the Two-Penny Act took place.) As a matter of fact, Jefferson usually spent his winters from this time on in Williamsburg, returning to his home in Albermarle County for the summers, releasing his mind from the drudgery of plodding through Bracton and King Alfred's Code and Anglo-Saxon law which had occupied his mind during the winter.

Patience had been require in these studies, for just as *Coke on Littleton* was difficult, so Bracton's Latin was medieval and obsolete. Only a trained and, indeed, a learned lawyer could understand it. But this Jefferson set out to be. Wythe had no patience with anything superficial—was, indeed, contemptuous of one who wished to skate lightly over the surface of learning. Wythe insisted that anyone coming under his training know both the civil and the common law deeply. Indeed, one could say—and this was true of Wythe especially in later life—that so determined was he to follow up the most obscure expressions and the most involved Greek and Latin references in the law and the most anti-quated Anglo-Saxonism therein that he became something of a pedant.

Very few men of that time and even fewer of our own can follow Wythe in some of his legal arguments, so involved, so filled with classical references, so complete with Anglo-Saxon precedents are they. Bracton, of course, was a con-temporary of the writers of the Magna Carta and if one would study him, then one likewise had to study medieval English history, medieval Latin, and the laws of England as they existed at that time, as well as the political theory which informed the medieval man. This in itself made for enormous erudition and it is not surprising that Jefferson himself became one of the foremost civil and common lawyers of his day. It would take at least five years for one to absorb all this knowledge.

Jefferson built up a strong distaste for the apprenticeship system. In later years he saw to it that would-be lawyers had an alternative system of training for their careers. For it was Jefferson who founded the law chair at William and Mary. Even though this formal system of training was now available, a young man who couldn't afford college training could still become an apprentice or a private student of an established lawyer, for the two systems of training contin-ued to exist side by side. Indeed, Jefferson took private students himself, viz., William Short and James Monroe. But when his own training was over, he reacted to the apprenticeship system strongly. Writing to Thomas Turpin on 5 February 1769, he declared:

> ". . . I was alwyas of opinion that the placing a youth to study with an attorney was rather a prejudice than a help. We are all too apt by shifting on them our business, to incroach on that time which should be devoted to their studies. The only help a youth wants is to be directed what books to read, and in which order to read them. . . ."[2]

When Jefferson began the practice of law, he was an immediate success, in his first year fighting some sixty-eight cases. In 1771, he had a total of some four hundred and thirty cases. This means that as a lawyer he was only less success-ful than Wythe himself and such others as Pendleton and Henry.

These two, however, had the edge on both Wythe and Jefferson for they were out-going expansive men, with a flair for oratory and an ability to move juries on a basis of emotion rather than reason. In no way could either be called intellectual, with the connotation, both good and bad, that the modern world reads into that word. However, intellectual was a word applicable to both Wythe and Jefferson. Naturally, they shunned the lurid criminal cases, working more along the quiet path of the civil law.

It was Wythe, again, who in 1767, introduced Jefferson to the practice before the Virginian General Court, the Supreme Court of the colony. This had its home in the Capitol, and the Judges were the Governor and the members of his Council. All had an equal vote, the Governor being no more than first. This was only natural for none of the Royal Governors were necessarily lawyers and even if they had been, they were Englishmen and thus unfamiliar with Virginian law. Even the members of the Council were often not lawyers, although they very well might have acquired a smattering of law through their earlier work on the County Courts.

In this same year of 1767, on the 9th of June, Jefferson had occasion to begin paying back to Wythe all the attention and devotion the older man had given the younger. For on that date, the young lawyer wrote a memorandum: "Gordon (a seafaring man) v. George Wythe (my friend). Defend him *totis viribus*. Take no fee." We have no idea of the circumstances of this suit. Evidently a sailor was suing Wythe, but what was the cause we do not know. We do not even know who won the suit. But of Jefferson's ardor to defend his former teacher there can be no doubt. The simplicity of the note itself tells of the heartfelt willingness of Jefferson to repay *"totis viribus"*—with all my powers—"George Wythe (my friend."

Nor was it in the practice of law alone that Wythe seconded Jefferson. For it was probably due to Wythe's influence that Jefferson entered politics at this time. It certainly needed no urging, since Jefferson was, above all, one to whom politics was the beat of the heart, the breath of life. Peter Jefferson, the Burgess and planter in Albemarle, had left his son (who came of age in 1764) some 1900 acres of land. The son began his practice in 1767, as we have seen, and jumped to the forefront of the profession in his work. In modern money Jefferson probably earned about $3000 a year from his practice. His Albemarle plantation, so lovingly cared for, gave him perhaps a further $2000. Thus with an income of $5000, he was a young man very well off indeed. The House of Burgesses met only at stated times each year—intermittently but for periods of not long duration. Thus, as Wythe himself had done, it was not difficult for Jefferson to enter the House and to practice law at the same time. The young lawyer therefore stood for election to the House in December of 1768, with his erstwhile guardian Dr. Thomas Walker as his colleague from Albemarle. John Page, a college friend of his (and who was no older than he) had just been put—through family connections—on the Governor's Council and this desire to at least begin to match Page's new eminence may very well have added urgency to Jefferson's natural love of politics.

Through the vagaries of Virginian politics, Wythe, when his young friend entered the Burgesses, was himself no longer a member of the House. Indeed his sole elective office was now Mayor of Williamsburg. Wythe's own career during the period when he was training Jefferson had been a busy one, but also one of some ups and downs. His friend, Governor Fauquier, had, despite his willingness to go along with the colonists, opposed them firmly whenever his position as agent of the King called on him to do so. In no area was this matter more pertinent than in that of the Colonists' everlasting desire to trade with the enemy—even during time of war.

This illicit trading with the enemy at the very time that the British were fighting for the life of their empire was well known in Britain and stuck in the Britisher's throat like a gnat, to be remembered with relish in the coming fight over the Stamp Tax. To this, of course, was added the perennial argument over paper money. And over all, of course, was the crushing burden of debt, which the English government had built up in the course of fighting the war and which it felt had been incurred as much in defence of the Virginians as of the English themselves. Therefore, it was quite within the nature of things that they should feel strongly that the colonists should help pay the cost of the war.

The English Parliament had already enacted the Sugar Act and this the colonists felt was heavy enough in its exactions. If the Stamp Tax were added to this, the colonists were set to fight it. They just were not going to pay such great sums to England. All the things the colonists had to import were taxed: raw sugar, foreign refined sugar, molasses, textiles, indigo, coffee, wines, iron, hides, silk, potash, etc. Since the colonists imported almost all their manufactured goods and since these were already taxed in England, the Americans knew full well that they were paying England's debts already.

The Stamp Act itself—or the quarrel over it—is one of the most confusing incidents of colonial history. It has been fought over by historians even more perhaps than it was fought over by those who lived through it. The members of the Committee of Correspondence, George Wythe among them, reacted with great alarm to the first hint of taxing the colonists. Wythe had been deputed with two others to write the first protest letter to the agent. The Stamp Act itself was preceded by the Declaratory Act, by which the English Parliament flatly declared that it had a complete right to tax the colonies and declared also that Parliament indeed *would* impose the Stamp Tax. This was in March of 1764. The colonists placed their defence on the constitutional position that they indeed admitted the right of the English government to regulate the commerce of the Empire—by placing duties upon it if necessary. But they had no right to tax internally. The difference may be specious to us but it certainly was not to the colonists. The fight was taken up by all the Americans, not just the Virginians. Nothing, not even the previous French War, ever united the colonists as did this struggle against the British Parliament.

In their anxiety, the Committee—with the apparent approval of the Burgesses—wrote to Montague that:

> ". . . to prevent a precedent of being taxed in this unconstitutional manner, it is supposed the Legislature of this Country would rather agree to lay on themselves any reasonable Apportionment of the Sum intended to be raised in the Colonies . . . ."

So great was their concern that they desired him

> ". . . if possible to get this Matter postponed 'till the Committee can furnish him with the sentiments of the General Assembly . . . which is to meet the 30th of October next."[3]

The Committee knew full well the extent of the danger, for they tried to warn the Parliament through Montague against stirring up ". . . a Storm so very replete with the most dangerous Consequences." This letter was composed 28 July 1764 by Blair, the Nelsons, Robert Carter, "Mr. Attorney," Wythe, Nicholas and Digges.

When the House finally met on October 30, autumn lay upon the land, the heat of summer being somewhat sated. The absence of this, however, was supplied by the heat of the Burgesses as they considered with indignation what was in store for them. The House set itself up as a Committee of the Whole to consider the affair and what should be done. On the 4th of November, the Committee of the Whole House resolved that a humble and dutiful Address be presented to his Majesty; that a Memorial be laid before the Lords, and that a further memorial be sent to the real seat of power, the House of Commons.

It should be noted that throughout the coming years in the interminable quarrelling with the English government, the colonists tried never to place themselves in the wrong as far as protestations of loyalty were concerned. They regarded themselves as Englishmen. Englishmen far away from "Home," but Englishmen nonetheless. And therefore loyal to the King. Never had an occasion of royal rejoicing gone by without a loyal address from the Burgesses—in fact, in 1762, when a royal child was born (the future George IV) George Wythe with others had been given the task of framing an address of congratulations. To George III, the colonists professed complete and loyal love. They were aware, of course, of the politician they faced. In his attempts to control the House of Commons, George III made English politics quite as venal and filled with bribery and corruption as any English king before him. But this did not cause revulsion on the colonists' part. They played the same game of politics, of interest and family connection, of political rewards and intrigue in their own country of Virginia. Even when the Revolution itself came on, the colonists fought the King—and protested their undying loyalty to him at the same time. Nor was this entirely hypocrisy—many Americans sincerely loved the British connection. (There were, of course, a good many who did not.) It was at this time that Richard Bland wrote a pamphlet, printed in Williamsburg, declaring that the only connection Virginia had with the British Empire lay through the Crown. Out of this struggle therefore came a sort of declaration of independence from the British parliament. Parliament, went this theory, had no more right to make laws for the Virginians than it had to do so for the German Hanoverians, whose King George III was likewise.

Oddly, this independence from Parliament implied a dependence on the King. For the extremists (and George Wythe was one) insisted with Bland that only the King connected Virginia and England. Indeed, said they, the two countries were two separate crowns with the same king—George Guelph. But all this lay as yet in the future. Jefferson later on declared that he could find only Wythe who held this theory with him. However popular the idea may have later become, it was not held by many during this crisis.

In their resolutions as to the Memorials to be sent to England, the Burgesses referred the writing of these to a Committee composed of Attorney Randolph, Richard Henry Lee, Landon Carter, George Wythe, Pendleton, Harrison, Cary and Fleming. These were all redoubtable men, who would place Virginia's cause firmly before the English, speaking out boldly and bravely but also temperately. They were ordered to tell the British Government ". . . with decent Freedom" about the

". . . Rights and Liberties of the People of this Colony as British Subjects; to remonstrate that laws for their internal Government, or Taxation ought not to be imposed by any Power but what is delegated to their Representatives, chosen by themselves . . . ."

The Virginians knew their power and hinted at it. Britain lived by trade, and if pushed to it, the Americans would attack with vigor this Achilles heel:

". . . the People are already taxed . . . so heavily . . . that an increase . . . would . . . divert . . . the Inhabitants . . . to manufacture what Articles they have hitherto been supplied with from the Mother Country and consequently one grand source of her wealth . . . will be stopped up."[4]

The various addresses of the House *ad hoc* committee were written and from the 6th of December to the 13th, the Burgesses were every day arguing over the wording. Wythe prepared the Address to the Commons but the House felt that it violated their injunction about "decent freedom . . ." so passionate must it have been.

In fact, Wythe's fellow Burgesses refused to condone his first draft since it had, to their eyes, "the aspect of Treason." They therefore smoothed its features to its present form. Jefferson himself is the authority for the statement that Wythe prepared this address to the Commons.[5] And certainly he ought to have known, even though he stated this as fact only in 1814, many years later. He was Wythe's student at the time of the Stamp Act crisis and the event would have bitten deep into his memory—few events of his youth could have been as vivid to him as the excitement of those days. Surely in so important a matter,

Jefferson must have talked it over with Wythe, discussing the affair at great length. Describing the matter, the student declared that his teacher wrote

". . . with so much freedom, that, as he has told me himself, his colleagues . . . shrank from it as wearing the aspect of treason and smoothed its features to its present form."[6]

But Wythe and his fellows might have saved their time and energy. For their addresses and memorials were not even read by the high and mighty Parliament. The Stamp Act was pushed through with little debate and less opposition.

From now on, all kinds of documents in use in America would be taxed. There were a total of 55 resolutions to this effect, and they decreed that not a college diploma, marriage license, a land deed,—in short, not a single legal document—was to be legal without paying a fee to the English government. The unanimity of the opposition can be understood when one realizes that this legislation hit not a special class, but all the people, since presumably almost everybody marries, owns land, etc. Likewise, in dealing with legal documents, it hit the lawyers who were both literate and articulate. These people could shout and they knew the ins-and-outs of the law. If the English parliament had deliberately tried to outrage the colonists, it could not have tried a better means or stirred up a more formidable set of antagonists.

Despite this, however much the colonists disliked it, when the law was passed it is probable that it would have been obeyed. After all, the Virginian leaders had done all they could do legally. Having lost, they would not resort to unconstitutional means to disobey the law. It was too bad the effort had failed, but failed it had. How could Virginia or any of the colonies stand against the might of Britain?

When the Parliament in the Home Country had passed the Act, it was specified that it should not take effect until November 1765. Thus almost a whole year was assigned the colonists as a cooling-off period. The Assembly, in the year 1765, had met in the Spring and Governor Fauquier, knowing the temper of the Burgesses, had quietly kept the news of the Act's passage to himself. The end of May was nearing and on the 31st the House would dissolve. It seemed better to Fauquier to let the members go quietly home. Dispersed over Virginia's wilderness, they could not thus excite themselves or stir each other up. If such was truly his plan, the jovial if cautious Governor had a surprise in store for himself.

For a long time now, the western people had been restive under the control of the ruling clique. The stage was set for the formation of a cabal against the group in power and now that cabal came into existence. The dissatisfied looked about for a leader and found Patrick Henry, the young lawyer who had made such a noise in the famous Parson's Cause. He had been a member of the Burgesses only about a month in that famous Spring session of 1765. The session was a somewhat dull one, with a large number of private acts being passed. The members were bored, anxious to return home. Most of them had already left—of the 116 members of the House, only 39 were in their seats when Henry rose in his place to present a set of resolutions on the Stamp Act. Tall, sloppy, dressed in crude homespun, the young man had heretofore excited little attention from the elegant tidewater Burgesses. What they did not know was that (as Paul Carrington wrote many years later) these resolutions had been prepared by the group backing Henry at the residence of Thomas Lewis, representative from Augusta. This group consisted of Henry himself and George Johnson, together with John Fleming of Cumberland and Robert Munford. It is possible that Richard Henry Lee was of this group, but we cannot be sure.

It is certain, however, that Lee later joined this cabal in his search for power. Yet he did not attend, apparently, this session of the House so it is probably true that he wasn't in on the framing of the resolutions. Henry in later years wrote that he himself had penned them.[7] But they follow in their wording whole passages of the resolutions offered by Wythe and the others in the addresses of the previous December which were sent to the English government. There were two differences, however. In addition to the resolutions of the earlier addresses, the group around Henry (or Henry himself) added two more. The timing was exactly right—or so the group thought. In three days, the House would rise. It had already approved the first resolutions in December. The group could force these through a second time and add the last two, giving themselves great prominence as the only ones refusing to accept English dominance tamely. These two final resolutions seem mild enough from our standpoint:

> "*Resolved,* That his Majesty's liege people of this most ancient colony have uninterruptedly enjoyed the right of being . . . governed by their own Assembly in the article of their taxes and internal police, and that the same hath never been forfeited or in any other way given up, but hath been constantly recognized by the King and people of Great Britain.
> *Resolved,* That therefore the General Assembly of this colony have the sole right and power to levy taxes and impositions upon the inhabitants of this colony; and that every attempt to vest such power in any other person or persons whatsoever, other than the General Assembly aforesaid, has a manifest tendency to destroy British as well as American freedom."[8]

Really, what Henry was saying had been said before, and by Robinson, Pendleton, the Randolphs and Wythe. But now the Stamp Act was officially law. And if Burgesses passed these resolutions now, it could very well be interpreted as rebellion—or at least as defiance of Britain. The ruling clique knew of other and better ways to force Britain to its knees. Open defiance by the little Virginian parliament simply could not succeed. In support of his resolutions, Henry uttered his vivid, flaming words which have echoed through the centuries to our own day and even now force one's admiration with their eloquence:

> ". . . Caesar had his Brutus, Charles Ist his Cromwell, and George the 3d . . ."
> "Treason! Treason!"
> "—may he profit by their example."

Thus he saved himself. It has been said that Wythe was one of those who called out Treason! Treason! when Henry spoke the foregoing.[9] And it probably was so, although in effect, Wythe would have been crying Treason against his own resolutions. And recall that these resolutions as offered by Henry were the Wythe resolutions of the previous December but watered down by the House, as Jefferson states. So Wythe's original resolutions must have been even more radical than Henry's. Wythe's opposition to these resolves was not therefore to their wording but rather to Henry's timing—what was before a mere protest, however strong, was now incitement to rebellion. In addition, Henry's action would result in breaking the power of the clique of which Wythe was a part.

Even with his fervid oratory and with the House reduced to a mere 39 present, Henry's resolutions barely got through. Indeed, the last passed by only a single vote.

It must be stated, however, that the story of this action is a confused one. It could not have come so completely as a surprise to the House as one might suppose, for the House had considered the resolutions behind closed doors the previous day. The day on which Henry made his eloquent and stormy defense was when they were put before the House for open debate. Nor was Henry the only one who spoke on the matter—George Johnson spoke strongly in their favor also.

There were 39 Burgesses who heard the Henry speech. None of the 39, as far as we know, wrote any account of it. But there were two spectators who were not only present but wrote down what they saw and heard. One was Wythe's student, Thomas Jefferson, who had left his law books to visit the House and watch the excitement. His account follows:

"Mr. Henry moved and Mr. Johnston seconded these resolutions successively. They were opposed by Messrs. Randolph, Bland, Pendleton, Wythe, and all the old members, whose influence in the House had, till then, been unbroken. They did it not from any question of our rights, but on the ground that the same sentiments had been, at their preceding session, expressed in a more conciliatory form, to which the answers were not yet received. But torrents of sublime eloquence from Henry, backed by the solid reasoning of Johnston, prevailed. The last . . . and strongest resolution was carried by a single vote. The debate on it was most bloody. I was then but a student and stood at the door . . . between the House and the lobby (for as yet there was no gallery) during the whole debate and vote; and I well remember that, after the members on the division were told and declared from the chair, Peyton Randolph (the Attorney-General) came out . . . where I was standing, and said, . . . "By God, I would have given 500 guineas for a single vote."; for one would have divided the House, and Robinson, was in the chair, who he knew should have negatived the resolution. Mr. Henry left town that evening, and the next morning, before the meeting of the House, Colonel Peter Randolph, then of the Council, came to the Hall of Burgesses, and sat at the clerk's table till the House-bell rang, thumbing over the . . . journals, to find a precedent for expunging a vote of the House, which, he said, had taken place while he was a member . . . . I stood by him . . . a considerable part of the time, looking on, as he turned over the pages, but I do not recollect whether he found the erasure. In the meantime, some of the timid members, who had voted for the resolution, had become alarmed; and as soon as the House met, a motion was made and carried to expunge it from the Journal. There being at that day but one printer, and he entirely under the control of the Governor, I do not know that the resolution ever appeared in print. I write this from memory, but the impression made on me . . . was such as to fix the facts indelibly in my mind. I suppose the original journal was among those destroyed by the British, or its obliterated face might be appealed to. And here I will state, that Burk's statement of Mr. Henry's consenting to withdraw two resolutions, by way of compromise with his opponents is entirely erroneous."[10]

In addition to Jefferson, there was also present at this time, as a spectator in the House, a French traveller. Jefferson wrote his account in later years, but the account of the Frenchman was written when the matter it described happened, that is, in 1765. It was not discovered, however, until 1921, having lain mouldering in French archives some 156 years. And it presents a far different Henry from that in the standard history books. This was a Henry who had perhaps imagined an easy victory with the almost-empty House. Carried away with his own eloquence, he was as taken aback by the cries of "Treason! Treason!" of the older members as they had been by his vehemence. In the words of the Frenchman:

"Shortly after I came in one of the members stood up and said he had read that in former times tarquin and Julus had their Brutus, Charles had his Cromwell, and he Did not Doubt but some good american would stand up, in favour of his Country, but (says he) in a more moderate manner, and was going to Continue, when the speaker of the house rose and Said, he, the last that stood up had spoken treason, and was sorey to see that not one of the members of the house was loyal enough to stop him, before he had gone so far, upon which the Same member stood up again (his name is henery) and said that if he had affronted the speaker, or the house, he was ready to ask pardon, and he would shew his loyalty to his majesty King. G. the third, at the Expence of the last Drop of his blood, but what he had said must be attributed to the Interest of his countrys Dying liberty which he had at heart, and the heat of passion might have lead him to have said something more than he intended, but, again, if he said anything wrong, he begged the speaker and the houses pardon. Some other members stood up and backed him, on which the afaire was droped."[11]

The group Henry headed had managed to push their resolutions through the Burgesses. They had prepared the two final ones which they decided not to offer. In part, they read

"That his Majesty's liege people . . . are not bound to yield obedience to any law . . . whatsoever, designed to impose any taxation upon them, other than the laws . . . of the General Assembly . . . ."[12]

This was defiance indeed!

Fauquier reported to the Board of Trade the passage of those resolutions which were presented:

"My Lords . . . On Wednesday the 29th of May, just at the end of the Session when most of the members had left the town, there being but 39 present out of 116 of which the House of Burgesses now consists, a motion was made to take into consideration the Stamp Act . . . I am informed the gentlemen had two more resolutions in their pocket, but finding the difficulty they had in carrying the 5th which was by a single voice, and knowing them to be more virulent and inflammatory; they did not produce them. The most strenuous opposers of this rash heat were the late Speaker, the King's Attorney and Mr. Wythe; but they were over-

powered by the young hot and giddy members. I have heard that very indecent language was
used by a Mr. Henry a young lawyer who had not been a month a member of the House;
who carried all the young Members with him; so that I hope I am authorized in saying there
is cause at least to doubt whether this would have been the sense of the Colony if more of
their Representatives had done their duty of attending to the end of the Session . . . ."[13]

Fauquier, who worked so well with his friend Wythe, with Robinson, with
the Randolphs, with Pendleton, and in general with the ruling clique, wanted to
help them keep their control. This was the reason he dissolved the House at this
time. New elections were necessary after each dissolution and Fauquier probably thought the radicals would be disowned by the people. If so, he was sadly in
error. For the people sent the same men back to the House—there were indeed
only four new members (George Washington was one).

Among those returned was George Wythe from his constituency of Elizabeth
City. He was not hurt by his opposition to Henry—Henry's strength lay not in
the tidewater but in the hills. In fact, Wythe now received more votes than any
other candidate—one hundred in all. Colonel Wilson Miles Cary and Captain
James Wallace were honored by the freeholders with 81 and 69 each. Wythe
himself, as a gesture of courtesy, voted for each of these men. (It will be recalled
that each freeholder could vote for two candidates.) In this election, Wythe's old
colleague, Wager—he of the ever-contested elections—received a grand total of
six votes.

Shortly after the dissolution of the House, the old Speaker-Treasurer, Robinson, died, and after him came the deluge. It is highly probable that Robinson's
death, with its subsequent scandal, broke the power of the old clique even more
than the work of the Henry-Lee cabal. The leadership of the colony now de-
volved directly on Peyton Randolph and his cohorts and they fought the Stamp
Act in their own way. The colonists had three principal weapons in their fight
against Britain. The parliamentary struggle having ended in failure, they began
an economic boycott. So effective was this to become that within a short time the
English traders themselves began to petition Parliament for the repeal of the
Act. A standing army would have been needed in America because the colonists
used all means in their power to enforce the boycott. Let a merchant be caught
selling English goods and he soon found himself riding around town on a pole,
lucky if he escaped a coat of tar and feathers. George III then decided upon
repeal. The British had found themselves in a peculiar position indeed. For the
Rockingham ministry began to work in July to repeal a law which was not to go
into effect until the following November. It was not actually repealed until 18
March 1766.

Besides the boycott, the second means of fighting the British was to close the
courts. Since legal documents needed the stamps to be legal, and since nobody
dared brave the fury of the mob by buying stamps, it is obvious that the law
courts could not be open. Even the British government finally discovered what a
nest of hornets it had disturbed, and proded by the merchants and goaded by

disobedience in America, it repealed the Stamp Act. The news arrived in May, 1766, and there was a feeling of joyous relief on both sides of the ocean.

To show their gratitude to the British for having done what they had forced them to do, the Burgesses decided to erect a monument to the British politicians. This was not sarcasm, for the Burgesses were truly grateful to those—surely, Pitt first of all—who had rescued them as well as the mother country from an ugly situation. On 4 December 1766, the House set up a committee

> ". . . to prepare Inscriptions for the Obelisk intended to be raised to express the Gratitude of this Colony to the several noble and Worthy Patriots who distinguished themselves, in both Houses of the Parliament of Great Britain in procuring the Repeal of the Stamp Act; . . ."[14]

The committee was an oddly assorted one, for acting with Landon Carter, Bland and Wythe were Munford, Henry (!) and Richard Henry Lee, along with Fielding Lewis, among others. The insurgents had shown their power and were, to some extent at least, being invited in.

By this time John Robinson had died and the great question was—who would get the power he had thus vacated? There was no question but that the chief man in the government would be Peyton Randolph. But who then would get second place? For when "Mr. Attorney" moved to the Speaker's chair, someone must get the Attorney General's place.

If Francis Fauquier had had his way, the second man in the Virginian government would have been his dear friend and dining companion, George Wythe. Fauquier pushed as hard as he dared (without seeming to interfer too openly in Virginian internal affairs) to get the position for his friend. About six weeks after Robinson's death the question was still undecided and Wythe tried to put leverage into his office-seeking by writing to Benjamin Franklin. One could not say that Franklin was a good friend—but he was an acquaintance and probably had been ever since the good Benjamin had journeyed some ten years before to Williamsburg to receive his honorary degree from William and Mary. Franklin himself was supremely the politican and he could build up political credit for himself in Virginia by interceding with the British government on Wythe's behalf. Franklin was then in London and one could never tell, maybe some day he would need a friend in Virginia. Wythe thus penned the following letter, redolent with scholarship and insight into human nature:

> "If our attorney ge [neral, Mr. Randolph, should be elected Speaker] of the house of burgesses, and thereby leave vacant the Attorney General's office as in all probability will be the case, the governor wants me to succeed him; and that recommendation, will be more effectual, were some of those great per [sons t] o whom it must be addressed, to know that such a promotion would be in any degree pleasing to doctor Franklin. If you incline to honour me with your patronage in this competition, you will perhaps be partly instrumental in procuring that rare phaenomenon a contented mind, at least in the article of fortune; and you shall find an exception to that observation of Tacitus; *"Beneficia eo usque lacta sunt, dum videntur exsolvi posse: ubi multum antevenere, pro gratia odium redditur."* Favors are

pleasant only to the extent to which they can be repaid; but when they have exceeded that, hatred is returned instead of gratitude."[15]

Wythe thus delicately translated the Latin, since he knew his Franklin—the latter was no Latinist. The connection between Wythe and Franklin was not close, it is true. But the two did have a mutual friend—William Hunter. Like Franklin, Hunter was a printer—indeed he printed the Williamsburg Gazette, a task he had begun on 3 January 1750. He was Colonel John Hunter's brother, Colonel John being a successful merchant and a very close friend indeed of Governor Dinwiddie. William was made (undoubtedly through the intercession of his powerful friends) Deputy Post Master General. Franklin, of course, was himself the head of the postal system in the colonies. William therefore was his assistant, an office he secured in 1753 and held for his lifetime. His tenure was not, however, long, for he died in 1763. He also printed the laws and the money of Virginia. In his will, Hunter provided that £100 was to be spent to purchase mourning rings

". . . to be presented as a token of . . . friendship to John Hunter, Esq., Mrs. Emelia Hunter, Benjamin Franklin, George Wythe, Nathaniel Walthoe, Robert Carter Nicholas, William Small, Benjamin Waller, Thomas Everard, and James Tarpley."[16]

Wythe in his letter to America's Postmaster General had gently and subtly nudged the arm of the celebrated Franklin. Fauquier was more blunt:

Williamsburg May 11, 1766
"My Lords: It is with great concern I am to inform your Lordships that His Majesty's Service has received a shock from the death of our late worthy Speaker. This event would have been a sensible loss at any time, but more particularly so now, as I had promised myself great assistance from him in the next Session of Assembly, to quiet the minds of the people and bring them to a just and proper sense of their duty. He was a man of integrity . . .

I have heard of two candidates for his offices, viz., His Majesty's Attorney General Mr. Randolph, and Mr. Lee. The first is . . . the best qualified . . .

. . . in the place of Attorney General I intend to nominate Mr. George Wythe to succeed Mr. Randolph *till his Majesty shall be pleased to appoint another.*[17] This gentleman has also exerted himself in support of Government particularly so in his opposition to the late hot and virulent resolutions which brought on the dissolution. . . . I cannot deny this truth, that I have conceived a love and esteem for these gentlemen, but if I know my own heart, it was at first generated and has been since nourished by my observing their conduct both in public and private life, which has been uniformly void in guile and steady in support of Government."[18]

More than this Fauquier could not do. The struggle for power was sharp and decisive. The Burgesses elected their Speaker—the Governor could not appoint him. And they choose whom they wished—that is, they elected the one with the most power. Even Robert Carter, whose lawyer Wythe was, had written to the London merchant firm of Hunt & Sons, on 20 November 1766, asking them to use their influence:

"The burgesses believe that the salary which they have annexed to the chair will now induce the speaker to vacate the office of king's attorney. The salary was £500. And if he should I hope you will assist to have my townsman Mr. George Wythe appointed to it. He is a member of the house . . . , a zealous advocate of government, a prevailing speaker, an able lawyer and a worthy man."[19]

Nothing, however, availed. The power of the Randolph family was too great. Peyton Randolph stepped into the Speakership. His brother John, who had been Clerk of the House, became Attorney-General. And for Wythe, as a sort of consolation prize, the vacant clerkship was left open. Strangely, he took it. This meant vacating his seat in the House, and this put him firmly out of political life. For as Clerk, he was now on the sidelines as a mere spectator. A more ambitous man would have rejected the job out of hand, but Wythe accepted it. Fauquier's letter is so worded, however, that Wythe had probably been the Attorney-General for a short time in the interval between Robinson's death and the receipt of orders from England giving the position to John Randolph. But of this there is no sure knowledge.

Before Wythe gave up his seat, however, some time went by. And the House teemed with excitement over the revelation—impossible to be hidden—of the great Robinson defalcation.

For years now, the planters of Virginia had been living beyond their means. Even the wealthiest had gone in debt to British merchants, buying the luxuries they loved: Fine furniture, wines, silks, even blooded horses—had been imported from England. To pay for these there was the soil of Virginia producing the wealth-bringing tobacco and to produce the tobacco, there were the slaves who toiled that the nobility might live in ease. But not all the toil of the down-trodden slaves could pay for the luxuries of their owners, especially when these were bought on credit. This credit had to be paid for at the rate of 25%—and even more. To this was added the exchange on paper money. And added to this were the high shipping charges. Small wonder, then, that the planters were ever more deeply in debt to the English merchants. This situation continued right through the Revolution and even after, when the South ultimately exchanged England for the North as its source of credit and manufactured articles. Right down to the Civil War, the planters of the South lived on borrowed money.

It is in this situation that is to be discovered the secret of Robinson's power, for it will be recalled that the Speaker was likewise the Treasurer. And as such he had control of the disposal of Virginia's paper currency. As far back as 1763, the Council had complained that the paper money was still in circulation after it was supposed to have been destroyed. The reason for this continued use—since the money was to have been burned—now became evident. Robinson had been giving it to his friends. They, perennially in debt, had applied to him for loans and he had bestowed the country's currency on them as largesse. This was done secretly, of course, for he had no right to loan the country's paper currency to anybody.

Wythe's part in all this certainly does him little credit, for he had been perennially on the committee to supervise the destruction of the currency. So serious was the fault of the ruling clique that Edmund Randolph could offer only the lamest of excuses:

> "The only apology, which can be framed for the supineness of the legislature in not more frequently and more minutely examining the treasury, is founded in human nature."[20]

The defalcation, when fully uncovered, amounted in present-day money to almost a million dollars—surely a sum so great could not be hidden from sight. Even a casual investigation conducted with ever so mild a questioning would have brought in evidence of Robinson's fraud. Wythe, together with Bland, Carter, Richard Henry Lee, Archibald Cary, Fleming, Patrick Henry, Blair, Carrington, Tabb, and Francis Lee, was one of the group ordered by the House to investigate after Robinson's death. Almost without exception, the foremost families in Virginia were found to be in debt to the Robinson estate. Again and again, they had applied to the Speaker-Treasurer and again and again, he had given them money which should have been burned.

To a very great measure, this affair can explain the subsequent unpopularity of Richard Henry Lee, an unpopularity which followed him all through his political life. The first families of Virginia never forgave one who by his investigation might have even earlier uncovered a defalcation which could have been their ruin. Years later, John Adams noticed the distaste with which the Virginian delegates in the Second Continental Congress treated Lee, and questioned Wythe about it.

> "Jealousies and divisions appeared among the Delegates of no State more remarkably than among those of Virginia. Mr. Wythe told me, that Thomas Lee, the elder brother of Richard Henry, was the delight of the Eyes of Virginia and far the most popular Man they had. But Richard Henry was not. I asked the reason, for Mr. Lee appeared a schollar, a Gentleman, a Man of uncommon Eloquence, and an agreeable Man. Mr. Wythe said this was all true but Mr. Lee had when he was very young and when he first came into the House of Burgesses moved and urged . . . an Inquiry into the state of the Treasury which was found deficient in a large Sum, which had been lent by the Treasurer to many of the most influential Families of the Country, who found themselves exposed and had never forgiven Mr. Lee. This he said made him so many enemies, that he never had recovered his Reputation, but was still heartily hated by great Numbers. . . ."[21]

When the defalcation was finally uncovered, it was found that there was hardly a prominent name in the country which was not involved. To their everlasting credit, the names of George Wythe, Peyton Randolph, and George Washington can not be cited as debtors to the Robinson estate. These, at least, had no part in the scandal.

The excitement over this matter will be seen in better perspective when we note that news of the repeal of the Stamp Act had come to Virginia only a week before Robinson's death and there was plenty of excitement over *that*. By the end of the month, the defalcation was apparent. The satisfaction over the repeal was tempered by the scandal and the fear of ruin. There was very good reason, therefore, for Fauquier to write, as he did a year later, to the Earl of Shelburne

". . . the . . . cool old members . . . will, I am in great hopes, regain that lead in the House which they formerly had, but at present it is lost."

The old leadership was discredited, and the new group, led by Henry, Richard Henry Lee, Johnson, and their cohorts was bent on taking over.

In November, 1766, Lewis Burwell, Wythe, John Blair the younger, John Randolph and Benjamin Waller were appointed a committee which was set up to examine in June and December of each year the state of the Treasury. They were taking no chances, for they ordered that the money burned was to be published in the Virginia Gazette. The treasurer now was the honest and devout Churchman, Robert Carter Nicholas. For the two offices, as Dinwiddie some ten years before had wished, of Speaker and Treasurer were now separate. An old associate of Wythe, Nicholas and he had worked on many law suits together in their private practice. They would work together now—Wythe continuing on the committee, with many notices in the Gazette, all during the years when he was no longer in the Burgesses. Apparently his usefulness was such that the Burgesses did not care that he was no longer a member, as he was not after 31 March 1768.

Notes to Chapter III

1. 10 February 1814. *The Writings of Thomas Jefferson—*. Paul Leicester Ford, ed., (New York, G. P. Putnam's Sons, 1892), Vol. 1, p. 360 fn.
2. Thomas Jefferson. *Papers of—*. Boyd ed., Vol. 1, p. 23–4.
3. Burgesses. *Journals, 1761–65*. p. 257.
4. Virginia Magazine—. Vol. 9, p. 364 et sequor.
5. *Ibidem*, p. 368.
6. Thomas Jefferson. *Writings of—*. Lipscomb ed., Vol. XIV, p. 168.
7. In his *Manuscript History of Virginia*, Edmund Randolph asserts that Henry didn't write his resolutions at all. Rather, says Randolph, John Fleming wrote them (or copied them from the previous resolutions, which they follow mostly word for word. (Manuscript History—. p. 107).
8. Burgesses. *Journals, 1761–65*. p. lxv.
9. Claude G. Bowers. *The Young Jefferson, 1743–1789*. (Boston, Houghton Mifflin, 1949), p. 41.
10. Burgesses. *Journals, 1761–65*, p. lxv–lxvi.
11. American Historical Review. Vol. XXVI, p. 745.
12. Burgesses. *Journals, 1761–65*, p. lxvii.
13. *Ibidem*, p. lxviii.
14. Burgesses. *Journals, 1766–69*, p. 53.
15. Benjamin Franklin. Manuscript Collection, American Philosophical Society, Philadelphia. Brackets inclose presumed wording in places where the paper has disappeared.
16. William and Mary—. First Series, Vol. 7, p. 13.
17. Italics mine.
18. Burgesses. *Journals, 1766–69*, p. xiv.
19. Magazine of American History. Vol. XXX, p. 129.
20. Edmund Randolph. *Manuscript History—*. p. 110.
21. John Adams. *Autobiography*. Charles Francis Adams, ed., Vol. 3, p. 31.

CHAPTER IV

Clerk of the House of Burgesses

Among the incidents which completed the ruin of the now unhappy Robinson family and which brought the faction which Robinson had headed to an almost complete reversal of its fortunes in the House of Burgesses and in the political life of Virginia was a most sad one which reflects upon the pride and high temper of the great aristocrats of Virginia. The incident concerns the melancholy murder of Routledge by Colonel John Chiswell, a tale in which Wythe himself is implicated, if only obliquely.

This Chiswell had been for many years one of the most prominent men in the Colony. He had married into the great House of Randolph, taking the daughter of William Randolph of Turkey Island, Elizabeth by name, as his wife. And his children, the issue of this marriage, likewise married well. For example, Susanna found her husband in Robinson, the Speaker.

Sometime in 1766, probably shortly after the death of his son-in-law John Robinson, Chiswell, possessed as he was of a high temper, got himself into very serious trouble indeed. Although is no proof of this, it may very well be that the quarrel was over the son-in-law's defalcation. This is pure conjecture, however. The story is given by the Virginia Gazette of 12 September 1766 from the deposition of a certain John Wayles, taken before:

"The Honorable John Blair, William Byrd, and Presley Thornton, Esquires, three of the judges of the Honourable the General Court.

This deponent saith . . . That it was proved that Routlidge assaulted the said Chiswell, by throwing a glass of wine in Chiswell's face. That Chiswell returned a bowl of bumbo at Routlidge. That a chair was taken up by Routlidge to throw at Chiswell, and Chiswell took up the candlestick to throw at Routlidge. That many angry and insulting words were used by both persons. That Col. Chiswell ordered his servant to bring his sword . . . . That the sword was brought by the servant, and Chiswell held it naked in his hand. That the people attempted to disarm Chiswell . . . . That Routlidge was taken by Joseph Carrington, in order to be carried out of the Room . . . . That upon something Chiswell said (as calling him fellow) the deceased turned suddenly round, and then Chiswell dropped the point of his sword, and held it with an extended arm without advancing. That when Routlidge sunk in Carrington's arms, he said he believed the man was dead; yes, replied Chiswell, you may take him away, I have killed him. The reason of saying which was, Chiswell said he felt him on the point of his sword, which no other man could know."[1]

Routlidge apparently was wildly drunk when the altercation took place. Chiswell, on the other hand, was sober, controlled in his actions not by liquor but by his passionate anger. The awful scene took place in a tavern in New Kent County, whether in daylight or evening time is not known. The community took sides in this affair with a passion equal to that which inspired the murder.

After the killing of Routlidge, Chiswell was taken to jail in Williamsburg and there held for a time to await trial. He was, however, released on bail by three judges of the General Court. The circumstances of this are not clear and the Virginia Gazette was filled with letters to the editor arguing the propriety of allowing Chiswell bail "out of term time." However, given bail or no, before the trail could take place, tragedy piled itself on tragedy. Chiswell, unfortunate as well as high-tempered, killed himself in his home on Francis Street in Williamsburg. And thus brought his part of the business to an end. But the affair continued long after. For the arguments in the newspapers waxed more and more fierce. Many people, both lawyers and non-lawyers, wrote their opinions to the Gazette. Of all the opinions thus volunteered, certainly we must give especial attention to that which Wythe himself gave. He was, of course, high in the counsels of that group which had formerly ruled Virginia with a strong and forceful hand. Wythe's letter appeared on the 1st of August 1766 and he coolly placed his matter on a legal basis and argued the point without using ridicule or emotion. From the context of the latter, it would appear that Wythe must have been applied to by the Judges for his opinion prior to the bailing-out, for he seems to be justifying his action in the matter.

"Gentlemen,

An opinion in a point of law on a late unhappy occasion having exposed the authors of it to censure, and the grounds of that opinion being required of us, I shall lay before the publick what governed me, and I suppose the Gentlemen with whom I concurred, in that affair, not that the question will probably be terminated by this method of discussing it, but lest a total silence may be thought to betray something we dare not openly avow, and add credit to calumnies which innocence alone is not a sufficient security against.

The Court of King's Bench in England have power to admit all offenders whatsoever to bail, even those accused of high treason and murder. . . . Several statutes were ordained to restrain the power of bailing, but they were confined to Sheriffs, Justices of Peace, and the Marshall of the King's Bench . . . . Since those statutes, the rule is, that so far as any persons are judges of any crime, so far they have power of bailing a person indicted before them of such crime; and this power . . . appears to have been exerted by single Justices of that Court. . . . The General Court are, equally with the King's Bench, judges of all high offences; . . . the powers of those Courts are the same within their respective jurisdictions;

and the example of that hath been always deemed warrant sufficient for any proceedings of this.

Our opinion thus founded was delivered without presuming to say whether it was proper to exercise the power in that particular instance, wherein it was not our province, and it would have been impertinently officious to interpose . . . I was indeed present at the bailment, and own it gave me pleasure to hear such a relation of the facts, which I knew no cause to discredit or suspect of partiality, as might comfort a family more distressed than perhaps their enemies wished them to be; a pleasure humane breasts cannot be strangers to the source of . . . .

Your very humble servant[1]
G. Wythe"

The legal merits of the admission to bail having been argued over and over again, the opponents of the Chiswell group satirized Wythe, Waller, Blair and the others who had supported the late Chiswell. In the Gazette of 8 January 1767, there appeared

"A SATIRE ON THE TIMES.
. . . Mankind would swear all language was forsworn———
That wisdom meant *mere folly,* folly *sense,*
High airs *observance,* meekness *insolence.*
Applauses *satire,* and invective *praise,*
Happy for blundering Ben would be such days;
Ben would be thought a sage, meant blockhead wise,
and fond of truth, were truth design'd by LIES
. . .

Respectful W– –e's evasion of a charge
Will be confession of the wrong, at large;
His – – – non-officious – – – counsels seem a snare
T'engage in measures strange H–, T–, B–.
. . .

Yet W– –e, I mean not to decrease your fame,
  Never shall my just satire brand a name,
  That glows with virtue; or if some defect,
Her nicer scrutiny, perchance inspect;
. . .

I love desert, and freely bow to thine:
Without a vice, with genius, science, stor'd,
You want but FORTITUDE to be ador'd;
Nor can cold CAUTION the defect supply,[3]
. . . ."

There was more, indeed much more. Thus the writer attempted to sting Wythe by imputing to him lack of courage and fortitude. Was Wythe angered by all this? We have no way of knowing, but we do know that he was not lacking in courage. The several events of his life to come will prove this amply.

Among the works undertaken by the public-spirited Wythe was to act at the end of the year of 1768 as Mayor of Williamsburg. He was elected 30 November, 1768, it being the Feast of St. Andrew, which was the day appointed by the Corporation of the City for the election of Mayor (it was in this year that his

friend Thomas Jefferson first entered the House of Burgesses). Williamsburg
had received a royal charter in the year 1722, and was incorporated as a munici-
pality with a mayor, recorder, aldermen and common council, these people
filling vacancies in their rank by themselves. It was, in other words, a self-
perpetuating political body. They had their meeting place in the Common Hall
on the Palace Green, and it is from this that they derived the name—the
Common Hall being synonymous for the government of the little city. The
various tasks with which they were entrusted were the regulating of fairs and
markets, supervising roads and buildings of the city, the establishing of a watch
(in 1722) which patrolled the streets from 10 o'clock at night until daylight,
crying the hours the while. They provided for a fire engine in case of fire, and so
forth. It was during Wythe's mayoralty that it was determined to build a
commodious brick courthouse in Williamsburg. A committee under Wythe was
set up and this was to supervise the letting of the contract for building. This had
been desired for several years, for in 1764 the Assembly had empowered the
Corporation to raise money by taxes to build it.

Both the City of Williamsburg and the County of James City shared the
expense and use of the building. In order that this might be, the Assembly of
Virginia changed the boundary between the two counties, York and James City,
which heretofore had been the Duke of Gloucester Street. A piece of York County, a small section of Market Square, was given to James City County that the
Courthouse might be built thereon. (It will be recalled that Wythe's friend, Ben
Waller, was the attorney for both counties.) The building is still there, and still
in its original form, despite the fact that its porch is and may never have been
complete, lacking as it does the columns which would ordinarily have graced its
front. It is, nonetheless, a building of some dignity and beauty. Since it was
begun during Wythe's time in office, one can regard it in a sense as one of his
accomplishments.

Some nine months before George Wythe was elected Mayor, there died at the
Governor's Palace, on the 3d of March, the Honorable Francis Fauquier. In the
words of John Blair,

> ". . . early this morning died at the Palace after a tedious illness which he bore with the
> greatest patience . . . Francis Fauquier."[4]

He was at this time some 65 years of age and was truly beloved by the people he
had governed in the name of the King for the past ten years. He had named as
the executors of his will William Nelson, Robert Carter, Peyton Randolph, and
George Wythe. Of the four he was probably closest to the last named and
Wythe took this onerous task as a duty to be performed—a last tribute to the
memory of his friend. The Governor—whether or not he had been most of his
life a Deist—did not die one. He was buried in the north aisle of Bruton Parish
Church, the Virginians giving him the most splendid funeral they could afford,
in testimony to his sweetness of disposition and gentleness of spirit. Beloved by

most Virginians, he was truly mourned.

For the next two or three years, Wythe and his fellow executors struggled to settle the estate of their late friend. And it indeed was an onerous task. Strictly speaking, the late Governor had two sets of executors. There was the group appointed to dispose of his property in Virginia, and also another which cared for his property in Britain. To his executors was to be given each a diamond ring, of the value of 25 guineas, which they were to wear

". . . not as a reward for their trouble I have given them . . . but which I desire they would wear in remembrance of a Man who once loved them and dies in the belief that they loved him."[5]

That the work was troublesome we know because Wythe declares it so. In his letter to Robert Carter, 29 May, 1772, he points out that he is anxious to be rid of this ". . . troublesome business." And he is sure Carter is also desirous of getting it over with. "Let us then endeavour to bring this matter to a speedy conclusion."[6] But four years after Fauquier's death, they were still attempting to clear up the estate. Indeed, the matter went on for two years more. It was all the more troublesome because the proceeds had to be sent across the ocean to England. And for help in this Wythe appealed to his English relative, John Norton, the London merchant:

"I beg the favour of you to deliver the packet . . . to Mr. Fauquier, and also pay him twenty five pounds sixteen shillings and eight pence more, . . ."[7]

Even by mid-1774, the estate had not been entirely disposed of, for again Wythe wrote to his fellow executor, Robert Carter, sending him a copy of the account of the estate. For Wythe felt guilty in his conscience; certain things had been mentioned in the inventory of Fauquier's possessions which could not be found. Wythe believed the servants had stolen them—indeed, Carter wished to make up the loss, but Wythe insisted on sharing the expense for

". . . if we were blameable, I was not less so than you. The next time we meet, I shall hope to finish this affair. Till then adieu."[8]

There still exists in Yale University Library a precisely figured account in Wythe's beautiful handwriting of the exact amounts taken in and expended by the Executors. And we can see thereby the trouble to which they had been put. They had not only to sell the property, but to pay all outstanding debts and to collect all money owed the late Governor. We even find under date of 14 November, 1772, "to cash paid for cleaning . . . the coach—£1/5/." By far the larger part of the work of the estate was done by Wythe, judging by such records as survive. It was the last duty he could perform for his friend.

The English government had now to discover a man to succeed Fauquier. The man they chose was one who became as beloved as Fauquier had been, Norborne Berkeley, Baron de Botetourt. Edmund Randolph in his *Manuscript*

History of Virginia gives an idea of what the men of that day thought of the new Royal Governor.

> "Always accessible on business, adhering without a single deviation to the humblest visitor in social circles, easy himself, and contributing to the ease of others, he was sincerely and universally beloved. . . ."[9]

During the 1760's, Wythe had been made—to add to his already numerous works—a Visitor of William and Mary College. He was therefore associated with Botetourt in this as in other duties, since the Governor was *ex officio* the head of the Visitors (Board of Trustees) of that College. A very strong friendship sprang up between Wythe and the new Governor, for they were both relaxed, easy persons. The latter was an immensely popular man. Short in stature, he had a knobby nose and a lack of beauty which may in itself have endeared him to the people. However, he was so amiable that he was without the necessary steel, acid, venom to make a successful politician. He believed the promises of the British government, which in itself says something about his innocence or unworldliness. Having been appointed Governor in October, 1768, he came to his duties after the trouble of the Stamp Act and before that of the Townshend Duties. It would seem to most people that the British had learned a lesson in the late attempt to extract coin from the Americans; however, it was to try again and this time by the Townshend Duties.

When the colonists learned of the new attempt to tax them, their temper and resentment equalled that of the reaction to the first try. Once again the mobs were called out. The Crown Officers were without the means to quell them and the provincial authorities did not even attempt to do so. A new Assembly met 11 May, 1769, after the imposition of the Townshend Duties. The Burgesses argued warmly against the taxes, finally deciding on various resolutions against them. That resolution which, before all others, was most important was worded thusly:

> ". . . The seizing any person . . . residing in this colony, suspected of any crime whatsoever committed therein, and sending such person . . . to places beyond the sea to be tried, is highly derogatory of the rights of British subjects . . . ."[10]

This was a protest against the attempt by the British to enforce the Revenue Acts. The Royal Officers knew well by virtue of experience that having found a person smuggling was one thing, and getting him convicted was another. The citizenry simply would not convict. Therefore, the Crown Officers hit upon the solution of taking the suspected smuggler to a colony—or to Britain itself—where more pliant jurors could be found. This, of course, would result in convictions. It would likewise break the teeth of the resistance movement. Thus the strong protest of the Burgesses.

Botetourt, with his spies in the House, had a pretty good idea of what the Burgesses were cooking up. And they in turn knew that he knew. Arguing over the wording of the Resolution, they sat late in the evening. George Wythe, their clerk, sat with them taking the minutes. The genial Governor, knowing the wrath that would descend not only upon the Virginians but also upon himself, had, no doubt, hoped that all would go smoothly during his tenure in Virginia. And here, at his first Assembly, things had already begun to go wrong.

Botetourt tried to get a copy of the minutes (probably from Wythe) that very evening, but Wythe contrived to put him off. The thing was not to be done so easily for the next morning the worried Governor sent the clerk of the Council, Nathaniel Walthoe, to demand the minutes.[11] Forewarned, however, the Burgesses had convened very early in the morning and, when Walthoe appeared, the doors were shut to him. After all, the House paid the salary of the door-keeper and he was answerable to them, not the Governor . . . . When the House completed the wording of the Resolution and Wythe had hurriedly writ-ten the same in the Journals, the doors were opened. Walthoe was admitted; his message was delivered; the Journals were brought to Botetourt in the Council Chamber where he perused them. Without hesitation, he made up his mind what to do. Summoning the Burgesses to the Chamber, he gave them a brief speech. Standing about the Council table, the Burgesses listened as he said:

> "I have heard of your deliberations and augur ill of them. They have made it necessary for me to dissolve you and you are accordingly dissolved."[12]

Thus succinctly and without ceremony, the Burgesses were supposed to be sent to their homes.

But the dismissal was not to be so simple. For they quietly marched down the street to the Raleigh Tavern and there seated themselves in the large banqueting room, over whose lintel was written *"Hilaritas sapientias et bonae vitae proles"*— "Joy, the child of wisdom and good living." This was the famous Apollo Room, and it was there that Peyton Randolph, as private citizen now that the House was dissolved—chaired the other private citizens which included Washington, Pendleton, Richard Henry Lee, Archibald Cary, and so many others. It is probable that Wythe was likewise present, although he did not sign the Non-Importation Agreement which the erst-while Burgesses framed there. It is difficult to say whether or not the colonists' boycott was very successful. One thing is sure. They made their point to the British government. For when the House met again, on 7 November, 1769, Botetourt reported that:

> "His Majesty's present administration . . . it is their intention to propose in the next session of Parliament to take off the duties upon glass, paper and colors, . . ."[13]

Notice that the duty on tea was not rescinded.

On 15 October 1770, having been in Virginia only two years, the worthy Botetourt died—without leaving a will. A bachelor, his heir was his nephew, the Duke of Beaufort. The late Governor's friends were assigned the task of working out the details of his estate and so George Wythe found himself given this also to do, at the same time as he was still caring for the details of Francis Fauquier's estate. The entire committee comprised William Nelson, John Randolph, Robert Carter Nicholas, Wythe, and John Blair. They wrote to the Duke of Beaufort on 30 October 1770 to acquaint him with the death of his uncle. Apparently the major part of the work of the settlement fell, not upon Wythe, but upon Nicholas. However, the whole committee shared the work. As late as 14 April 1772, they advertised in the Gazette that all those indebted to the late Governor should make up their debts at once, the Executors being desirous of closing their accounts.[14]

Besides his private practice, Wythe filled his life with many activities. It was in the year 1769, while Clerk of the Burgesses and also Major of Williamsburg that Wythe, with his co-workers, Peyton and John Randolph and Robert Carter Nicholas, finished the arduous work of preparing a complete collation of Virginia's laws. Wythe and the others had been given this job in 1765 and had accordingly worked on it for the past four years. Now at last it was finished, the workers being paid £100 and given the official thanks of the government for their efforts. This was not the first time that Wythe would struggle with the work of giving Virginia a unified code. There would be three more attempts to bring order into the legislative chaos—but all that lay far in the future.

Wythe's work as clerk of the Burgesses was not really very arduous. He had none of the heat of the parliamentary battle but could act as a sort of elder statesman, advising both groups. Meanwhile, his legal work continued and he kept busy as Visitor of William and Mary (which was a hotbed of controversy and quarrelling), as Alderman of Williamsburg (1771), and as Vestryman of Bruton Church. He likewise had his Back River estate to care for and the executorships of both the Fauquier and Botetourt estates. His personal life, spent for the most part in his lovely home in the city, visiting with his wife every now and then the Chesterville estate, must have been pleasant and enjoyable indeed.

His Clerkship must have been not the least part of that happy life. It had been the very first item of business in the House on Thursday, 31 March, 1768, to swear in George Wythe 'Gentleman' as the clerk. In the procedures of the House, whenever a new-elected Assembly convened, a new Speaker had to be chosen. Of course, Peyton Randolph was always the successful candidate. Until he was chosen, however, it was Wythe who, as clerk, called the House to order. Those who wished to speak, addressed themselves to the clerk and he, pointing to them silently with his finger, gave them the floor. As clerk, Wythe was paid the munificent sum of £125. By way of comparison, Nathaniel Walthoe, Clerk of the General Assembly, received only £60. (The General Assembly included both the House and the Council.)

As clerk, Wythe not only took the House's minutes, but also concerned himself with gathering the taxes, as is shown by the advertisement in the Virginia Gazette of 2 December 1773:

"Ordered that the clerks of several county courts in this Colony do transmit to the Clerk of this House in the first part of every meeting of the General Assembly a list of all tithables in their counties, containing the names of such tithables and that they transmit also at the same time a list of the public charges of their respective counties. G. Wythe C H B"[15]

All through their history the Virginians have been exceedingly careless of their public records, so it causes no surprise that the Burgesses should have no record of their proceedings of the early days. It was only people like Jefferson who carefully and meticulously gathered together and preserved such records that had not been by his time lost. But even here the attrition of the decades since has destroyed much of his good work.

In the early part of 1700, Jefferson found the need of providing himself with living quarters. For his old house of Shadwell had burned. This was a serious loss since the younger man lost many of his books and a large number of papers in this fire. He found it difficult to continue his cases in the law courts, for many of the lost papers pertained to suits then pending. Wythe tried to encourage him in his loss, writing him:

"G. W. to T. Jefferson.
    I send you some nectarine and apricot grafts and grape vines, the best I had; and have directed your messenger to call upon major Taliaferro for some of his. You will also receive two of Foulis's catalogues. Mrs. Wythe will send you some garden peas.
    You bear your misfortune so becomingly that, as I am convinced you will surmount the Difficulties it has plunged you into, so I foresee you will hereafter reap advantages from it several ways. *Durate, te vosmet rebus servate secundis.*   9 Mar 1770"[16]

Jefferson had already begun to level the top of the mountain on which he was to build Monticello. And by March, 1769, when everyone else was concerned about Non-Importation and the Association (as was Jefferson himself), he began his orchard there. This was where he planted Wythe's gift of apricot and nectarine grafts, and also the grape vines. He was about to commence also the building itself and did so. But when he married, on 1 January 1772, Martha Wales Skelton, there was available to the young lawyer and his bride only one building in which, despite a snow-storm, they yet made themselves comfortable. While there is a tradition that a large Chippendale table which is yet to be seen in the dining room at Monticello was a wedding present from Wythe, there is no proof of this. However, it is certain that Wythe gave the table to Jefferson.

Wythe was evidently in high prosperity and, probably at the urging of Mrs. Wythe, felt himself able to order a chariot.

"To John Norton
Dear Sir, If you will be so good as to procure for me a well built handsome post-charriott, I will remit the price of it in due season. Some thing like the enclosed device may be put upon it. Of the several articles I have lately wrote for, the glasses, balls and other apparatus, such as are used by the house of commons in balloting and the duplicates of our journals, I am most anxious about and earnestly desire your particular attention to. The journals especially

would be of considerable advantage to me. I am, Dear Sir, your sincere friend and well wisher

George Wythe Aug. 8, 1768."[17]

Along with the multitudinous duties of his public life, Wythe was often caught up in private activities in which his probity and good sense, as well as the respect accorded him by the public, was a valued thing. His conduct had been one of complete honesty—in fact, he was known as "the honest lawyer." His prestige in this respect, as in other things, was enormous; indeed, to have him party to an undertaking was to secure the confidence of the people at large. He would never be a popular hero in the sense Henry was. But despite the satire of Curtius, his contemporaries knew him to be a good, honest, decent and learned man. It is not strange, therefore, that he was sought after to act in such things as the lottery which Mann Page established (lotteries were very common things in those days—they were, in fact, a favorite way of raising money, in public as well as private works). Page had 146 lots of land in the town of Hanover, the least valuable being £20. The advertisement in the Virginia Gazette declared that

"The consideration money will not be required of gentl'men willing to become adventurers . . . until April next. Robert Carter Nicholas, George Wythe, T. Everard, John Thompson, Jerman Baker being the managers."[18]

The lottery was to be drawn at Mr. Anthony Hays, that is to say, Hays Tavern in Williamsburg on 4 April 1768.

Even the government of Virginia took part in lotteries. One of the largest ventures of this kind was that gotten up to enlarge the navigable portion of the Potomac River. Some 20,000 tickets were offered to the public, which was fond of gambling. More than 8,000 prizes were the enducement to take up these tickets. Wythe was among the fourteen public men (most of them members of the Assembly) given the task of conducting this lottery.

Ever since his assumption of the office of clerk, Wythe intended to do his job well. Thorough-going and painstaking, he was always mindful of a good performance. Basic to his job was knowledge and for this a library was essential. He tried to gather one for the House and was constantly ordering books from Norton, the London merchant. On 15 May, 1768, he wrote to

"Mr. John Norton, Merchant, in London
Dear Sir, I beg the favour of you to send me the printed journals of the house of commons from September 1766 (until which I have them complete), and of every future session so soon as they are published, an handsome large inkstand fit for a public office, a treatise concerning money-matters, (I think the title is "Of Civil economy" written by sir James Stewart, and Fawkes's Theocritus. I am Sir Your most obed. serv G. Wythe'[19]

He wanted the Commons' Journals for the House and the "handsome large inkstand," one presumes, for his own office as clerk. Wythe's workroom and office, where he kept his records and the books of the House of Burgesses, was in the Capitol. It was a large, comfortable room, commodious enough for two people, Wythe himself and his assistant, Jacob Bruce (who did most of the drudgery of copying documents and transcribing minutes).

Within a fortnight, Wythe was again writing Norton:

> "Dear Sir, I shall be obliged to you if you will send me eight or ten gallons of the best arrack in carboys properly secured, and some garden seeds. Your son left us this morning. He is in very good health and spirits. He was going to Hanover court. With my best wishes for yours and your family's happiness, I am Dear Sir . . . ."[20]

In the absence of catalogues by which far-away customers order from modern mail-order houses, the people of those days had to be vague. They relied on the intelligence of the merchants in England to select for them what was needed—hence Wythe did not specify what type of garden seeds he wanted. A delightful insight into the needs of the Virginia family, so far from the source of supply, is seen in his letter to Norton of 8 August 1768. The time of the Non-Importation oath of the Associations formed in reaction to the Townshend duties was getting very close. In his letter, Wythe intermingles articles for his own consumption and for the use of the Burgesses:

> "Dear Sir, I wrote many months ago to messrs. James Buchanan and company for an elegant set of table and tea china, with bowls of the same of different sizes, decanters and drinking glasses, an handsome service of glass for a dessert, four middlesized and six lesser dishes, and three dozen plates of hard metal, 100 skins of writing parchment proper for enrolling our acts of assembly on, several bundles of best quilt, two pieces of blanketing and so many of rolls for servants, 10 or 12 pairs of shoes and two slippers for myself, and one or two other articles which I do not recollect. At that time there was due to me about thirty pounds, I believe, for I have mislaid their last account current; and besides I had shipped four hogsheads of tobacco to that house. The goods have not come to hand, neither have I yet an account of sales of tobacco. If they have not been sent, nor design to send the goods I desire you will be so kind as let me have them, with a bonnet for mrs. Wythe and present the enclosed order and receive the balance. A few days since I desired you would procure for me an handsome well built charriot, with the device now sent painted on it, for which you may depend on a seasonable remittance. I again beg the favour of your attention to the affair of the journals. If they are not to be procured let me be informed what 120 copies of them to the year 1752 will cost. If they do not exceed the sum I suppose, the assembly, I doubt not, will defray the expense. The prospect of a benefit to me, I flatter myself, will not only excuse the earnestness and frequency of my importunities but stimulate your endeavours to serve me in this business. You will oblige me by sending a copper plate, with the arms of Virginia neatly engraved and some impressions of them to be pasted on the books belonging to the house of burgesses. If any additions are made on the plate in consequence of what is proposed within, I will cheerfully pay the extraordinary cost. John Hatley Norton left us a day or two in good health. I forgot to mention that I had drawn bills on Mssrs. Jas Buchanan and company for about sixteen pounds payable to mr. James Cocke, I am, Dear Sir, Your Sincere friend and well wisher. Williamsburg. G. Wythe. Aug. 18th, 1768"[21]

The difficulties of securing the appurtenances of the beautiful life in 18th Century Virginia, far from the source of supply, can easily be seen in the above letter. The means by which the Virginia planter expected to pay for the goods was by sale of tobacco which, of course, Wythe produced from his Chesterville estate. The vagueness with which he ordered "a bonnet for Mrs. Wythe" must have given that lady some annoyance.

A fascinating insight into the difficulties of being well-dressed in colonial Virginia is given by the following letter from Robert Carter to his London tailor in 1765:

> ". . . the clothes you sent my neighbor George Wythe fitted him much better than my last suit did me. My size and shape of body resemble Captain William Fauquier of the Guards."[22]

Norton indeed had his employments for, as before noted, Wythe engaged him to remit money to Francis Fauquier, the son and heir of Wythe's dear friend. In the same letter dated 29 May 1772, he engaged Norton to secure for him a proper robe, to be used in his duties as Clerk of the Burgesses. Nor would just any robe do, for Wythe wanted one

> ". . . such as is worn by the clerk of the house of commons, but better than the one I had before from Mr. Child, which indeed was scandalous."[23]

Wythe was building, as ever, his library, for he ordered at the same time that the works of Theophilus ". . . in Greek and Latin two volumes in quarto, published at the Hague in 1751, . . ." be sent him. Norton was further to procure for him Glanville, Bracton, Britton, Fleta. These were legal works, and added thereto was Lamb's *eirenarcha,* Erasmus' *adages,* and the *Book of Common Prayer* in Greek. Wythe's accomplishments in the ancient languages has been noted before and his purchases in this regard show that he was no amateur. But food for the body was also needed, since at the same time he ordered "two pipes of Madiera wine."

That Wythe was one with the Associators in 1769 in refusing to buy any of the taxed articles of the Townshend Duties (lead, paper, tea, paint, glass), can be seen by a letter written 4 August 1769. The colonists were to bring the merchants of England to their knees by importing only the necessities and the paucity of Wythe's order on this occasion shows that he went along with this attempt.

"To John Norton Esq. Merchant in London
Dear Sir I beg the favour of you to send me the articles undermentioned. Capt. Robinson will deliver you nine hogsheads of tobacco, which are all that I made. Pray give mrs. Wythe's and my best respects to mrs. Norton and all your good family, and believe me to be
                                              Your sincere friend G. Wythe
2 pieces of sheeting linen not exceeding 2s per yard.
2 pieces of Irish linen for shirts 2 s per yard
1 piece of ditto ditto 1/3 per yard
1 piece of dark coloured Russia drab.
Debates of the Parliament in Ireland
Journals of the house of commons since 1766

some best razors and pen knives.
a genteel Man's saddle, bridle & blue housing to be
made by Pennymen ord. in J.H.Ns. Letter of 4th August."[24]

Upon his undertaking the duties of his job as clerk, Wythe decided to change
some of the routines of the House. One was in the method of voting. Hitherto
members had, in the way of voting, either remained in their seat or had left the
chamber, depending on whether they approved or disapproved of the measure
before them. But as the membership of the House became larger and the chamber thus more crowded, this was awkward. So Wythe decided to imitate the
ways of the English House of Commons. He accordingly ordered balloting
glasses by means of which to take the votes. Wythe was still very much at this
time the Virginian Englishman:

> "I have paid to my cousin J. H. Norton thirty seven pounds and ten shillings for which he
> will desire you to to credit my account with thirty pounds sterling. I have also given him
> orders for four hogsheads of tobacco to be shipped to you. Be pleased to send me a piece of
> cambrick and another of lawn, one pair of satin and five pair of callimancho or lasting shoes
> with high full heels and a satin cloak for mrs. Wythe, and a piece of irish linen 2/6 per yard,
> two large damsk and four small huckaback table cloths, six pair of cotton stockings and two
> of black silk for myself, a dark tie wig and a sett of balloting glasses such as are used in the
> house of commons. Mr. Waldron may send me two pairs of black Manchester velvet
> breeches and a suit of very fine light cloath fit for our hot summers with a silk waistcoat and
> pair of silk breeches besides. With my best wishes for your and all your family's health and
> prosperity . . . ."[25]

There is preserved in the hairdressing shop in Williamsburg today a large
box on which is written in large letters: MR. WYTHE. This contained his wig.
One of the more startling of the customs of Wythe's time is that of the gentry in
the matter of wigs. For the nobility of the time shaved their heads completely
free of hair. They then put on their wigs. Only the gentry wore these, for they
cost a good deal of money—indeed, one could rent a house for two or three
months for the price of a good wig. These wigs were sent from time to time to
the hairdressers to be cleaned and furbished. A white wig was apparently more
expensive than one of dark hair, and to make it whiter, talc was freely applied.
Nor did Wythe shave himself. His bill for one year's shaving came to £2/3 in
1771. That same year it cost him exactly the same sum to have the hairdresser
dress and refurbish his wig. So ran the account book of Wythe's barber, Edward
Charlton, wigmaker and barber.

Later in life, Wythe would wear his own hair, probably in revulsion against
aristocratic pretensions. But at this time, he wished to cut a good figure and he
could afford to do so. He was a successful lawyer, the Clerk of the House, had a
beautiful home and an accomplished wife, and so could live well. He entertained
such people as Fauquier, Botetourt, Jefferson, Washington, the Randolphs, his
in-laws the Taliaferros, and others. Naturally he drove a chariot, wore a wig,
and dressed himself in velvet breeches.

To be clerk of the House was also in effect to be librarian: that is, to keep the records and journals of the House. The Burgesses possessed a complete set of their journals (in manuscript) from the year 1751 on. Wythe wrote to Norton on 13 June, 1768 seeking his aid in getting the journals of an earlier time. He declared that Virginia's Governors had, by command of the King, sent to the English government "two or more duplicates" of the House journals. On the long and perilous voyage over the sea, it was quite possible that one copy might be lost. Hence the duplication. Norton was asked to seek Montague's help in influencing the British government to give up one copy of these from the founding of the colony in the first part of the 17th Century down to 1752. If they could not be pried loose from the British officialdom, then could copies be made? ". . . so as it be not made public, nor attended with great expense . . . ."[26]

The closeness of the Wythe family to the Nortons comes from the fact that John Norton, the English merchant, had lived in Virginia earlier in his life. While there he had courted and married Courtney Walker, the daughter of Jacob Walker, Wythe's uncle on his mother's side. John Hatley Norton, their son, often visited the Wythe home in Williamsburg, and indeed was nursed back to health on one occasion while there. This had occurred in the summer of 1767, as William Nelson wrote to John Norton:

> "Your son has been sometime confined Sick at my neighbor Mr. Wythes but is now pretty well recovered and gone to York."[27]

John Hatley Norton had been a member of the House and connected Wythe in some measure with the Nicholas family, since he married Sarah Nicholas, daughter of Robert Carter Nicholas.

Of all the work that George Wythe did, his greatest repute came not from his clerkship but from his legal practice. Any account of Wythe as a lawyer must begin, first of all, with the statement that he was pre-eminently a just man. Justice, in the Aristotelian sense, means the giving of that which is strictly due. It was Wythe's habit to be just to his clients as he expected them to be just to him. That is to say, he expected his clients to tell him the whole and complete truth. He would take an oath from his client if it happened that he thought his client was in any sense lying to him. If, during the course of a lawsuit, he discovered that, despite this oath, he had been deceived, the fee was returned and Wythe would refuse to continue the case. The favored name for Wythe among his contemporaries was "Aristides," that Greek who was known as the "Just."

Wythe began his law practice, as we have seen, in the courts of Orange County, practicing both with and against his father-in-law, Zachary Lewis in 1746. He continued in the law as one of Virginia's most eminent practitioners until the courts were shut down by the Revolution in 1777. From the various county courts, he went on to the Supreme Court of Virginia, namely, the General Court. It is a matter of some dispute as to when he actually began to practice before this Court. Composed of the Governor and his Council, it was the court of last resort for Virginians, save the Royal Privy Council in England. It is Hemphill who points out that Wythe must certainly have been admitted to this bar at least before May of 1755. Only members of that bar and the judges thereof could belong to the Board of Examiners which tested the aspirant as to his knowledge of the law—as we have seen in the case of Patrick Henry, being tested by Peyton Randolph, Pendleton, Carter and Wythe.

There is in the records the statement that Paul Carrington had his license signed by the two Randolph brothers, Peyton and John, and George Wythe in the month of May, 1755. Thus it is apparent that Wythe had begun his work in the General Court at least by this time.[28] This Court met in Williamsburg, the Spring session beginning in April, and the Fall session in October, with each session lasting two weeks. (The Court of Oyer and Terminer met in Williamsburg in June and December.) The General Court met in the Capitol itself, in a courtroom especially made over to it. Thus Wythe frequented the Capitol not only as legislator, as clerk of the Burgesses, but also as lawyer.

Notes to Chapter IV

1. Virginia Gazette (Purdie & Dixon). 12 September 1766.
2. *Ibidem.* 1 August 1766.
3. *Ibidem.* 8 January 1767.
4. William and Mary—. First Series, Vol. 8, p. 29.
5. Magazine of American History. Vol. 3, p. 133.
6. Manuscript Collection. New York Public Library.
7. Norton, John. John Norton and Sons Papers, Colonial Williamsburg, Inc., Williamsburg, Virginia.
8. Manuscript Collection. J. P. Morgan Library, New York City.
9. Edmund Randolph. *Manuscript History—.* p. 55.
10. Burgesses. *Journals, 1766–69.* p. 214.
11. Tyler "George Wythe" in *Great American Lawyers—.* p. 60.
12. William and Mary—. First Series, Vol. 16, p. 27–8.
13. *Ibidem.* p. 30.
14. Virginia Gazette (Purdie & Dixon). 16 April 1772.
15. *Ibidem.* 2 December 1773.
16. Thomas Jefferson. *Papers of—,* Boyd ed., Vol. 1, p. 38.
17. Norton, John. John Norton and Sons Papers, Colonial Williamsburg, Inc., Williamsburg, Virginia.
18. Virginia Gazette (Purdie & Dixon), 20 June 1766.
19. Norton, John. Opus citatum
20. *Ibidem.* p. 53.
21. *Ibidem.* p. 58.
22. Magazine of American History. Vol. 30, p. 127.
23. Norton, John. Opus citatum
24. *Ibidem.* p. 101.
25. *Ibidem.* p. 50–1.
26. *Ibidem.* p. 54.
27. *Ibidem.* p. 141.
28. William Hemphill. *George Wythe, The Colonial Briton: A Biographical Study of the Pre-Revolutionary Era in Virginia.* Doctoral Thesis, University of Virginia. 1937. p. 77.

CHAPTER V

From the House of Burgesses to the Continental Congress

As a lawyer, Wythe competed at the bar of Virginia against such men as Thomson Mason and Edmund Pendleton: men who were among the foremost lawyers of their day. Wythe may have been—and at this time one cannot say with certainty—a lawyer equal to if not better than Pendleton in point of law. It is a fact, apparently, accepted by Pendleton's biographers that the latter was able to best Wythe in those cases where the two opposed each other. While Wythe had more information than Pendleton, the latter was ". . . rather a great advocate than a deep lawyer." The rivalry between the two went deep. But the world judges by external appearance and here Pendleton had the advantage, for he was tall and strikingly handsome. He was possessed of a fine voice and pleasant manners.

It was Call who summed up the difference between these men:

> "In debate Mr. Pendleton was more captivating, Mr. Wythe more argumentative. 'Caesar ne priorem, Pompeius ve parem,' was a question which produced no animosity between them; but which the world never decided."[1]

This, of course, was not true, for the astute Pendleton, more worldly-wise and calculating, managed often to bring off the prize. And this rankled in Wythe's heart. The story is told that Wythe, annoyed that his rival should have won some preference over him, spoke in sharp annoyance of giving up the political world and entering the ministry. The rejoinder came from his listener—"Don't do that, for he'll follow you even into that and beat you there!"

In their legal encounters, it is Tyler who says that Pendleton was ". . . cautious and conservative, Wythe . . . bold and aggressive." This is strange, for it seemingly should be the other way about. Jefferson it was who declared that in ". . . pleading he [Wythe] never indulged himself with an useless or declamatory thought or word . . ." And this is the aspect of a cautious, conservative man. Pendleton was a tall, strong man, facile of tongue and very elegant. A man of high intelligence. Jefferson called him one of the ablest debaters he had ever faced, and Jefferson should have known, since he tangled with him in the Virginia Assembly many times during the Revolution. Juries were swayed by Pendleton, as they were by Henry, not so much by the subtle points of law which either Wythe or Jefferson might put forward, but by the silver oratory, the quick wit, the easy speech of Wythe's rival.

Wythe was a lawyer in an age when giants ruled the Virginia bar. Pendleton, Robert Carter Nicholas, Patrick Henry, John Blair, Peyton and John and Edmund Randolph—these were the men who shone as the stars in the Virginia legal firmament. And certainly in the estimation of Washington and others, Wythe was behind no one—not even Pendleton—in legal acumen and ability. Indeed, during a large part of his legal career, Wythe handled much of Washington's legal business. He began to do Washington's legal work, in the mid-1750's, when the future general was still fighting as a young colonel of militia in the French and Indian War.

One of the most interesting cases wherein Wythe defended Washington's interests was in a case involving Charles Carroll of Maryland. The beginnings of the suit may be traced in the Chancery Suit Papers in the University of Virginia Alderman Library. These are various legal papers signed or attested by Ben Waller, Charles Carrol, John Mercer, Henry Tyler and others. The suit is entitled "Ignatius Digges Assignee of Charles Carroll, William Digges, John Addison v. William Clifton and Elizabeth, his wife." On 22 January 1755, Digges, Digges & Addison won the case. However, they seem to have continued the Chancery Suit against Clifton for many years after that.

The substance of the case is that in 1740 William Clifton borrowed money from Charles Carroll and Ben Tasker of Annapolis. John Addison joined Clifton in giving a bond, 2 September 1740, for £200 payable to Tasker. The money was not repaid. In 1753, Ignatius Digges married a lady with money claims on Charles Carroll and the latter called on Clifton to repay the money he had borrowed. Clifton either couldn't or wouldn't do so. Carroll had the recourse of foreclosing on the mortgaged lands owned by Clifton, but Clifton's wife had dower rights to this land. She, however, conveyed these rights to her husband and the land was subsequently auctioned off, but at this auction there were unfortunately no bids by outsiders.

The creditors seemingly made bids against each other (apparently by concert) and so they got the land. But the price they paid for it did not cover the whole sum due them, and they therefore sold Clifton's house. There was still not enough money recovered to pay the debt. In fleecing the lamb Clifton's creditors pushed too hard for Clifton angrily refused even to try to pay the sum still due. Seemingly the lamb was tougher than had been expected, for Clifton refused even to leave or give up the house (in which he probably was living). He declared the sum was unjust and started a suit in Chancery Court. Since he had previously sworn that the accounts of his debt were true, there could be no dispute over the actual money due. However, the truth of the matter lies in the fact that interest on the debt had accumulated until Clifton owed a sum enormously inflated from what he had originally borrowed. Wythe came into the case in 1756, to be joined in it a year later by Robert Carter Nicholas. The case was still going strong in March of 1759, for on the 29th of that month a letter was written by William Digges and John Addison, the burden of which is that the lands in question were not as good as Clifton had originally claimed and therefore the value thereof was really insignificant. Could they therefore have the rents on what property remained to Clifton secured to themselves in order to make up the difference?

Washington joined in this imbroglio, again involving Wythe, on Tuesday, 20 May 1760 when in his *Diaries* he notes that it was a Court Day. Washington, ever expanding his land holdings, attended, for

> ". . . Mr. Clifton's Land in the Neck was exposed to Sale, and I bought it for £210 Sterling, and under many threats and disadvantages paid the money into the Commissioners hands and returned home at Night with Col. Fairfax and fam'y Captn Dalton . . . ."[2]

Washington evidently had second thoughts as to the wisdom of this purchase, for he wrote the next day to "Messrs Nicholas & With for advice how to act in regard to Clifton's land. Sent the Letter by the Post." The land he bought wasn't cheap, and in addition he settled the claim of others against the property to the tune of more than £368. He hadn't bought this land on the moment's spur for he wrote in his *Diary* for Tuesday, 1 April, 1760:

> "Recd a Letter from Mr. Digges, inclosing a Packet for Messrs Nicholas and Wythe which he desired I would send under Cover to some Friend of mine in Williamsburg as it was to go by Clifton, suspecting that Gentleman would not deal fairly by it."[3]

In the wretched communications and poor postal service of that day, it was a common thing to send letters by anyone who might be travelling. And such people did not scruple to open anything they thought might be of interest to themselves or others. This sociable custom was the reason why Digges wanted Washington to send the material (which evidently concerned Clifton) under another envelope, since apparently Clifton would be carrying his antagonists' evidence. It is apparent from this that Washington planned to buy the land some weeks before he actually did so.

The lawsuit boiled merrily on, as we see by the letter the elder Carroll wrote on 26 April 1763. As a pebble thrown into a pond spreads ripples, so this lawsuit spread its waves against more and more people.

"Dear Charley: . . . Dulaney . . . sued me for his part of the money I received of Wright and Frazier. The suit hangs . . . if . . . he does not drop the action, and he and my other partners do not pay me the damages I have suffered by Mercer's suit I shall prefer a bill in chancery against them. . . . I do not think it worth my while . . . to appeal against the decree of Clifton and Mercer."[4]

That Mercer himself some years later had his troubles is evident from the letter George Washington wrote to John Taylor on 12 March 1776. The nature of the letter is astonishing, considering the state of affairs at the time. For Washington wrote from Cambridge where he was then besieging the town of Boston, Gage's Redcoats being at that time locked up within. Not even a war could stop a lawsuit.

"Dear Sir: . . . I do not know a better hand than Colo. Francis Peyton to collect the Money due to the Sales of Colo. Mercers Estate, when collected, if the Situation of Affairs will admit of any intercourse with Great Britain. . . . What lawyer to . . . engage . . . I know not, . . . Mr. Mercer it cannot . . . be, because he is a party, and I believe has engaged both Mr. Pendleton and Mr. Wythe on his side. . . ."[5]

In other words, the best lawyers had already been engaged by the other side. And, as Washington well knew, these were Wythe and Pendleton. The two were not always rivals, but indeed at times worked together on various cases. For example, Pendleton noted triumphantly to William Preston about another lawsuit he and Wythe fought together:

"23 Apr 1773 . . . Mr. Reid totally defeated all his petitions being dismissed with costs. Had mr. Wythe's Assistance in the petitions. . . ."[6]

But perhaps the most important case Wythe handled for Washington was one engaged in when the Revolution was about to break out. The Wythe-Washington friendship was of long standing—Washington often noted in his *Diary* that he had visited Wythe at his home and had lunch there. In the year 1769, Washington, a Burgess, lunched at the Wythe house three times while the House sessions were going on. Washington apparently loved the theatre for at the same time as he visited Wythe, he spent the evening at play-going. Those were the days when Miss Hallam, a celebrated London actress, enlivened the stage and the social life of Williamsburg.

Despite his love of play-going, Washington was in earnest about his guardianship of John Parke Custis. He wanted to satisfy the importunities of his ward and step-son, and so he bought for him the plantation known as "Woromoroke" or "Romanoke" in King and Queen County. This land was between the York and Rappahannock Rivers, about half-way between Williamsburg and the Washington estate of Mt. Vernon. This property was bought from a certain William Black and the resultant tangle of legal matters vexed Washington exceedingly. Before buying the property, he, evidently knowing with whom he had to deal, secured the opinion of Wythe as to Black's right to sell. When Wythe assured him of the validity of Black's title, (in a document which exists today and is so complex that few modern lawyers could begin to explain it), Washington bought the land and appurtenances. As earnest money of his intention, Black gave a bond of £11,000. Then came a complication, for Mrs. Black had dower rights in the property, and evidently on the urging of her husband refused to execute the deeds. Washington himself had given earnest money of some £5,000. However, Black refused to give up possession until Washington surrendered his (Black's) bond. This business occupied the years 1773–4. On 7 February 1774 Washington burst out in a letter to Bartholomew Dandridge about the affair. Of William Black in particular he says:

> ". . . that worthless sc-----l, who seems to be adept in every species of artifice & Rascality—that he should expect the bond which was given for the express purpose of compelling him to surrender possession . . . free from any encumbrance of Dower . . . before he would give up the [property] . . . is such a masterpiece of impudence, as I thought no man could be guilty of . . . ."[7]

And in justification of this, he quotes Wythe's legal opinion. Washington wrote to Wythe on 17 January, 1774:

> ". . . I Find my trouble is not like to be at an end with Mr. Black; Mrs. Black (by his procurement I think . . .) has refused to execute the deeds you drew from them to me . . . Please drop me a few lines, with your sentiments on this matter by the Post to Alexandria . . . please to let the Speaker know how the matter stands between Black and myself that they may not be imposed upon by him; as I believe he will stick at nothing to carry his points."[8]

Washington, however, was not the only man whose lawsuits Wythe handled. Perhaps more important to him in the matter of steady, year-in, year-out work was that which he did for Robert Carter.

Wythe collected Carter's rents for him, and from time to time gave him legal assistance in the management of his estates. These totaled some 50,000 considerable acres. This Carter was a member of the Governor's Council later in life, a position which he pre-empted by virtue of being the grandson of "King" Carter. Carter called upon Wythe to do more than collect rents, however, as the following letter shows:

4 October 1772

"Dear Wythe, A few days ago I receiv'd a Letter dated 14th of last month, September, subscribed John Hough, who is my Steward—part thereof is in these words 'Parson Charles Mynes Thurston in Frederick is erecting a Mill on the Line near thy Conveniency on Shenadon Tract, has obtained an Order of Court to condemn & by a Jury has condemned an Acre to cut his Tail-Race through—This I apprehend is not according to Law as the Line crosses the stream—this Breach will greatly interfere with yr conveniency—This Hint I thought it proper to communicate—J. Hough.' The Conveniency spoken of in the above . . . , belonging to me, is a rich tract of land lying in Frederick County containing about 5 thousand Acres, and a very ordinary Mill thereon—there are several Families now living on that Tract who pay Rent to me, that part whereon the Mill is erected, is not rented, I having often refused to rent the same, intending to erect mills for different Purposes there. I think that a writ shou'd be issued immediately toward obtain:g an Enquiry, in the Genl Court touchg the Propriety or Impropriety of the Order of Frederick Court, granting leave for Mr. Thurston to build a mill—I will go myself up to Frederick County next spring and if the Neighbourhood there really want a Grist-Mill, I will order one to to be built, provided the Order of Court mentioned above shall be set aside—The Indisposition of several of my Children, & three upper Servts I apprehend will confine me here some time, pray present my Compliments to Ld Dunmore and all the Gentlemen Attendants, who shall attend the approachg Term of the General Court, from which I must absent myself, I am, Dear Wythe, Your . . ."[9]

As will be noted from the letter, Carter, by virtue of being a member of the Council, was also a Judge of the General Court. One wonders again and again at the fact that a conflict of interest did not seem to bother the Virginians. For Wythe, a lawyer practicing before the General Court, had one of the judges thereof as his client.

Just as in his early years as a lawyer, Wythe had opposed his friend and associate Zachary Lewis in many law cases, so Jefferson came to oppose his friend and associate and former teacher, Wythe. In 1780, Jefferson, now Governor of revolutionary Virginia, on the 1st of June, sent to a certain young man, William Short, to whom he stood as Wythe had stood to him, that is as teacher and guide, the digests of a case in which he and Wythe had been opposing each other. The matter is too long to quote here, but Jefferson gives Short the advice that he should read both opinions (for Jefferson sent both his own and Wythe's) carefully. The case was Bolling vs. Bolling, and Jefferson makes the chivalrous remark that Wythe's arguments are ". . . valuable in themselves, the latter to none by myself." Let Short take good care of these papers. And above all, Jefferson recommended to Short that he learn to set his arguments in ". . . a methodical and strict arrangement . . . . The best arguments are lost without this." Jefferson, now opposing Wythe, seems to have given this the most careful and minute preparation of any of his cases—he would have to, for he was up against the most thorough lawyer of his day. Wythe's argument is a long one, and carefully reasoned. He states the matter in question, which is one of emblements. Is, for example, wheat standing in the field, a part of the freehold or is it chattel personal? Wythe gives the various positions which may be taken. And then he cites the objections to each. For each position taken he gives the authority, the title of the work and even the page and paragraph number. In its digest form, the opinion is difficult to understand, but it is apparent that this was simply a sort of brief to be followed by Wythe as he stood and argued the case slowly and carefully, without a useless word and without any wild inflammatory oratory. He brought into his argument all manner of facts, citing, for example, under

". . . 4. it was not an adjudged case, but an extra-judicial opinion. Vau. 382. Sr. Coke was then but 27 years old. see his life by Sr. Harbottle Grimstone."

Just what the fact that the great Coke was "but 27 years old" when he pronounced an opinion had to do with the case is not now apparent, but it must have meant something to Wythe and, consequently, to his hearers.

That Wythe tried to anticipate the arguments his opponent (in this case, Jefferson) might use is obvious from the statement which follows:

> "Having made these particular remarks upon the books that probably will be cited by the def's counsel, I shall now shortly review them, and subjoin an observation or two upon the same subject."[10]

In almost the whole of Wythe's argument, one thing stands out pre-eminently. Wythe, at this stage in his legal work, relied almost exclusively in a case of this type on English precedents. The brief is argued with exhaustive learning and careful reasoning. It is a fine example of the way in which the man fought his cases at this time in his life.

It was during this time, also, that Wythe now took on his second pupil, St. George Tucker. Evidently his relationship with Jefferson had been so pleasant that he was willing now to continue to teach law while he practiced it. His new pupil was a member of a Bermuda family who had come to Virginia about 1770. Tucker, born in 1752, was a little more than 20 years old when he became Wythe's law student in 1773. He proved a very able student, for in somewhat more than a year he was licensed to practice in the county courts of Virginia. And a year after that Wythe led him to practice before the General Court itself, on 10 April 1775. When the Revolution broke out, Tucker, despite his Bermuda birth, took the part of the rebels and became Aide-de-camp to General Thomas Nelson, serving with great distinction in battles against the British. After the Revolution, he settled down to practice in Williamsburg, living as neighbor to Wythe and himself taking on law students. His career was a noble one, for in 1789 he became professor of law at William and Mary College, and in 1803 was appointed the presiding Judge of the Court of Appeals of Virginia.

But not all of Wythe's time was spent in law suits or in his clerkship. As an 18th Century man of the upper classes, Wythe was fascinated by the latest developments in physical science. All his life he would have a "philosophical apparatus," from the aelophyle of his early days as clerk in the Burgesses' committees to the end of his life when, old and honored, he experimented with an "electrical apparatus." He had ordered a telescope from John Norton and was, of course, in his friendship with Jefferson, caught up with one who was head over heels in love with science. For Jefferson concerned himself with such things as mastodon bones, or the birds and fishes of his native Virginia, or even the mechanical works of his friend, Rittenhouse, whose orrery yet exists in the library of Princeton University. In May of 1773, there was formed in Virginia the Society for the Promotion of Useful Knowledge, of which Wythe was a founding member.

It was in line with his membership on the Burgesses' Committee to promote manufacturing, and his joining in the group which promoted Estave's vineyard venture in Williamsburg, that he should join this Society, one of the first acts of which was to bestow a sum of money and a gold medal on a certain John Hobday, the inventor of a threshing machine. This machine, capable of threshing 40 bushels of wheat a day, was so simple to construct that any mechanic could build one. Invented before the society was organized, it may be that the invention itself gave impetus to establishing the society. Be that as it may, the Society apparently had its origin on 20 November 1772 with eight original members. They chose the great Virginian botanist, John Clayton of Windsor, as President. John Page of Rosewell became the Vice-President, while the Secretary was the Reverend Samuel Henley, Professor of Moral Philosophy at the College. Wythe's law student, St. George Tucker and David Jameson of Yorktown shared the job of Treasurer. At Clayton's death, the Honorable John Page (who was on the Council) was made President on 15 June 1774. George Wythe was then made Vice-President, while there were two secretaries, Mr. James Madison who, while now professor of Natural Philosophy at the College, was in a short while to be a law student of Wythe, and the Reverend Robert Andrews, a clergyman of York.

Corresponding members of the Society, which may have been modeled after Franklin's Philadelphia Society, were Dr. Franklin himself, Dr. Lettsom of London, the Reverend Thomas Baldwin of Chester in England, Dr. William Smith, the Provost of the College at Philadelphia, Dr. Morgan, Dr. Benjamin Rush and Mr. Rittenhouse of Philadelphia, Edward Foy, Esquire, of New York, Dr. Stewart of Bladensburg, Maryland, and Dr. Smibert of Boston.

The founding of the Society came at a difficult time, for the Revolution, with its disruptions, was in the offing. It is significant that it might very well have done some good work if politics had not prevented. Three of its members would be signers of the Declaration of Independence (Wythe himself, Franklin, and Rush). John Page would be Lieutenant-Governor of Virginia during part of the Revolution, and the others likewise would be caught up in the political tempest of the times. The Society lasted for approximately eleven years and was more a promise of what might have been than a reality of what was. The tie-in of the Society to politics is obvious when one sees that the meetings took place when the Burgesses were in session, for this was the only time when the requisite type of men were in Williamsburg. At any rate, it did award the first medal to be given by an American society for an invention—that given to Hobday.

After the death of the amiable Lord Botetourt, the British government appointed a most remarkable man to fill his place, John Murray, the Earl of Dunmore. In any assessment of this man's character, one must discount the reports of many of his contemporaries, since these were very prejudiced. Indeed, in the course of his activities in the Revolution, Dunmore came to be so hated that even Wythe, gentle as he was, rejoiced at Dunmore's misfortunes. In this connection, it is interesting to note that this is one of only two instances ever recorded of antipathy between Wythe and any other man. The two must have heartily disliked each other, as the following instance of biting wit on Wythe's part will reveal.

Dunmore as Governor was presiding over the General Court in the Capitol. Wythe, with a colleague, was opposing Pendleton in the case. Pendleton's associate, Thomson Mason, was late. The Court was ready to start, and Pendleton asked for a delay until his partner should arrive. Pendleton obviously did not wish to argue against *both* Wythe and his co-councillor, Robert Carter Nicholas. However, Dunmore replied from the bench—"Go on, go on, Mr. Pendleton, you'll be a match for both of them." At this Wythe replied "—with your Lordship's assistance." accompanying this reprimand with a low, courtly, 18th Century bow. The onlookers who reported this incident also noted that his Lordship was obviously stung by the sharpness of the retort, as well he might have been.[11]

In the political arena, the British government was becoming alarmed at the aspect of affairs in America and well it might be for nothing but trouble seemed to come from that continent. Then came the Boston Tea Party, a jovial affair (for the Americans) which was duplicated in many another American seaport. Now the British were really incensed. For once again the Americans had hit the British where their hearts were—in their fortunes. The great East Indian Company owned the tea, and would have to stand the loss if the Americans were not forced to pay. And the magnates of Britain owned the India Company. No one was going to take money away from the English ruling class and get away with it. And so, until the tea was paid for and Boston made proper restitution, the port of Boston was closed. Boston had been singled out for punishment, although it was not alone in the tea destruction. Those obstreperous Puritans had caused England so much trouble that it would be just fine if a good example were made of them.

The Boston Tea Party had taken hilarious place on 15 December 1773—a Christmas present as it were for the English. But it did not cause much excitement in Virginia, where the real news was the preparation by Governor Dunmore to march against the Shawnees. The news of the Boston Port Bill arrived in Virginia in late May. And this did cause excitement. Indeed, the House set aside a day of public fasting, prayer and humiliation as a protest against the closing of the port of Boston. Dunmore, who was busy with his warfare preparations, closed the House within the next two days, giving the Burgesses just such curt notice as another governor had earlier:

> ". . . I have in my hand a paper published by order of your House, conceived in such terms as reflect highly upon his Majesty and the Parliament of Great Britain, which makes it necessary for me to dissolve you; and you are dissolved accordingly."[12]

The Governor's action, cold and unsympathetic as it apparently was, did not seem to cause resentment in one Virginian, at any rate. For the very evening that Dunmore dissolved the Assembly George Washington spent at the Palace, dining with the Governor.

The next day Washington rode out to the Governor's farm with him for breakfast. The following evening he attended a ball at the Palace which the

Burgesses gave for Lady Dunmore, who had just arrived in Virginia. The future general stayed on in Williamsburg for a meeting on 15 June of the Society for Promoting Useful Knowledge and so may have voted for George Wythe who was then elected Vice-President of the Society.

Just as they had under Botetourt's governorship in 1769, the Burgesses marched to the very same room in the Raleigh Tavern and there again under the "hilaritas" motto, the now-dismissed House set upon the expedient of calling a general congress of the colonies to consider what should be done about the state of their affairs. Eight or so years before, when the Stamp Act Congress had taken place, Virginia had not been represented because Fauquier (who was no fool) had not let the Burgesses come into session. He knew what they might do. So at that time there was not even a semblance of a House which might send delegates. But on this occasion, the House itself, though dissolved, was entact, all its members gathered from the distant corners of Virginia. The instrument lay at hand and the Burgesses took it—the calling of the 1st Continental Congress, Peyton Randolph, the Speaker, being made head of a committee to arrange this. A few days later, 29 May 1774, the full import of what closing Boston meant came to the Burgesses with the letters that had arrived from that city, especially one from Sam Adams, imploring help. Most of the Burgesses had gone home, but 25 did remain, Washington among them. So angry was the Potomac planter that he on this occasion declared that he would raise 1000 men at his own expense and march with them to relieve Boston. The assembled Burgesses did not know quite how far to go with this, and so, wanting the advice of their absent fellows, called for a Convention of the former members of the House to meet in August. When it met, it was to send to the Congress in Philadelphia the Speaker Peyton Randolph, Richard Bland, George Washington, Edmund Pendleton, Richard Henry Lee, Benjamin Harrison and Patrick Henry as delegates for Virginia. This group was, save for Henry and Lee, almost wholly conservative. Notable is the absence of Wythe. Again, he was on the sidelines of politics.

From now on the real government of Virginia would be the Conventions, of which there was a series lasting until May 1776. The last of these declared Virginia independent and urged the 2d Continental Congress to do likewise for all the colonies. These Conventions, of course, were really the House of Burgesses under another name.

The first one met in the City of Williamsburg on 1 August 1774. Thomas Jefferson, a delegate from Albemarle County, described his action in this Convention:

> "I prepared a draught of instructions . . . to the Congress . . . the ground that . . . the only one . . . tenable, which was, that the relation between Great Britain and the colonies was exactly the same as that of England & Scotland, after the accession of James and until the union . . . In this doctrine, however, I had never been able to get anyone to agree with me but Mr. Wythe. He concurred in it from the first . . . ."[13]

The signs of war were looming fast, for in October, 1774, the Earl of Dartmouth wrote to the various colonial governors that the King had seen fit to prohibit the exportation from Britain of gunpowder or any arms or ammunition. The governors were admonished to secure ". . . any Gunpowder, or any sort of arms or Ammunition . . . under your Government . . . . Dartmouth."

And Dunmore, in a famous incident to be related, would try to do just that. At the present time, however, Dunmore was getting his army ready near the Great Kanawa River. His own war was going on apace, too, since the power of the Indians must be broken.

In the events which came swiftly now in anger, it should not be overlooked that the courts were shut. As a lawyer, this concerned Wythe deeply. The Burgesses were empowered to regulate the fees which lawyers might charge. This was always a renewed bill, being passed with each new Assembly. When the Assembly didn't meet, the Act for regulating the fees automatically expired. This meant Court actions were pretty much suspended, save for criminal cases. This meant that at this time also the debts owned British merchants could not be collected.

Before the August Convention met, the patriots set up committees in each county which passed resolutions of support for Boston and urged, generally, that non-importation resolutions be passed. It was not, strangely, until 23 December 1774 that the people of Williamsburg elected its Committee of Safety: Peyton Randolph, as ever, had the place of honor, while Robert Carter Nicholas, Ben Waller and George Wythe, with others, completed the roll. Although no records have come down to us, one can suppose that this group did just what the other committees did: inspected the merchant's books, hunted down violators of the Non-Importation Agreement, published them to public scorn, etc.

So worked up was George Washington over the boycotting of the British that he wanted especially to know how effective it was. To discover this, he asked Wythe for a list of the "taxables" (slaves of a certain age on whom were placed taxes).[14]

Dunmore called the Assembly to meet, appointing a date in Late November of this year of momentous happenings, 1774. He prorogued it quickly enough, however, when he discovered that its members were entirely in favor of all that the Convention (and the first Continental Congress) had done. They should have been, for they were simply the same people meeting under a different name. But even if Dunmore, to stiffle opposition, refused to call the Assembly after this for some time, the Virginian patriots could still meet in convention. And this they did again in March, 1775, the 20th of the month, at Richmond, where they were far enough away from Dunmore and any threat of interference.

Although Wythe was in the thick of the agitation against Britain as a member of the Williamsburg Committee, he was not chosen by the voting freeholders to attend the 20 March 1775 Convention. When it met, the question was not what shall we do? But how shall we do it? The delegates knew that they must put the colony in a state of defense. But should they set up a regular army, or should they simply call out the militia? The latter course would usurp the Governor's prerogative, but who cared? Robert Carter Nicholas favored the setting up of a permanent army and, as Nicholas was a conservative, this was quite a step. Some historians have maintained that Wythe likewise favored this, supporting Nicholas. However, there is not a single trace of evidence that Wythe was even present. It is true that he may very well have been, for tradition relates that it was at this time that Patrick Henry, speaking of Wythe, pays him a splendid compliment: "Shall I light up my feeble taper before the brightness of his noon-tide sun?" And answering himself he continued: "It were to compare the dull dewdrop of the morning to the intrinsic beauties of the diamond."[15] Henry, of course, wanted the defence to consist of militia. Such a plan would not take the people away from their farms too long, and this in an agricultural community was important. The need for arming the country had been made apparent fully well by Henry's blood-stirring peroration:

> "It is in vain, sir, to extenuate the matter. Gentlemen may cry Peace, Peace—but there is no peace. The war is actually begun. The next gale that sweeps from the North will bring to our ears the clash of resounding arms! Is life so dear, or peace so sweet, as to be purchased at the price of chains and slavery? Forbid it, Almighty God! I know not what course others may take; but as for me, give me Liberty, or give me death!"

The convention decided in favor of Henry's plan. It further chose delegates to the Second Continental Congress, sending Peyton Randolph and others to Philadelphia. Among the others was young George Washington. If there was to be fighting, it would be well to have a warrior in Congress . . .

Dunmore's war against the Indians, which had taken place the previous Fall, had been occasioned by greed for western lands. The Privy Council in England now decided to change the old method of granting land, and Dunmore knew that this would anger the colonists who were beginning to question by what right the British, many thousands of ocean miles away, could high-handedly dispose of Virginia's lands. Accordingly he did not proclaim the law at once and when he did so, the Convention took exception to it.

Jefferson at this time applied to Wythe for help in preparing the Colonial position. What he needed was the wording of the original charters in the matter of land-granting and Wythe, as Clerk and so custodian of the Colony's documents, gave him what help he could. He found one charter, signed by Charles II, and copied it out for Jefferson. The colony's agent, Montague, had years earlier sent copies of other charters, and Wythe promised to send copies of these for his friend. The very next day he discovered that these had already been printed as an appendix to Stith's *History of Virginia,* so all Jefferson had to do was look therein to get his information.

Meanwhile back in Williamsburg, Dunmore was laying his own schemes. He intended to carry out the orders of Dartmouth as to keeping powder and ammunition away from the colonists. In the center of the Green in Williamsburg there exists today, after many vicissitudes, a small octagonal brick building. Within this structure were stored the arms and munitions and powder which belonged by right to the colony. A British Ship of War, probably at the urging of Dunmore, had dropped anchor in the James some distance below Williamsburg. And the resourceful Earl, calling to his aid some fifteen British Marines, quietly removed in the darkness of the night of 20 April all the powder.

So angry were the citizens that they formed under Harry Innes—an usher of the College—and George Nicholas, a student,—a military corps of their own. It may possibly have been on this occasion that George Wythe, incensed at the turn matters had taken, put on a hunting shirt, grabbed his musket and joined the younger men in their military exercises.[16] He was 48 at the time, and really couldn't take the active life of a soldier. Used to a more sedentary occupation in law and the House, he was gently told that his services were not needed. Indeed, it is reported that Wythe often took part in the military assemblies of the day.

> "He was one of the most active men of the time in favour of the revolution; wore a hunting shirt, carried a musket, and joined the military parades, which took place at Williamsburg, during the latter part of lord Dunmore's government."[17]

Dunmore, as we have seen, stole the citizens' powder on 20 April, 1775. Only the day before, on 19 April 1775,—that "famous day and year"—the citizenry of Lexington, far to the North in Massachusetts had likewise had an instance of an attempted theft of powder. For Gage had planned to take that stored at Lexington. And he failed. Revere's famous ride through the night's darkness had warned the farmers in time, and they, as minutemen, stood off the British regulars. Now, indeed, the gale that swept from the north brought to their ears the clash of these arms resounding on the hillsides of Massachusetts Bay, for the Virginians got the news of the fighting some nine days later, on 29 April 1775, from the Virginia Gazette.

On 1 June of 1775, in the capitol at Williamsburg, the House of Burgesses met and the members came from Richmond to take their seats. The new members had the oaths administered by the Council, George Wythe "Clerk of the House of Burgesses, attending according to his duty." He had with him the book with the list of the new members and the writs certified by the Clerk of the Secretary's office. After the oaths the new members repaired to the Burgesses' Chamber. The play went gravely on, with all the ritual of the past. The Governor commanded the presence of the House in the Council chamber and the members all crowded in, standing around the large table at which sat the Governor and his Council. There was the solemn choice of Speaker with the usual ritual when the members had left the Governor's presence. Henry Lee addressed himself to Wythe who stood up, silently pointed at him with his finger and then sat down. Lee moved that Peyton Randolph should be the Speaker and so he was, elected without opposition. The Mace which before lay beneath the table was now solemnly moved to the place of honor on top of the table and the play went solemnly on.

Of course, Peyton Randolph had but lately come with the others from Richmond, where he had been President of the Convention which had resolved upon arming Virginia to oppose Dunmore. Returning to the Council Chamber, the Burgesses listened to the Governor's speech, just as if the March 20 Convention for arming the militia hadn't taken place—or Henry's Liberty or Death speech!

Then, returned now again to the House chamber, they resolved to make legal their late doings in Convention:

> "Resolved *nemine contradicente,* That this House do entirely approve the Proceedings and Resolutions of the Convention of Delegates . . . ."[18]

In all the maneuvering and tacking about, Wythe must have been discretely but deeply caught up. As Clerk of the House he took the minutes and was, naturally, in that capacity a passive instrument. But outside the House, when heads were gathered together in the corridors he was undoubtedly in the middle of the intrigues—now become almost Byzantine—which sought always legally, always blandly, to put Dunmore in the wrong. Wythe's part in this, had the documentation survived, would have showed him as one of the extreme party, intent on reducing Britain's power in America (or at least, in Virginia) to almost nothing.

Another Convention met in July of this year, coming together on the 17th of the month in Richmond and lasting until 26 August. (Richmond would not always be safe from British depredations!) In this July Convention, it was thought wise to set up a Committee of Safety which from now on ruled the Colony whenever the Convention was not in session. (Dunmore had by now fled to the warship the *Fowey,* anchored in the James River.) The Virginia delegation in Congress had now a vacancy, for on 16 June 1775, delegate George Washington was chosen as the Commander-in-Chief of the military forces of the United Colonies. Washington took command of the Massachusetts forces fighting the British and integrated these into the combined Continental Army of which Congress assumed the direction. A delegate from Virginia was now needed to replace Washington. And in a letter of George Mason we discover who was chosen:

> "To Martin Cockburn, Richmond, July 24, 1775
> The Convention will tomorrow appoint a delegate to the Congress in the room of General Washington, when I believe Mr. Wythe will be almost unanimously chosen."[19]

And so he was. Thus, of the original delegation, Washington and Henry were out, since Henry was given command of the military forces of Virginia. Richard Bland also resigned, Francis Lightfoot Lee getting his place. So the delegation stood as Peyton Randolph, Richard Henry and Francis Lightfoot Lee, Thomas Jefferson and George Wythe. The inclusion of Wythe was a great honor for him, since the Convention did not ordinarily reach outside its own membership to appoint a Congressional delegate.

The same Convention was really controlled by Edmund Pendleton. And he was also the head of the Committee of Safety. Thus he was the virtual ruler of Virginia. From now on until the depths of the Revolution, the radicals (Wythe and Jefferson) had no chance to take over. Pendleton had been extremely clever, making Henry a military nonentity and sending the strongest of the progressives far away to Philadelphia.

It was reported in the Virginia Gazette, published by Pinckney (now that Hunter's Gazette was suspected of Toryism—and rightly so!), on 31 August 1775 that:

> "Last Sunday morning the honorable PEYTON RANDOLPH, esquire, left this city to attend the continental congress and on the succeeding morning GEORGE WYTHE, esquire, set off for the same laudable purpose. The LADIES of the above gentlemen accompanied them. The volunteers, as usual, paid every mark of distinction on this occasion."

Thus Mayor Dixon's Independent Company accompanied on each successive departure the delegates to the Congress, marching with them four or five miles out of town on their way. No explanation has survived to show why Wythe and Randolph didn't travel together. But each had his wife, and surely Mrs. Wythe was company enough for her husband. These journeys to the Congress at Philadelphia were the only times, as far as we know, that Wythe—or his wife either, for that matter—ever left the confines of Virginia.

Unknown to either Wythe or Randolph some few days before—on the 23d of August—King George III had proclaimed the colonists to be in rebellion.

George Wythe, journeying north across the flat lands of Virginia on his way to Philadelphia with his lady, was entering on one of the most hard-working and enjoyable periods of his life. He was going on that Monday, the 29th of August, 1775, to the foremost city in America, a city far surpassing little Williamsburg. A city with beautiful and impressive buildings—with the mansions of the wealthy fully on terms of equality with those of the nobility of Virginia. If Wythe followed the route Jefferson often took, the way led him north to Hobbes Hole, where there was a ferry across the Rappahannock River, up through Maryland crossing the Chesapeake at Baltimore to Rock Hall on the eastern shore. Then across the flat lands to Chestertown, thence up the eastern shore of Maryland to the Delaware, following that river up to Philadelphia. Arriving there, he hired lodgings for himself and Mrs. Wythe in a house opposite the Indian Queen, where many of the Congressmen stayed. The delegates worked long hours—but Wythe was used to that. There were convivial dinners, with many pleasant pipes to be smoked while discussing events and possible measures.

Wythe met the foremost men in the Colonies and worked with them on terms of friendship. It is notable that the irascible and often petulant John Adams, sarcasm itself when it came to his colleagues, never breathed an unpleasant or ugly word about George Wythe. But it was truly hard and dangerous work. Since George III had declared the colonies in rebellion, the Congressmen were in danger of being hanged if the British caught them. And the Congressional delegates were all of them very headstrong men. They argued, as stubborn people will, a great deal. And this is the reason they got so little done—they talked too much. As George Read wrote to his wife:

> ". . . I prepare in the morning for the meeting at nine o'clock, and often do not return to my lodgings till that time at night. We sit in Congress generally till half-past three o'clock, and once till five o'clock, and then I dine at the City Tavern, where a few of us have established a table for each day in the week, save Saturday, when there is a general dinner."[20]

Exactly when Wythe and his wife reached Philadelphia is difficult to determine, but it must have been at least by the 14th of September, since Josiah Bartlett wrote a letter on that date saying, among other things, "Mr. Wythe is come to Congress." Wythe may, however, have reached Philadelphia before that date. In John Adams' diary, that truculent person notes:

> "15 Septr Friday Thomas Nelson, Esquire, George Wythe, Esqr., and Francis Lightfoot Lee Esq., appeared as Delegates from Virginia."[21]

All during the month of September, Dunmore, now actively engaged in war on Virginia's people, continued raiding the river-side plantations.

> "To Thomas Jefferson   16 November 1775
> Last week the King Fisher and four tenders full of men came up to Burwell Ferry and made several attempts to land during three days stay, but never came nearer than to receive a discharge of the Rifles, when they retired with great precipitation, and 'tis supposed the loss of some men. . . . Our last Accounts from Ld. Dunmore are that he daily expects to be recalled. May the Intelligence be speedy. . . . A happy period to the Campaign in Canada, should we be lucky enough to obtain it, may go a great way in hastening peace. Nor do I think Ld. Dunmore will be so sanguine about his Piratical War, as he was, since he finds that small Arms in the hands of a few Men will keep numbers from landing. . . . I had only to mention our friend Wythe to the Town. It met their Warmest Wishes and he will be chosen, and I fancy Jos. Prentis will be his Substitute, unless Mr. Everard will accept it. Greet him and his good Lady, Colo. Lee's, Colo. Harrison, Colo. Nelson and Lady, Mr. Willing, Mr. Mease and all my worthy acquaintances in the City . . . ."[22]

In this above letter, Pendleton shows his control of affairs in Virginia. For, as he says, he had only to mention Wythe to the Town—that is Williamsburg, and the Freeholders thereof elected him as their delegate to the 4th Virginia Convention which was to meet in Richmond on December 1, 1775. Of course, Wythe was now in Congress, so the citizens elected Joseph Prentiss as his alternate. The reference to the "Campaign in Canada" is, of course, to the attempt by the Congress to seize Canada—an attempt which would drag on for many months and end in failure. Pendleton, of course, had been in the First Continental Congress and so had made many a "worthy acquaintance in the City."

Benjamin Rush served in Congress at about the same time as Wythe, and he had a good deal to say—as did also John Adams—of the pridefulness, the arrogance, the quarrelsomeness which took up so much of the energy and time of these strong and stubborn characters. Concerning, for example, Robert Treat Paine, Doctor Rush wrote:

> "He was educated for a clergyman, and afterwards became a lawyer. He had a certain obliquity of understanding [wonderful way to put it!]. He seldom proposed anything but opposed nearly every measure that was proposed by other people. And hence he got the name of "The Objection-Maker." His temper was amiable, and his speech and conversation often facetious . . . . He was remarkable for his regular and punctual attendance."[23]

Of course he was. It is not often that a stupid man can hold up the deliberations of so august a body as the Second Continental Congress. What an opportunity for a chatterbox! And Rush goes on to describe Elbridge Gerry

> ". . . a respectable young merchant, of a liberal education and considerable knowledge slow in his perceptions and in his manner of doing business and stammering in his speech."[24]

Rush remarked of George Wythe:

> "A profound lawyer and able politician. He seldom spoke in Congress but when he did, his speeches were sensible correct and pertinent. I have seldom known a man possessed of more modesty or more dovelike simplicity and gentleness of manner. He lived many years after he left Congress, the pride and ornament of his native state."[25]

Rush next described that stormy petrel of Massachusetts, Samuel Adams. Declaring that he was

> "Near 60 years of age when he took his seat in Congress but possessed of all the vigor of mind of a young man of 5 and 20. He was a Republican in principle and manners, he once acknowledged to me 'that independence of the United States upon Great Britain had been the first wish of his heart seven years before the war.' He considered national happiness and the public patronage of religion as inseparably connected."[26]

These then were some of the men with whom Wythe was to work during the next few years.

Notes to Chapter V

1. Virginia. Supreme Court of Appeals. *Reports of Cases Argued And Decided in the Court of Appeals of Virginia.* Edited by Daniel Call. (Richmond). Vol. 4, p. xiv.
2. George Washington. *The Diaries of—.* Vol. 1, p. 163.
3. *Ibidem,* p. 147.
4. Kate Mason Rowland. *Life of Charles Carroll of Carrollton.* Vol. 1, p. 55.
5. George Washington. *The Writings of—.* Edited by John C. Fitzpatrick. Washington, 1931–44), Vol. 37, p. 521–2.
6. Preston Family Papers. Manuscript Collection. Library of Congress.
7. Manuscript Collection. Virginia Historical Society, Richmond.
8. Washington. *Opus Citatum.* p. 174.
9. Manuscript Collection. Duke University Library.

10. Jefferson. *The Papers of*—. Boyd ed., Vol. 15, p. 586.

11. Virginia Supreme Court of Appeals. *Opus Citatum.* Vol. 4, p. xiv, footnote.

12. Burgesses. *Journals, 1773–76.* p. 132.

13. Jefferson. *The Writings of*—. Lipscomb ed., Vol. 1, p. 12.

14. Richard Henry Lee. *Memoir of Richard Henry Lee.* (Philadelphia, Carey, 1825) p. 105–6.

15. Virginia. Supreme Court of Appeals. Opus Citatum, p. xiv.

16. Edmund Randolph. *Manuscript History*—. p. 79

17. Virginia Supreme Court of Appeals. *Opus Citatum,* p. xiv.

18. American Archives. Edited by Peter Force. (Washington, M. St. Clair Clarke & Peter Force, 1837–53) Fourth Series, Col. 1195.

19. Helen Day Hill. *George Mason Constitutionalist.* (Cambridge, Harvard University Press, 1938), p. 122.

20. George Read to Mrs. Read, 18 May 1775, in *Letters of the Members of the Continental Congress.* Ed. by Edmund Cody Burnett. (Carnegie Institution of Washington, 1921–36), Vol. 1, p. 92.

21. John Adams. *Diary,* in *The Works of*—. Charles Francis Adams ed., Vol. 2, p. 422.

22. Edmund Pendleton to Thomas Jefferson, 16 November 1775, Williamsburg, in: Thomas Jefferson. *The Papers of*—. Boyd ed., Vol. 1, p. 260.

23. Benjamin Rush. *Autobiography of*—. Ed. by G. W. Corner. Princeton University Press, 1948), p. 155.

24. *Ibidem,* p. 147.

25. *Ibidem,* p. 151.

26. *Ibidem,* p. 139.

CHAPTER VI

At Work in the Continental Congress

The expedition to conquer Canada was already underway. A week after the Congress opened in the opulent and comfortable city of Philadelphia, the members taking their ease and pleasure amidst their squabbles, the great general Benedict Arnold, a man who showed his fortitude and patriotism in this campaign as no other would, had started up the Kennebec River to Quebec. For this was to be a two-pronged attack—the one under General Montgomery up Lake Champlain through the Sable River, to Montreal and then up the St. Lawrence to the fabled city of Quebec, the other under Arnold through the wilderness and forest fastnesses along the Kennebec through the swamps, the cold, the hunger, the floods to Quebec also. Arnold began his tortured journey with his heroic men on 13 September—a journey which equaled in hardship and perseverence the marches of military men anywhere. From now on, the main struggle Congress had was to keep this army supplied with men, food, ammunition. This was a task in itself equal to the actual fighting, for the way—even by the Champlain Lake—was roadless, through the endless forest, and even more difficult in winter than in summer.

Washington had laid siege to Gage in Boston. The Battle of Bunker Hill had taken place 17 June, 1775 and the New England men had proved they could defeat the British forces. This was more than the Virginians had yet done, for Great Bridge in Virginia did not take place until December 8th. In Congress, a motion was put to seize Governor Tryon of New York, who was gathering troops after his defeat in North Carolina (where he had been Governor). Again, an even greater need was to stop the constant torment to which Dunmore, raiding along the shores of the Chesapeake, was subjecting both Virginians and Marylanders. In the course of his depredations, Dunmore had a considerable fleet at his disposal: four men of war, the Liverpool, the Otter, the Kingfisher and the Dunmore. There were, in addition, several cutters and small craft. A resolution, aimed at Dunmore but applicable to any Tory causing mischief, was framed by Congress:

> "Resolved, that it be recommended to the several provincial Assemblies . . . to arrest and secure every person . . . whose going at large may, in their opinion, endanger the safety of the colony, or the liberties of America."

Chase, who came from Maryland, one of the assaulted colonies, lamented that the resolution did not go far enough.

> "Lord Dunmore has been many Months committing Hostilities against Virginia and has extended his Piracies to Maryland, I wish he had been seized, by the Colony, Months ago. They would have received the Thanks of all North America. Is it practicable now? Have the Committee any naval Force? This order will be a mere Piece of Paper. Is there a Power in the Committee to raise and pay a naval Force? Is it to be done at the expence of the Continent . . . ."[1]

Chase here fingered the rub. To take a pirate, ships were needed and that meant money. Lee, of Virginia, who knew Dunmore well and hated him greatly, pointed out a weakness:

> "I wish Congress would advise Virginia and Maryland to raise a Force by Sea to destroy Lord Dunmores Power. He is fond of his Bottle and may be taken by Land, but ought to be taken at all Events."

(The thought process here escapes one.)

Another Congressman, Zubly of Georgia, broke in to say that he thought the plan to be "vile, abominable and infernal" but he was ". . . afraid it is practicable." The fear was expressed that by touching an officer of the Crown, the King would be made even angrier than he was. This delicacy towards the King's royal temper was not sarcasm—the delegates (or many of them)—really revered His Angry Majesty.

Eliphalet Dyer[2] of Connecticut realistically answered:

> "They cant be more irritated at home [note the word!] than they are. They are bent upon our Destruction."

A note of satisfaction came in—Dunmore was intimate with the Royal Family, was powerfully connected in England. What a prize to catch!

> ". . . his Connections in England are such that he may be exchanged to Advantage. [Ethan Allen was presently in chains in England.] Wentworth [Governor of New Hampshire] is gone to Boston. Franklin is not dangerous [Benjamin's illegitimate son, Governor of New Jersey], Penn [of Pennsylvania is not]. Eden [Governor of Maryland] is not."

Again and again, reconciliation was the keynote, and again and again the delegates, actively fighting the King with musket and cannon, feared to go too far. Johnson of Maryland stalled for time:

"Five or six weeks will give Us the final Determination of the People of Great Britain. . . . A renunciation of all connection with Great Britain will be understood by a step of this Kind."

That is, if the colonists tried to arrest the Royal Officers, the English would take this as a Declaration of Independence. Lee, desperate with concern for Virginia, hurled back the arguments:

"Virginia is pierced in all parts with navigable Waters. His Lordship knows all these Waters and the Plantations on them. Shuldam [an English Admiral from whom Dunmore had requested naval support] is coming to assist him in destroying these Plantations. We see his Influence with an abandoned Administration [that of Lord North] is sufficient to obtain what he pleases. If 6 weeks may furnish decisive Information, the same Time may produce decisive destruction to Maryland and Virginia. Did We go fast enough when we suffered the Troops at Boston to fortify."

This was a dig at New England, where the Congress had adopted the New England troops and gave them support.

And things kept getting mixed up. Seizure of Royal Officials, trading with the world, opening some of the custom-houses or shutting them all, could the Colonies afford a naval force? Did they need one? And now Zubly gave breath to the underlying fear which nagged at the secret mind of the members:

". . . The Motion was . . . to apprehend Governor Tryon. We have not yet conquered the Army or Navy of Great Britain. A Navy consisting of a Cuter, rides triumphant in Virginia. There are Persons in America who wish to break off with Great Britain. A Proposal has been made to apply to France and Spain—before I agree to it, I will inform my Constituents. I apprehend the man who should propose it would be torn to pieces like De Witt."

At this point, Wythe broke through the hysteria with common sense and calm words:

"It was from a Reverence for this Congress that the Convention of Virginia neglected to arrest Lord Dunmore. It was not intended suddenly, to form a Precedent for Governor Tryon. If Maryland have a Desire to have a Share in the Glory of seizing this Nobleman, let them have it. The 1st objection is the Impracticability of it.—I don't say that it is practicable but the attempt can do no harm. From seizing Clothing in Delaware, seizing the Transports &c., the Battles of Lexington, Charleston, &c every Man in Great Britain will be convinced by Ministry . . . that we are aiming at an Independency on Great Britain. Therefore We need not fear from this Step disaffecting our Friends in England. As to defection in the Colonies, I cannot answer for Maryland, Pennsylvania, &c., but I can for Virginia."[3]

At this point, Francis Lewis, of New York, moved:

". . . that it be recommended to the Council of Virginia, that they take such measures to secure themselves from the practices of Lord Dunmore, either by seizing his person, or otherwise, as they think proper."

Another position in which the Congressmen found themselves was a rather anomalous one. For they had retaliated against the British by forbidding trade with them. But by so doing—stopping trade—they also prevented the supplies they needed to run the army and fight the war from reaching America. All the colonies, save New York, North Carolina, Delaware and Georgia had these non-importation measures. When it was proposed to shut all custom-houses (since they were offices of the Crown), Georgia objected strongly. Zubly, of that Colony, was on his feet once the proposal was made:

> "New England . . . may live without trade; the money circulates . . . they may live. Without trade *our people must starve;* we cannot live, we cannot feed or clothe our people. . . . I would do and suffer any thing, rather than not be free; but I am resolved not to do impossible things."[4]

He was seconded in this by John Jay of New York, where the New York Assembly had refused to join the Continental Association. Indeed the merchants of that town, ever loathe to sacrifice their trade, even sold supplies to the British army in Boston. Jay's comment was a parable:

> "If a man has lost his teeth on one side of his jaws, shall he pull out the teeth from the other, that both sides may be upon a footing? Is it not realizing the quarrel of the belly and the members? The other Colonies may avail themselves of the custom-houses in the exempted Colonies."

Chase of Maryland felt the debate had need of another sort of truth:

> ". . . if [Zubly's] position is true, and his advice followed, we shall all be made slaves. If he speaks the opinion of Georgia, I . . . lament they ever appeared in Congress. They cannot, they will not comply! Why did they come here? Sir, we are deceived! Sir, we are abused! . . . There will be jealousies, if New York and the other exempted Colonies are not put upon a footing."

At this point, Wythe tried to bring order and reason to the argument. Jay had pointed out that the proceedings were irregular, that the debate was wandering. And Wythe agreed with him, trying to get to the real point. He urged that the safety of America depended on a union of the people in it. Was it possible that the Union would continue if four members of it were allowed to do things forbidden to the others? Wythe had a good memory, and he pointed out that once before New York had refused to join with the other colonies. This had caused dissention, and Wythe, with a classical instance always in mind, recalled that

> ". . . when Attica was invaded by the *Lacedemonians,* Pericles ordered an estate be ravaged and laid waste, because he thought it would be exempted by the Spartan King."

In other words, let all suffer alike. Wythe gave the answer to Jay:

> "Nothing was ever more unhappily applied than the fable of the stomach and the limbs."

But Jay was not silenced, continuing to attack what seemed to him to be contradictory about Congress' action.

> "Lest your produce fall into the hands of your enemies, you publish a law that none go from the Continent; yet to get powder, we keep a secret law that produce be exported. Then come the wrangles among the people. A vessel is seen loading,—a fellow runs to the Committee."

Lee answered that:

> ". . . the people may be quieted by the committees of safety."

And Wythe rejoined the argument:

> "The only persons who can be affected by this revolution, are those, who, on the other side of the water, will be called smugglers. Consider the danger these smugglers will run; liable to seizure by custom-house officers in the port they go to. What can they bring? Cash, powder, or foreign manufactures? Can't see the reason for restraining our trade, as little can be carried on. My opinion, we had better open our trade altogether. It has long been my opinion, and I have heard no arguments against it."

And there Wythe stood. To open trade altogether. Away with the sophistry of to shut or not to shut the custom-houses. But his arguments did not prevail for Zubly again on the next Saturday presented Georgia's case:

> "We can't do without powder, intelligence, drugs. Georgia must have an Indian war, if they can't supply the Indians. The Creeks and Cherokees are in our Province. . . . Eighteen millions of dollars is an enormous sum of money . . . We are to pay six millions now, twelve millions more presently, and have no trade. I could bear the character of a madman, or that of an emissary of Lord North, rather than believe it possible to pay eighteen millions of dollars without trade. Can we make bricks without straw? We can live upon acorns, but will we?"[5]

Wythe apparently supported this, and to protect trade argued for an American navy:

> "Commerce, whether we consider it in an economical, a moral, or political light, appears to be a great good; . . . Why should not America have a navy? No maritime power near the seacoast can be safe without it. . . . America is one of the wings upon which the British eagle has soared to the skies. . . . The British navy will never be able to effect our destruction. . . . Why should we divert our people from commerce, and banish our seamen? Our petition may be declared to be received graciously, and promised to be laid before Parliament, but we can expect no success from it. Have they ever condescended to take notice of you? Rapine, depopulation, burning, murder. Turn your eyes to Concord, Lexington, Charlestown, Bristol, New York; there you see the character of Ministry and Parliament. . . ."

But the running debate over trade was for a moment interrupted by another of the worries of Congress. Allied to the matter of the arrest of the Royal officials who had conducted raids against the colonies was the matter of the raids themselves. A spirit of anger was building up and the Congressmen came to feel that the British should be made to pay for what they were doing. Hence Silas "Ticonderoga" Deane, John Adams, and George Wythe were made a committee to secure

> ". . . a just and well authenticated account of the hostilities committed by the ministerial troops and navy in America, since last March . . . with evidence of the truth . . . the number and value of the buildings destroyed . . . vessels inward and outward bound . . . also the stock taken by them. . . ."[6]

In relating the news of the committee to his wife Abigail, John Adams described Wythe as

> ". . . a new member from Virginia, a lawyer of the highest Eminence in that Province, a learned and very laborious man; so that We may hope this Commission will be well executed. . . ." [7]

Appointed on Wednesday, 18 October, they got right to work, for the next day the Committee sent out a letter to the New Hampshire Committee of Safety asking for information. Shortly, they were flooded with details about the British destruction. Indeed, the rumor evidently went around that the Congress was to pay for this, and claimants even sent in bills for damages wrought by the American army itself. In the end, however, it was labor lost, for nothing apparently was ever done with the information collected.

The various *ad hoc* committees, such as this was, could find their own time to work—in the odd hours of the night or whenever the Congress was not in session. But this was seldom, and, as usual, the weeks-long debate over exporting continued. On 20 October, Chase picked up with

> ". . . We have letters from Guadaloupe, Martinique, and the Havana, that they will supply us with powder for tobacco. . . . The proposition is for exporting for a special purpose,—importing powder. . . . I would restrain the merchant from importing any thing but powder. . . ."[8]

Jay of New York contradicted this:

> "We want French woollens, Dutch worsteds, duck for tents, German Steel, &c. . . . Shall we shut the door against private enterprise?"

Here Peyton Randolph broke in to point out:

> "We are making laws contradictory in terms. We say nobody shall export, and yet somebody shall, Against all rule."

Finally, on 30 October, we find in the Journals of Congress the laconic statement by Ross of Pennsylvania:

> "We can't get seamen to man four vessels. We could not get seamen to man our boats, our galleys. Wythe, Nelson, and Lee for fitting out four ships."[9]

Randolph had, as above noted, argued that the Congress was "making laws contradictory in terms." He should have known, with his many years of experience as Speaker of the House in Virginia. But this observation was to be one of his last. Before the week-end was out, he was dead, cut down suddenly and sadly. As Richard Henry Lee wrote to Washington:

> "Tis with infinite concern I inform you that our good old Speaker Peyton Randolph Esquire went yesterday to dine with Mr. Harry Hill, was taken during the course of dinner with a dead palsey, and at 9 o'clock at night died without a groan—Thus has American liberty lost a powerful Advocate, and human nature a sincere friend."[10]

There were other consequences as well, for in Virginia the political power Randolph thus vacated was seized by Edmund Pendleton. Peyton's brother John was a Tory; John's son, Edmund, while brilliant and able, was very young. Wythe was in Congress, as was Jefferson, and the two Lees. Nicholas was a conservative and the Treasurer besides, Henry wanted to be a warrior and was sulking in his tent, Bland was old and growing blind and so Pendleton assumed complete control without much struggle.

If it wasn't one thing, it was another. Burdened with work and saddened with this death as Wythe was, a further worry intruded. The Western lands claimed by Virginia were always of concern to Wythe—the winning of Virginia's great western empire was in no small part due to him. By the terms of the original charter which James I of Scotland and England had given to the London Company of Merchant Adventurers who had founded Virginia, the colony was to stretch from sea to sea—that is, from the Atlantic to the Pacific. Of course, it wouldn't really, for eventually it came to the territory claimed by Spain—the trans-Mississippi Valley. But Virginia did claim the lands presently encompassed by Wisconsin, Michigan, Ohio, Indiana, Illinois, Kentucky and West Virginia. Now a company had been formed in North Carolina which, leaping back over the centuries, tried to set up a proprietorship in Virginia's western lands. This was called the Transylvania Company, and it assumed title to lands in Ohio by virtue of purchase from the Indians. The leading spirits in this were Richard Henderson, Thomas Hart, John Williams, John Luttrell, William Johnston, James Hogg and Leonard Bullock. Virginia strongly contested their claim, but they didn't give up easily. They even sent their own embassy to Congress. This was James Hogg, who tried to interest John Adams in supporting him. He arrived in Philadelphia 22 October and both Samuel and John Adams advised him to

> ". . . sound the Virginians, as they would not choose to do anything . . . without their consent. . . . All the Delegates were . . . so much engaged in Congress from Morning to night, that it was some days before I was introduced to the Virginians, and before that was informed that some of them had said . . . they would not consent that Transylvania should be admitted as a Colony and represented in Congress until it originated in their Convention and should be approved by their constitutents. Some days after that, I was told that Messrs. Jefferson, Wythe and Richard Henry Lee were desirous of meeting with me, which was accordingly brought about . . .
>
> They seriously examined our map, & asked many questions. They observed that our purchase was within their Charter . . ."[11]

The business over Transylvania, despite the optimism of Hogg, was a bone for the Virginians to gnaw at their leisure over the coming years. Eventually, Virginia conquered the territory for itself, a conquest in which Wythe was to have a very important part.

Work increased rather than diminished during the month of October, for on the 23d, Wythe, Johnson, Jay, Edward Rutledge, Samual Adams, Jefferson and Franklin were appointed to investigate the rumor in Philadelphia that certain persons had refused to take as legal tender the money printed by the Pennsylvania Assembly. And on 28 October, the committee on Salt Petre, an essential ingredient in gunpowder, having lost two members, Peyton Randolph and John Morton, got three new ones: Wythe, Robert Treat Paine and Charles Humphreys.

Just as Georgia had feared the menace of Indians left without trade goods, so did New York. The situation was made more ominous because the Tory leaders of the Upstate Country, Sir John and Guy Johnson were friends and patrons of the Indians, having their loyalty and love. A treaty had been made with the aborigines by the Congressional Commissioners of the Northern Department somewhat earlier, when Congress was trying to appease the Iroquois—for those were the Indians in question. This was essential, for the great Indian empire which they controlled stretched from Canada down through Kentucky. Mostly they were attached to the English side, but the Americans did have some few ploys to attract them. A letter of 6 November, from an Albanian with the improbable name of Vokert P. Douw, was read in Congress on 11 November:

> "Hon. J. Hancock:
> Sir:. . . Mr. Deane . . . informs me that the Cayuga, Mohawk, and Senecas, who went with Colonel Johnson, are returned from Canada, and informed their brethren that they had taken up the hatchet against the Colonies, at the request of Colonel Johnson, in Canada, which their brethren, who had been on the treaty here, were much displeased with, and insisted that they should bring said hatchet to the Commissioners at Albany, to be buried. . . ."[12]

This was bad news, for if "said hatchet" were really taken up, the frontier would be boiling with smoke and fire and blood once again. It was especially bad since the Iroquois (or at least, the Mohawk tribe of that Confederacy) lay athwart the route to Canada by which supplies could be sent to the army there, presently besieging Montreal.

In an effort to keep the route open and prevent the Indians from attacking, Congress set up a committee made up of Wythe, Franklin, Sherman of Connecticut, James Duane of New York and Cushing of Massachusetts. The celebrated missionary to the Oneida Indians, Samuel Kirkland (founder of Hamilton College) had brought Vokert P. Douw's letter to the Congress. The Committee conferred with him and concluded that, Deists though the Congressmen may have been, Christianity did have its uses. The missionary was given money that he might return to his Indians "for the propagation of the Gospel . . . and conciliating their affections to the United Colonies. . . . ." A week later, on 22 November, Wythe's committee gave a further report, that trade goods should be sent to the Indians, Congress itself to provide the goods. Also, General Schuyler, the commanding general at Albany, was to give the Indians powder "if he can spare it." Some $750 was to be spent by the Northern Commissioners to entertain the Indians (more than they gave Kirkland to convert them) and somehow blacksmiths were to be provided who should live and work with the Indians.

These latter were especially important as the Indians needed iron workers, they themselves not knowing how to operate a forge.

Much of Wythe's work in Congress (and the same was true of the other members) was made up of the commonplace drudgery of administration. For the Congress was all three branches of government—executive, legislative, judicial. An instance of judicial work comes from Washington's request for directions from Congress on how to treat such enemy vessels as they might capture. Wythe, Rutledge, John Adams, Franklin and Wilson were made a committee to decide on this. Wythe was especially concerned, for he and Wilson were two of the greatest lawyers in the land, and Wythe, far back in his very young days when he had been Attorney General of the Virginian province under Dinwiddie had also been by the same office the Judge of the Vice Admiralty Courts. His good friend Ben Waller was to have this office now and for many years to come. As the Americans came to wage war on the sea, this work became ever more important. Wythe's committee recommended that prize courts be set up. For once, Congress did not delay, for on 25 November they were duly erected.[13]

Some twelve days before this happened, far to the north in Canada, Arnold had come to the end of his agonizing trek through the Maine wilderness and now stood in awe before the towering citadel of Quebec—awe enhanced by the glittering spires of the churches which sent their narrow crosses heaven-ward. Now the siege began—one of the most heroic in the bloody story of American warfare. Arnold proved himself over and over again a hero, devoted to the American cause as few of his compatriots were. Certainly, the cool patriots sitting at their ease in the coffee-houses in Philadelphia debating the course of events knew little of the suffering Benedict Arnold's frozen, starving band was enduring before the walls of the old city.

The siege had hardly begun, however, when Carleton, having fled from Montreal, managed to scuttle into the town, his presence putting a ramrod up the spines of the besieged inhabitants. The fighting there might be bloody and cruel, but elsewhere the earnest charade of loyalty to the King went on. Even the generals indulged in it. When he heard of the fall of Montreal to Montgomery, Schuyler trumpeted a letter to Trumbull, Governor of Connecticut:

"May Heaven . . . prove propitious and Britons and Americans once more regard each other with the fond tenderness of a parent and child."![14]

Within a few days, however, news came to the Congress which stopped the endless debating of the Congress on the matter of ships, naval action, whether or not to arrest Crown officials, etc. For the Committee of Safety of Northampton County, in Virginia, wrote to say that Lord Dunmore had proclaimed martial law, seized Norfolk and the County of Princess Anne, started to enroll the slaves in his army, commenced a Loyalist Association, and begun to export goods to the West Indies in contradiction to the Non-Exportation Agreement. Dunmore offered freedom to any slave joining his army. This was on 17 November.

Now the time for leniency towards Dunmore was past. Pushing the foot-draggers out of the way, the Congress told Virginia to set up a new government—this in itself was not really new, for Congress had given the same recommendation to Massachusetts the previous June, as it had to New Hampshire and South Carolina. On 2 December Congress decided that the two ships it had recently acquired should be sent against the Scotch Lord. Pilots who knew Virginia's waters were sent for and two of these actually arrived in Philadelphia. However, two British warships arrived in the Chesapeake and the Congress, fearing to risk its vessels, decided not to help Virginia.

But again, it it wasn't one thing, it was another. For years there had been a now-smouldering, now-burning quarrel between Connecticut and Pennsylvania. The whole of the northern part of that state, namely the Wyoming Valley, was claimed by Connecticut. Fighting had broken out in 1775 in real earnest when a certain Plunkett of the Pennsylvania forces attacked a Connecticut settlement. After this he was given a force of 700 men and he continued his attacks on the Connecticut settlers who, however, ultimately defeated him. Throughout the Revolution, Connecticut's military supremacy went unchallenged. Thus, although the various colonies could not find the men to fight the British, they were able to find the men to fight each other. Congress gave the question of settling this dispute to a committee composed of Wythe, John Jay, William Hooper and others. This was on 27 November. At this point, the Second Continental Congress resembled the old woman who lived in the shoe, having so many children she didn't know what to do. From fighting Dunmore in Virginia, to keeping the peace between Connecticut and Pennsylvania, to supplying Arnold and Montgomery before Quebec's citadel—the Congressmen were busy. And above all, despite the Tories and semi-Tories in Congress, the idea of independence would not be silenced. And yet the old dependence on Britain remained a powerful thing. Like the Israelites looking back on the Egyptian flesh-pots, the reluctant Americans hated to give up their old attachment to "home"—the mother country.

Over in the Jerseys, but a few miles from Philadelphia, in Burlington, in fact, the Provincial Assembly, William Franklin still being the Governor, prepared to send yet another petition to the King. No matter how contumaciously or scornfully the petitions of past months had been received by the King, Lords and Commons, perhaps yet another laid with proper servility at the feet of his Graciously Angry Majesty, Farmer George, might set awry matters aright. But the Congressmen thought this would never do. If a new petition were sent to England, the English surely must interpret this as weakness on the part of the Americans. Congress therefore sent a three-man committee: Dickinson (himself a temporizer and no friend as yet to Independence), Jay (of New York, a most reluctant colony indeed), and Wythe to plead with the Jerseyites not to petition the English government any more.

Our only knowledge of what was said comes from intercepted letters of the Tory Governor Franklin. The latter wrote to Lord Dartmouth:

"After the draught of an address was prepared, which would probably have passed the House, a committee of the General Congress at Philadelphia came in great haste to Burlington, desired admittance into the Assembly, which being granted, they harrangued the House for about an hour on the subject and persuaded them to drop the design."[15]

According to Franklin, Dickinson said that it was needful that the British be made to understand that the colonists were in earnest, that they would fight (indeed were fighting), and that all the colonies should act in concert. Dickinson emphasized that the colonists should not appear as a "rope of sand" to be scuffled apart. Jay seconded him, telling the Assemblymen that we had "nothing to expect from the mercy or justice of Britain." And Wythe followed up the remarks of his colleagues with more of the same.

The New Jersey Assembly gave balm to its pride by simply letting the petition die, reasoning that since other petitions were still before His Majesty, an answer to those should come before yet another was sent floating across the Atlantic.

On 9 December Wythe was again back in Philadelphia where he was put on a committee to consider General Schuyler's problems, his fellows in this matter being Dickinson and Thomas M'Kean. From now on, relations with Schuyler, considering his problems, getting him supplies, etc., would fall mainly on Wythe; whoever else was on the committee in regards to Schuyler and the Northern Army, Wythe was invariably a member.

The old business of how far the Colonists were to be allowed to prey on British shipping came up again in December, as it would constantly and intermittently in the year to come. When news arrived from General Washington, 19 December, that Massachusetts sailors had taken two more British ships, Wythe airily proposed that any person should have full and complete leave to seize all British ships, where ever on the surface of the sea found. This was reprisal with a vengeance. Sadly, it lost by five colonies against four. It was finally decided that only those vessels found to be aiding the British in any way were liable to seizure.

Events were now developing with frightening swiftness. The Canadian expedition was an everlasting worry. The troops had enlisted for only one year; when that year was finished they would vanish homeward. The small-pox kept great numbers of the troops on the sick list, food was in ever-dwindling supply, the Quebecois were not at all enthusiastic about their Protestant invaders (the Clergy having been warned by the Bishop not to support the Americans) —everything was in short supply except hardship and hostility. Schuyler had earlier warned the Congress that something must be done, but Congress temporized as usual by sending a committee to Albany to talk with the General.

This returned to Congress and Congress appointed yet *another* committee to confer with the previous committee! On this were put Dickinson, McKean, Wythe, Hooper, Jefferson and Langdon.

The situation was urgent, for during this very last week of December, 1775, the American army, unbeknownst to the Congress at Philadelphia, was readying itself for the frontal attack on the heights of Quebec itself. Sick, tired, hungry, the weak American army dared to do what Wolfe himself had not done. For Wolfe had fought his battle on the heights before the citadel, the Plains of Abraham. What Arnold and Montgomery would try to do was to storm the lower town along the river's edge, and then climb up the precipitous hill to the upper town. Surprise was an essential element, but if the British were alerted, then the Americans would have to fight hand-to-hand up the steep precipices.

And so it came about. Montgomery hurried to the attack, knowing that some of the soldiers were due to return home the very next day—their enlistment period was up. And nothing, nothing could induce them to endure any more of the freezing, cruel cold, and the vicious, weakening hunger. On the morrow, they would start back home. No one and nothing could stop them. Save death itself, and some would meet just that in this midnight battle on New Year's Eve. On the night of 31 December, in the icy cold of the Northern Winter, in a swirling snow-storm, the American army attacked. The attempt came within a fraction of victory, but before the action was over, brave Montgomery lay on the battlefield dead. And Benedict Arnold's leg was shattered by mustket-fire, while most of the attackers who had entered the lower town were captured. And the American army fell back in the cold to their camp, maintaining now only the pretense of a siege. Before long, they had to abandon even that and make their agonized retreat down the treacherous St. Lawrence to an only-too-temporary haven in Montreal.

But all this fighting was, at present, unknown to Wythe and his colleagues in the City of Brotherly Love. For on 1 January, 1776, the day after Arnold and Montgomery were defeated, Congress placidly took note of a letter from General Washington. There were aspects of satisfaction in it, for the General announced the capture of the sloop *Betsey,* a vessel sent by Lord Dunmore loaded with Indian corn, oats, potatoes, as supplies for the British army in Boston. Some of this food may very well have come from Wythe's own plantation of Chesterville, for his dishonest, rascally and Tory overseer was hand-in-hand with Dunmore and often supplied him with food from Wythe's property, unbeknownst, of course, to Wythe.

But Dunmore had himself got his just desserts on this New Year's Day, being forced to evacuate Norfolk. The news came to the Congress on 8 January. It was early in January likewise that the Americans got the news that the King had graciously declared them to be in a state of rebellion. It arrived on the same day that Thomas Paine gave an answer to King George in the form of a pamphlet entitled "Common Sense." Yet such was still the fear of the bugaboo word "Independency" that Paine published his work anonymously.

On the next day after Paine's pamphlet came out, James Wilson, of Pennsylvania, came into Congress with an address to counteract Paine's work. He held a copy of the King's speech at the opening of Parliament wherein His Majesty charged the colonists with working for independence. Now that Paine's pamphlet was out, it would certainly seem that the King was right. Yet what a fool George III was, when so many of the Americans right in Congress were trying with every desperate means to keep America within the empire! Wilson, anxious to overcome the stigma of independency, moved that a committee be appointed to explain to the world what were the true intentions of Congress—and those intentions certainly did not aim at independence. There were many who supported Wilson, and among these were Cushing and Robert Treat Paine, John Adams' colleagues from Massachusetts! So angry were the Forward Men that, stung by the success of Wilson's move, they declared that ". . . if a Foreign Force shall be sent here, they are willing to declare the Colonies in a State of Independent Sovereignty."[16] And this, of course, only proved the accusation the Accommodation people had been hurling at them was true. They really did want independence.

But despite this Congressional quarrel, it was necessary to govern the Army. In this matter, one of the strange details of the Revolution concerns Negro troops. As we have seen, Dunmore was willing, indeed, anxious to use them in Virginia. He had issued a proclamation (antedating Lincoln by some 90 years) freeing the Virginian slaves that would join him. Indeed, we know that there were serious proposals by patriot leaders (for example, Laurens of South Carolina) to enlist slaves in the American army, giving them their freedom in exchange for fighting. Indeed, in Virginia there are cases where this did happen. But what about persons of color who might be free already and wish to fight for American liberty? For there were many such in the American army, as foreigners noted. On this subject, Washington now wrote to the Congress, 31 December 1775:

> "It has been represented to me, that the free Negroes who have served in this Army, are very much dissatisfied at being discarded. As it is to be apprehended that they may seek employ in the Ministerial Army, I have presumed to depart from the Resolution respecting them and have given license for their being enlisted. If this is disapproved by Congress I shall put a stop to it."[17]

The question was given to a committee composed of Wythe, Samuel Adams and Wilson. The question had arisen before, Edward Rutledge having worked to compel the discharge of the colored soldiers. However, the Wythe Committee reported favorably to Congress, and that body gave grudging assent: ". . . that the free negroes who had served faithfully in the army at Cambridge, might be re-enlisted therein but no others."[18]

From now on, most of the committee work regarding Washington and his army would involve Wythe. All kinds of administrative problems thus came to

Wythe who, together with others on his committee, tried to settle them. For example, Washington referred to Congress and Congress referred to Wythe and his fellows the matter of the Massachusetts soldiers—four companies of them. The province wanted Washington to pay them but the General was puzzled—were these men part of his army or not? This was a matter of some moment to the two Adamses, Samuel in particular wishing to see ". . . justice done to the colony." Also referred to Wythe, Adams and Wilson was another letter of Washington, written on 31 December 1775.[19] The General was now more concerned about the pay for the whole army than merely for a couple of provincial companies. He noted rather curtly that he had written Congress on 25 December, but had had no reply. He wanted money to pay the troops up to at least the first of January, and since no funds had been forthcoming, the army was murmuring. Every month the army expenses were about $275,000. The clothing heretofore sent the army did not outfit even half the men in uniform. And so on. The Commander-in-Chief had even written to Schuyler in Albany to send him clothing, piously hoping that Montgomery could take care of himself. Washington's last news from Quebec had come by a Captain Freeman, who had left that place the day before Christmas, and thus he didn't know what had befallen Arnold in that blinding year's end midnight. But he soon would, and so would Congress, for on 18 January Captain Antill completed his torturous journey from Quebec. They had received letters the day before from Schuyler giving his news—but after the defeat of Arnold, Antill was sent to report directly to the Congress and to plead for help from that distant legislature.

Following the snowy banks of the frozen St. Lawrence, he reached Montreal, then down the course of the Sorel River to St. Johns, across the icy fastnesses of Lake Champlain, the low Adirondacks glowering against the cold winter sky, and on to Albany. Thus far by foot and horse. Now after a short rest in the Dutch warmth of the old city on the Hudson, by sleigh down the reaches of the river. Skirting New York, he travelled over the Jerseys in their cold lonely desolation to reach Philadelphia. He was at once closeted with the Congress, where the delegates gave him silence and attention. He told them of the death of the brave Montgomery in the coldest winter in ten years in Canada, explaining that the British guards on the walls of the citadel could stand guard duty for only a half hour at a time, so fearful was the cold. American sentries, on the far edges of the Plains of Abraham were sometimes found dead, frozen at their posts.

Antill went on to describe how Arnold with his men had attacked the lower town and had even entered it. Then the musket shot had crippled the General's leg, the swirling snow had confused the men, the British, under cover of the houses, began a counter-attack and the Americans already in the town were cut off, Arnold himself barely able to escape capture—and now the troops, far away in a hostile country, were even worse off than before, for the natives now knew they were defeated, and would not supply them with food or firewood.

Now the business was up to Congress. Brave men had fought and died while they talked. Would they at last act, or would they talk even more?

So serious was the news that some in Congress even proposed to wear mourning—and well they might. But this would alarm the populace and give solace to the enemy. Optimism must be presented to the world. Now was the time for courage, not weeping. Congress, shaken from its usual temporizing, gave the matter to a committee, as usual. It had, however, at least the grace to keep a man like Dickinson out of it, giving the chairmanship to Sam Adams, and associating with him Wythe, Lynch, Sherman and Ward. These were all Canada-men, who wanted to support the troops there as much as possible. This committee put forth many resolutions regarding what should be done, but writing resolutions and getting their colleagues to act upon them was another thing indeed. Congress did not act until Arnold, beaten, was forced to retreat from Quebec down the St. Lawrence, hoping to reach Montreal before Carleton could catch him. All that winter until the early Spring, Congress argued on the matter.

But even in the midst of a war for freedom, the matter of servitude intruded. On 27 January, Wythe was put on a committee of three to report on the practice of enlisting apprentices and persons in debt into the army. The rule was that servants (i.e., apprenticed persons) were not allowed in the army. It is interesting to note here that some white persons at this time were in a sense slaves, just as were Negroes. Of course, the Negroes were slaves for life, while indentured persons were slaves only for a stipulated time, and owed service under certain conditions. Nonetheless, such servants could be bought and sold, just as slaves were. There are several instances of Washington selling his white servants when it suited his purposes.[20] It was strictly forbidden to receive them into the army, of course. And this was what Wythe and his associates were to look into.

At about the same time, Wythe's own personal life intruded into his business in the Congress. For by this time Dunmore had retreated from Norfolk and many of the unfortunate Negroes who had joined him were now wandering around the countryside derelict. Some of them he had taken with him, where they sickened and died of camp fever. But he didn't apparently have food enough for all, and so when he abandoned Norfolk, many of his colored hangers-on were simply shaken loose. Of these we find in a report of the committee to inquire into the prisoners in the goal of the Virginia Convention, Wednesday, 17 January 1776,

". . . Many negroes—those who bore arms under Dunmore—to be sold in the West Indies . . . or Bay of Honduras . . . And that *Neptune* belonging to George Wythe, Esq. was taken up as a runaway. . . ."[21]

The slaves were advertised in the *Virginia Gazette,* their owners to have them on payment of the jail costs. If they weren't claimed, then they were to be sold at public auction, and the money was to be given to the owners. Thus the Virginia Convention in the War for Independence. What action Wythe took is not known, but certainly he was too busy in Philadelphia to do more than give his private affairs glancing attention.

The dog days of February were now here. Dull, overcast with winter's frown, Philadelphia then as now was not a cheerful place in Winter. But the Congress worked on, Wythe doing his industrious share. At this time, 9 February, Wythe and the others who wished independence had the aid once again of John Adams, that stalwart Bostonian, who had just returned from his leave. While home (or as close to it as he could get, since Boston was besieged), he participated in Washington's war councils. Now he was back in Congress and the Congressional fight for independency went forward with renewed vigor.

On 9 February, another letter from Washington was turned over to a committee on which Wythe sat, together with Chase, John Adams, Penn and Rutledge. (By now it is axiomatic that Wythe was on any committee which concerned Washington and his army, or any which considered the state of the Canadian expedition, whether the letter concerning it was from Schuyler, Arnold or any of the other generals.) Once again, Washington pointed out his needs:

> "No man upon earth wishes more ardently to destroy the nest in Boston, than I do; no person would be willing to go greater lengths than I shall, to accomplish it. . . . But if we have neither powder to bombard with, nor ice to pass on, we shall be in no better situation than we have been in all the year; we shall be worse, because their works are stronger."[22]

So beset with lack of arms and powder was the General that, having asked the various New England States for supplies and been disappointed, he had sent "as the last expedient" officers into the country ". . . with money to try if they can buy."

But Washington wasn't the only one without arms for his soldiers. Schuyler also wrote on 14 February that General Wooster in Canada had applied to him for military stores since there were none in that country. To which Schuyler replied that he couldn't help, for there were none at Albany either. Schuyler asked for money for the Canadian expedition, and complained that the two Pennsylvania companies which had been sent to him had neither mittens or moccasins. He petulantly added that the various colonies ought to supply their troops with necessaries before sending them out on military duty. But the troops in Canada didn't have shoes either, and would Congress please sent some money to pay such Connecticut troops as were on duty at Albany?

All through this sad winter, Wythe and his fellows argued for reinforcements for the Canada expedition, but the rest of the Congress were obdurate. It was forever a matter of never enough supplies, money, ammunition. Finally, on Saturday, 17 February, John Adams, Wythe and Sherman were selected as a committee to prepare instructions and a commission for the delegation the Congress had decided to send to Canada. For it was determined that Congressmen should go to see for themselves the situation there. It was not, however, to be as simple as that, for weeks were to go by after the committee had prepared its draft of instructions, weeks in which the delegates argued over the precise extent of the delegation's authority.

John Adams reported with glee on 18 February, the next day, to James Warren in Massachusetts that Dr. Franklin and Chase of Maryland were selected as the Congressional Commissioners to go to Canada. These were strong liberty-men, all interested in the Canadian venture. Not only had the Congress selected these, but the forward wing, of which Adams was naturally one, had managed to include in the delegation a Mr. John Carroll, who was a Roman Catholic priest (later the first Bishop of the Catholic Church in America). He was to try to counteract the influence of the Bishop and clergy of Quebec. And Adams continued:

> "The Unanimous Voice of the Continent is Canada must be ours; Quebec Must be taken. . . ."

And he added from 3 Jeremiah 12:

> "Go proclaim these words towards the North. Return thou backsliding Israel and I will not cause my anger to fall upon You, for I am merciful and will not be angry forever."[23]

Next occurred an instance, once again if one were needed, which demonstrated how the gnat of independency stuck in the throats of the reluctant ones. For the Provost of the College at Philadelphia, Dr. William Smith, was asked to deliver a Sermon during the Memorial service which Congress held for the late General Montgomery.

In his sermon, Smith maintained that the Congress was in favor of continuing dependence on Britain. William Livingston later moved in Congress that Smith be thanked and that his eulogy be printed. That would be a public assertion in print that everything the Forward Men in Congress wanted was frowned on by that body, so Wythe, John Adams, Chase, Rutledge, Wolcott and Sherman fought it ardently. So angry were they, indeed, that William Livingston finally withdrew the motion. The strength of the conservatives is apparent when one reflects that this happened as late as 21 February 1776, when it should have been apparent to all that dependence on England was a shattered dream.

Thus even in the midst of pushing the action in Canada, the Forward Wing was trying to shake Congress loose on the matter of trade. The interminable argument about opening the ports and trading with all the world was still going on. Even Sherman of Connecticut was afraid that American trade, if allowed, might be at once crippled by the power of Britain's navy. But he did concede that if trade were opened, it would be needful to set up a treaty with a "foreign power" in order to protect American shipping.

Wythe broke into the debate, as usual, with common-sense realism. By the terms of the Association, the ports were to open 1 March, anyway, when the Association ended. The question was then what to do?

"*Faece Romuli non Republica Platonia.*
Americans will hardly live without Trade. It is said our Trade will be of no Advantage to
Us. because our Vessells will be taken, our Enemies will be supplied, the West Indies will be
supplied at our Expence. This is too true, unless We can provide a Remedy. Our Virginia
Convention have resolved, that our Ports be opened to all Nations that will trade with us,
except Great Britain, Ireland and West Indies. If the Inclination of the People should
become universal to trade, We must open our Ports. Merchants will not export our Produce
unless they get a profit. We might get some of our Produce to Markett, by authorizing
Adventurers to Arm themselves, and giving Letters of Mark—make reprisals. Secondly, by
inviting foreign Powers to make Treaties of Commerce with us. But other Things are to be
considered before such a Measure is adopted."

And now Wythe went to the core of the argument:

"In what Character shall we treat, as subjects of Great Britain—as Rebells? Why should
We be so fond of calling ourselves dutifull Subjects. If we should offer our Trade to the Court
of France, would they take Notice of it, any more than if Bristol or Liverpool should offer
theirs, While We profess to be Subjects.—No. We must declare ourselves a Free People."[24]

And so there it was—out in the open. Independency. And that was where
Wythe stood. And this had to be serious. It was a forever thing, not a temporary
measure. For:

"If We were to tell them, that after a Season, We would return to our Subjection to Great
Britain, would not a Foreign Court wish to have Something permanent."

Furthermore, Wythe went on, a fleet was needed. This was an old proposal,
one he had argued for far earlier, when he had first come six months before to
Congress. The belief that an American fleet might bankrupt the Continent was
nothing to Wythe, who believed that America could have as strong a fleet as it
wished. At this point Wythe moved a resolution—in fact, he moved several. The
first resolution was to the effect that the Colonies had a right to set up alliances
with foreign nations. Immediately, the conservatives, Dickinson, Wilson,
Hooper, Duane and all, began their objections. This was in fact, said they, "Independency." So strong were they that the Congress, acting during all this as a
Committee of the Whole, was asked if the question should even be considered.
By 7 to 5 votes, the radicals won.

The next day the argument broke out afresh.[25] Independence was advocated
openly and strongly. And what would be the benefits of this? The answer came
back strong and forthright:

"A free and unlimited trade; a great accession of wealth . . . a vast influx of foreigners . . .
a proportionable rise in the value of land; . . . where encouragement is given to industry,
where liberty & property are well secured. . . ."

And suppose the war should continue six years . . . ?

"We cannot pay too great a price for liberty."

Notes to Chapter VI

1. John Adams. *Diary,* in, *The Works of*—. Charles Francis Adams, ed., Vol. 2, p. 458, et. sequor.

2. It was of Eliphalet Dyer that John Adams said: "A very long winded and roundabout, obscure and very cloudy . . . tedious, yet an honest, worthy man, means and judges well . . . ." In *Letters of the Members of the Continental Congress.* Vol. 1, p. 194–5.

3. Second Continental Congress. *Journals,* Vol. 3, p. 482.

4. *Ibidem,* p. 490 et sequor.

5. *Ibidem,* p. 500 et sequor.

6. *Ibidem,* p. 298.

7. John Adams to Abigail Adams, 17 September 1775, Philadelphia, in *Family Correspondence,* Adams Papers, Series 2. Edited by Lyman H. Butterfield. (Cambridge, Harvard University Press, 1963), Vol. 1, p. 303–4.

8. Second Continental Congress. *Journals,* Vol. 3, p. 495.

9. *Ibidem,* p. 311.

10. Richard Henry Lee. *The Letters of*—. Ballagh ed., Vol. 1, p. 153.

11. *American Archives*—. Fourth Series, Vol. 4, Col. 544.

12. Second Continental Congress. *Journals.* Vol. 3, p. 350.

13. *Ibidem,* p. 358.

14. *American Archives*—. Fourth Series, Vol. 3, Col. 1603.

15. *Ibidem.* Col. 1874.

16. Richard Smith. *Diary,* Tuesday, 9 Jan 1776, in, Burnett. *Letters . . . of the . . . Continental Congress.* Vol. 1, p. 303.

17. Washington. *The Writings of*—. Ford ed., Vol. 3, p. 307.

18. Second Continental Congress. *Journals.* Vol. 2, p. 24–27.

19. Washington. *The Writings of*—. Ford ed., Vol. 3, p. 305.

20. Washington. *Writings of*—. Fitzpatrick ed., Vol. 3, p. 261.

21. *American Archives*—. Fourth Series, Vol. 4, Col. 128.

22. Washington to Congress, 24 Jan 1776, Cambridge, in, *The Writings of*—. Ford ed., Vol. 3, p. 371.

23. John Adams. *Diary.* Butterfield ed., Vol. 2, p. 233.

24. John Adams. *Diary,* in, *The Works of*—. Charles F. Adams, ed., Vol. 2, p. 486, et sequor.

25. *American Archives*—. Fourth Series, Vol. 4, Col. 1168 et sequor.

CHAPTER VII

Wythe between Philadelphia and
Williamsburg

But again the Congress seesawed between Independence and Canada. The committee on which Wythe worked so incessantly considered the needs of the expedition under Arnold as reported by Schuyler and tried to satisfy them. The General at Albany had reported that the troops being raised in Connecticut for Canada had no blankets and few arms. Each colony should supply its own men, but, said Schuyler, since Connecticut couldn't, he would take from his own scanty supply for these troops. With some impatience, he spoke his mind to Congress: "I hope none of the officers will receive any other commissions than those from Congress." Evidently, state commissions were a source of trouble! In addition, one-half of the Pennsylvania troops had defective guns. These needed repair. Even getting the troops to Albany was difficult. Why couldn't each district through which they passed supply the troops with necessities as they went through it? Reverting again to the Pennsylvania soldiers, the harried Schuyler reported that they had much venereal disease. Would it be possible to send a ship to Portugal, maybe, to get medicine? Not only that, but the army at Albany needed steel.

On the last day of February, Wythe's committee reported that enough steel should be sent to the General, and that the New Jersey delegates should provide it. As to the other details, Hancock, president of Congress, wrote a letter to Schuyler regretting the fact that he was ill, and praising him for his patriotic work as General.

This apparently was all the Congressmen had time to do as far as Schuyler was concerned, for trouble came to the radicals from the usual source—the anti-independency conservatives. A certain Lord Drummond, a young man erstwhile resident in New York, and seemingly a sort of pacific busybody, had proposed himself as an intermediary for peace. He approached Washington, and that General sent on his proposals to Congress in a letter which was referred to, as usual, Wythe, Chase, John Adams, Penn, Rutledge—all strong independence men.

> "Sir: . . . lay before Congress the enclosed letter from Lord Drummond . . . as I have never heard of his Lordship being vested with power to treat with Congress. . . . I confess it surprised me much . . . his conduct . . . is premature and officious, and leading to consequences of a fatal and injurious nature to the rights of this country."[1]

Drummond had evidently been to Congress at Philadelphia, or had had correspondence with the conservative members, for he had written to Brigadier General Robertson at Boston on 5 February from New York that he had every reason ". . . to think them most seriously disposed towards reconciliation." The conservatives knew what was in the wind, and now that Washington's letter to Congress, even disapproving as it was, had made the matter open to the delegates, they joyously sniffed out reasons why this avenue of inquiry should be opened up. Drummond had been working through Thomas Lynch, of South Carolina, and he had also lately been in England where he had discussed the American situation with the ministry.

It was on 5 March, less than a week after it had been received, that Wythe, with the help of the other Forward Men, attempted to defeat Drummond's plan. To have gone through with it at this juncture, when Congress needed all its attention, if not for Independence, or foreign trade, or foreign alliances, or the needs of Washington's troops, then at least for the Canadian expedition, would have been disastrous. And Drummond's proposal would be useful as a delaying action for a good two weeks. Without hesitation then, Wythe moved, as Congress sat as a Committee of the Whole, to the effect that ". . . no public Bodies or private Persons other than the Congress or the people at large ought to treat for Peace." Yet Wythe's motion went down to defeat, by a vote of 8 to 3. The conservatives were stronger than the Forward Men had thought. On the other hand, a motion by William Livingston to call Drummond to the Congress to explain himself (and thus give him a chance to push his peace movement forward) also was defeated. This at least was some balm to the Forward Men.

But Canada once again interrupts. Returning to the first week of March, the day before Drummond's proposal was laid before Congress, Wythe, John Adams and Sherman were made a committee to which was referred a letter from General Wooster in Canada. This had been written 11 February, and had seemingly taken some long time to reach Philadelphia. Wooster, a fat, rather alcoholic man who loved bumbo, sent trouble in his letter to the delegates. He pointed out what they already knew, that General Arnold had only one-half the troops the enemy had and had yet kept up the blockade of Quebec. Wooster

added that it was impossible to depend on the Canadians. Then he got down to
business. General Schuyler had insulted him. In fact, Schuyler had written him
that he (Wooster) had written him (Schuyler) with "unbecoming subacity."
Wooster went on to declare

> "He began to insult me immediately on my joining the Army . . . merely to indulge his
> capricious humour, which . . . he has dealt out very liberally . . . ."[2]

Evidently the insults had been going back and forth between the two generals
for some time, a sort of long-distance quarrel which boiled on merrily. On the
very same day, the committee received a letter from Schuyler. This submitted
the flat ultimatum: either Wooster or I will have to quit this department.
Schuyler added that he would continue his duty regardless of the quarrel, but
the situation was nonetheless plain: the committee could choose either Wooster
or Schuyler. It thus appeared that if these two generals couldn't fight the enemy,
they could at least fight each other.

Faced with a fight between the officers of the army, the committee apparently
didn't know what to do. So for the present they ignored it and busied themselves
with further preparations for the reinforcement of the army in Canada. Without
ado, Congress voted supplies for the soldiers in the Northland. But what was
difficult was securing the passage by Congress of the instructions for the Commissioners to Canada. Wythe and his fellow committeemen brought in these
instructions on Saturday, 9 March. They were immediately ordered to lie on the
table, that the delegates might look them over. As John Adams put it, ". . .
these instructions were opposed by our antagonists with great zeal. . . ."[3]
And the Forward Men gave them equally zealous support.

The instructions were debated for a week, but before they were accepted, the
Congressmen had plenty of other things to discuss, the most important of which
was a proposal by George Wythe. Evidently he followed the maxim: to attack,
and attack and attack. The matter was as always: to cruise or not to cruise, to
trade or not to trade. To trade meant to be attacked on the high seas by British
vessels, and the consequence of this was to grant letters of Marque and
Reprisal; that is, to give permission for Privateering. Let commercial vessels be
armed, and let them take British vessels wherever and whenever they can. It is
Richard Smith's *Diary* which gives us the window through which we can watch
Congress at work:

> 13 March 1776
> ". . . R. Morris informed Congress that a Tender was sent from New York . . . from 12
> o'clock till 4 the Congress was in Committee Governor Ward in the Chair. On the Petitions
> for allowing Privateers to cruize against the English, Chase offered a Sett of Propositions
> and Wythe a Preamble. . . . the Determination was left till Tomorrow."[4]

While Wythe's preamble on this occasion is not given, its nature was probably the same as that which he offered again on 22 March, together with Richard
Henry Lee, stating that the King of England was ". . . the Author of our Mis-

eries." This was now attacking the King directly. Hitherto, the colonists had, in their official pronouncements at least, pretended that George III was the unwitting victim of bad advice on the part of his ministers. Now the ground shifted radically. However, Wythe and Lee managed only to get the Congress to condemn the King mildly for having scorned their petitions. But a victory did come on 23 March, for John Adams wrote to Horatio Gates:

> "The Continental ships-of-war, and Provincial ships-of-war and Letters of Marke and Privateers are permitted to cruise upon British Property, wherever found on the ocean. This is not Independency you know, nothing like it. Independency is a Hobgoblin of so frightful Mien, that it would throw a delicate Person into Fits to look it in the Face."[5]

This was really Wythe's victory, for it was he who had fought so hard for permission to attack British commerce.

It was probably just about this time that John Adams wrote his pamphlet on government which, he at least claimed, had such effect on the governments of North Carolina and New York, as well as New Jersey. As he himself told the story:

> ". . . according to my best recollection. In January, 1776, six months before the Declaration of Independence, Mr. Wythe of Virginia, passed an evening with me at my chambers. In the course of conversation upon the necessity of independence Mr. Wythe, observing that the greatest obstacle in the way of a declaration of it, was the difficulty of agreeing upon a government for our future regulation, I replied that each colony should form a government for itself, as a free and independent State. "Well," said Mr. Wythe, "what plan would you institute or advise for any one of the States?" My answer was, "It is a thing I have not thought much of, but I will give you the first ideas that occur to me;" and I went on to explain to him offhand and in shorthand my first thoughts. Mr. Wythe appeared to think more of them than I did, and requested me to put down in writing what I had then said. I agreed, and, accordingly, that night and the next morning wrote it, and sent it in a letter to him. This letter he sent to Richard Henry Lee, who came and asked my leave to print it. I said it was not fit to be printed . . . , but, if he thought otherwise, he might, provided he would suppress my name. . . ."[6]

John Adams, in his ideas on government, thought strongly that the War for Independence was really a war for the protection of property rights. And he may very well have been right—for the colonists were protecting their property rights. They did not want the British government to take away their money in taxes. When he came to frame a constitution, Adams and many others of his generation buttressed property with as many forms of protection as possible. Basic was the franchise. In Massachusetts this was narrowed.

In his *Thoughts on Government,* Adams gave the results of his illiberal thinking to Wythe. There is absolutely no reason to believe that Wythe was impressed with them, for Wythe was, with Jefferson, one of the great democrats of Virginia, while Adams ultimately was a pillar of the Federalist party. There is one point in Adams' disquisition which is worth quoting, however, for its own sake. Wrote Adams to Wythe:

"You and I, my dear friend, have been sent into life at a time when the greatest lawgivers of antiquity would have wished to live. . . . I hope you will avail . . . your country [Virginia] of that extensive learning and indefatigable industry which you possess, to assist her in the formation of the happiest of Governments, and the best character of a great people."[7]

This is advice which Wythe certainly took.

Now that the British had evacuated Boston, Washington was leaving for New York, in the fear that that city might be the next target of British attack. And he was right in his fear. Meanwhile, Wythe certainly had plenty to do. He was given, along with Braxton and Jay, the task of preparing a resolve by which Tory Americans who helped the British capture American vessels or goods were to be made liable for the damages. He was likewise put on a committee to consider the state of the "Eastern Department"—that is, New England. All sorts of busy work were found for the man; he was put on the standing committee for Indians Affairs (which had just now been created). He was also appointed to investigate an oath Governor Tyron was supposed to be extracting from passengers bound for England, that they should disclose American news to no one save the Ministers of King George.

In Canada, despite the best efforts of the Congress to supply the expedition with men, money, and supplies, the outlook was dreary. The troops before Quebec hadn't ten days' provisions. In all of Canada, there were only 3000 troops, and many of these had small-pox. On 5 May, Thomas, who had taken Supreme Command in the northern province, and Wooster held a war council and decided that their position before Quebec was untenable. The very next day a British fleet appeared. A brief battle, and all was over. The fresh British troops chewed into the tired Americans. Now what should have been an orderly withdrawal became a wild retreat.

The Americans fell back along the St. Lawrence in disorganized groups, only their uniforms distinguishing them from a mob. Now it was "Save himself who can" as the colonials scattered pell-mell along the banks of the river, trying wildly to reach Montreal. Only the dilatory action of the British still at Quebec in not following up the rout saved what was left of the American force. But Carleton knew that victory was his if he could reach the Americans in their flight. The only fortress in the way of stopping Carleton was about 30 miles above Montreal, a place called the Cedars. If that could hold out, there was still a chance of saving Montreal and with it the entire expedition.

The commander at the Cedars was a certain Major Butterfield, who was soon attacked by a Major Forster with 100 Canadians together with perhaps 300 Indians. Forster summoned Butterfield to surrender after a short play of cannon fire. And surrender Butterfield did, on 18 May. He and his men, nearly 400 strong, with cannon, powder and food enough to have withstood a siege, meekly gave up. Forster must have been astonished at his easy victory—certainly the Continental Congress was when it heard of it, for Wythe and his committee, to whom the surrender was referred, reported to Congress that Butterfield should be cashiered and the surrender terms disavowed. But all the anger and disgust in far-away Philadelphia could not change the fact that Carleton's way to Montreal was now open. Soon disaster followed on the footsteps of disaster, for on 2 June, General Thomas died of small-pox. On 8 June, the last army protecting the retreat was crushed, when General Sullivan was defeated in the middle of a bog near Three Rivers.

Arnold knew what to do and did it—on 15 June, he abandoned Montreal, the Americans reeling back through the forest to their homeland.

Meanwhile, far away in Philadelphia, the Congress sat placidly on. The day-to-day administration continued. On 6 May, John Adams noted in his Autobiography what was the matter:

> ". . . sundry resolutions, which, as they stand on the Journal, will show the art . . . with which the General's letters, Indian affairs, revenue matters, naval arrangements, and twenty other things, . . . very trivial, were mixed . . . with the great objects of government, independence and commerce . . . . We could only harrangue against the misapplication of time. . . ."[8]

Congress simply was not able to be all three branches of the government: legislative, executive, judicial. An example of the trivia is in Wythe's committee work. He and his fellows had to receive the petition of Captain Delaplace, the British commander of Ticonderoga who had a year earlier been taken prisoner by Ethan Allen. He had been kept a prisoner in Hartford, Connecticut, and was now inquiring about his property at Ticonderoga . . .

Nor was this all. The petitions continued. A Colonel Easton who had fought valiantly in Canada was now in prison—for debt! To Wythe and his committee came Easton's letter:

> Philadelphia   8 May 1776
> "Honourable Sir:
> . . . I have been in jail three weeks . . . I now humbly apply to your Honour, having no friends to assist me in this part of the world. I am sued for £1500, York Currency . . . I ought to be on my way to Canada . . . May not my honour be taken till I can go to New York; . . . to settle my affairs . . ."[9]

And there was more of this trivia. In fact, much more. But just as events were reaching a chaotic climax in Canada, so in Virginia the climax—not so chaotic—was likewise mounting. All during the winter the colony had been ruled by the Committee of Safety of which Edmund Pendleton was the Chairman.

They had managed to keep Dunmore at bay, and had kept down the Tories, collected taxes, etc. Now elections were ordered for the fifth and final Convention, due 6 May, which would sit in the old Capitol in Williamsburg. This Convention included all the old leaders of Virginia, save Washington, who was commanding now in New York, Peyton Randolph, who was dead, John Randolph, who was a Tory safe in England, and the members of the Congress—Wythe, Richard Henry Lee, Jefferson. These would hurry home, however, as soon as events in Philadelphia would let them. Even though Wythe, being in Congress, did no electioneering, he was chosen as representative for Williamsburg, his alternate being Edmund Randolph.

The Virginian Congressmen, having done everything they could to bring on independence, now turned to the Virginian Convention, thinking that perhaps action by that body would shock the national Council in Philadelphia to the point of a decision. Richard Henry Lee wrote to Patrick Henry urging him to move. As Lee put it:

> "Ages yet unborn, and millions existing at present, may rue or bless that assembly on which their happiness will so eminently depend."[10]

The date of this letter is 20 April, 1776, one year almost to the day since the Battle of Lexington.

But the man who actually put the resolution to the Convention was not Henry—it was Pendleton. This took place on 15 May, and the Union flag was run up over the Williamsburg Capitol as soon as the voting was done, for now Virginia had officially told its delegates in Congress to propose independence. These were anxious days for the Congressmen—their ears were straining for news of what was happening in Virginia and their heads were full of the trivia of Congress. On 14 May, Jefferson had returned to Congress from Virginia, not knowing what the decision had been. He was terribly anxious, however, since so much of his ambition lay in his own country.

The Convention was going to set up a constitution for his beloved Virginia, and he wanted to be there to help frame it but the conservatives were clearly in power—Pendleton, Bland, Nicholas, and the others. This made Jefferson so anxious to return to Virginia that he proposed that the entire delegation should also return. (By the system of rotation, Jefferson would be the last man to go on leave from Congress. Therefore, that he might get back where his heart and mind lay, he wanted them all to go back.) Such an action would have been fatal to independence at this juncture, since every vote would be needed for such a measure. Surely Wythe, who wanted also to leave as soon as he could, must have urged this consideration on Jefferson.

Nor was this the only anxiety, for the colonies were quarrelling—as usual. For years a long and angry fight had been going on between what is today called Vermont (then the New Hampshire Grants) and the colony of New York, the latter claiming the area as part of its territory. Of course, Massachusetts and New Hampshire also claimed the land, but the Vermont people were anxious to be free of all these states. Led by Ethan and Ira Allen, they had fought off the land claims of the citizens of New York—prominent among which were those of New York's delegate in Congress, James Duane. For the moment, the Vermonters were content to petition the Congress for help.

Although the membership list of the committee which considered these petitions has been lost, the report which it submitted is in the handwriting of George Wythe, and therefore he was probably a member, together with Rodney, Harrison, Hewes and Lynch. The best these could suggest, not daring to offend the powerful New York group (Duane was a lukewarm independence man at best) and yet knowing that the Canadian expedition needed all the help it could get, Vermont lying athwart the route between Montreal and Albany, was that "for the present" the Vermonters should submit to New York.[11]

But the moment was critical. There was not time to haggle over Vermont, for Howe, having abandoned Boston, was now about to attack New York City. Congress needed the support of the people. It therefore resolved to publish an animated address to stir up the ardent patriots, to overcome the lukewarm. Chase, Jefferson, Wythe, Samuel Adams and Rutledge were to prepare this address but due to the press of business, it was not completed. But a fragment of it does exist, and that is in the handwriting, again, of Wythe. Its noble words, inspired by the danger of the moment, may have come from the mind of Jefferson or of some other man. Wythe himself, who could write strong prose when he chose, may have composed it. Its stirring words can still excite:

> ". . . If the enemy conquer, we must be wretched; if not, we may be happy. . . . Uniting firmly, resolving wisely, and acting vigorously, it is morally certain we cannot be subdued. Those among us . . . who will not join with us . . . are as contemptible for their numbers as for their baseness of soul. This is the season when others may prove that love for their country . . . Those who fall cannot die in a better cause, nor can those who survive with victory earn a nobler triumph. . ."[12]

So desperate did affairs seem, and so awful the rush of bad news from Canada, that the Congress, through the Standing Committee for Indian Affairs, ordered ways to be found to enlist some 2000 Indians in Canada, a wild straw which, thrown into the face of the ill wind, came to nothing. Far more pressing was a letter of Washington, referred to Wythe, Sergeant, Francis Lightfoot Lee, and Button Gwinnett.

The general had heard that the troops at Boston were on the edge of mutiny for lack of pay—". . . several months of which are now due."[13] Now letters rained in upon Wythe and his colleagues: some twenty from Schuyler, one from the Commissioners in Canada, one from Herman Allen, three from General Thomas, who at this moment lay dead of smallpox, three from Brigadier General Arnold, one from General Thompson . . . .

And in the middle of it all, on the 7th of June, Richard Henry Lee, obeying the order of the Virginia Convention, presented the resolution for Independence to the Congress.

Now came the first great moment of fame for Thomas Jefferson. For he, with his burning pen, was chosen to write the Declaration. Not that the Congressmen had yet agreed to Independence, oh no! Let us delay a month or so . . . But the thing might as well be written, just in case . . . And so, while on the northern reaches of Lake Champlain, Benedict Arnold was trying anxiously to throw together a clap-trap fleet of boats to stop the British invasion, in Philadelphia the delegates threw together a committee to help Jefferson write the paper.

The question of independence was really one of timing. Those who opposed it most strongly were Rutledge, Robert Livingston, James Wilson, John Dickinson. They, as the debate ripened on Saturday, 8 June, declared that they were not really against independence. But they came from colonies which had not yet instructed their delegates to vote for it, or had expressly forbidden them to do so. And the reason, really, was that the time was not yet right, said they. The answer to this came from the forward group, the delegates from the New England states and Virginia. These, of course, were John Adams, George Wythe, Richard Henry Lee, and Thomas Jefferson. Their main argument was that the Congress might just as well recognize the situation as it existed—how much more independent could one country be than to wage war against another? Furthermore, no European country would come to help America, as George Wythe had often pointed out, if it did not declare itself free. In addition, the people wanted it. This last, of course, was a gratuitous supposition. For nobody at all had ever really asked the people if they wanted it. The people never voted on independence, and in fact never even voted for the men who did vote for independence. The delegates were elected by their respective assemblies, which often were controlled by a handful of powerful and wealthy men.

By this time, so sure was Wythe that the measure was going to pass and so anxious was he to get home to Virginia for the making of Virginia's constitution that he left while the debate was going on. Jefferson made copies of the Declaration (giving therein the changes as made by Congress) and gave them to Wythe, Lee, the Italian Mazzei, and Edmund Pendleton. In addition, Jefferson gave Wythe a copy of his idea of what Virginia's new constitution should be—Wythe was to introduce this to the Convention and urge its adoption.

Wythe having left Philadelphia, the Congress continued to sit on into the hot month of July, bothered by the sting of the horseflies from the nearby stables. In the beginning of the month, the great measure was passed, and some months later, when the various delegates now on leave replaced their colleagues who then were allowed to go on rotation, they all signed it. Wythe himself would not do so until he returned to Philadelphia in the early Fall.

Mr. and Mrs. Wythe, leaving Philadelphia on 13 June 1776, made their way southward to Williamsburg, Wythe carrying with him Jefferson's two documents. We can date Wythe's arrival and departure precisely: He left a voucher of expenses which has come down to us.

"Travelling from Williamsburg to Philadelphia 300 miles, and returning with ferriages cost $33.00. From 5 September 1775 to 12 June 1776, 281 days at 45s . . . 623s/o."[14]

Thus Wythe, precisely honest, must have left Philadelphia on the morning of 13 June, 1776. It is probable that Richard Henry Lee joined the Wythes in their journey homeward, for Lee wrote Washington a letter on 13 June, 1776:

> "This day I set off for Virginia, where if I can be of any service to you, it will oblige to command me."[15]

He did not, in his letter, mention Wythe as travelling with him, and one would think he would have, of course. He may, however, have been writing in too much of a hurry to do so. At any rate, both he and Wythe could turn homeward with light hearts. The battle in Philadelphia was now won, the battle in Virginia was soon to begin. Would the radicals win there as they had in Congress?

Exactly when Wythe reached Williamsburg is not known. He was going to a Convention which was in great confusion, as Edmund Randolph wrote to his friend George Baylor on 21 June, 1776 (which was just a few days before Wythe probably arrived in Williamsburg):

> "We are in confusion beyond parallel: no government is in existence but such as is vested in the hands of the Convention. This august body yesterday elected delegates for Congress and rejected colonels Harrison and Braxton. . . . It was determined we should have only five. The fortunate candidates were Wythe, Nelson, Jefferson, Richard Henry Lee and Thomas Lee. We are engaged in forming a plan of government. God knows when it will be finished. It is generally thought the contest will be between President Nelson and Mr. Henry, who shall be governor . . ."[16]

Unfortunately for both Wythe and Jefferson, their dreams of building a better Virginia by means of a good constitution were shattered for by the time Wythe arrived, the thing had already been written. We find him writing to Jefferson on 27 July:

> "When I came here the plan of government had been committed to the whole house. To those who had the chief hand in forming it, the one you put into my hands was shown. Two or three parts of this were with little alteration inserted in that."[17]

This was truly a crushing disappointment for Jefferson. He was now denied his chance to mould his country at this time. Both he and Wythe had to work long and hard to undo the work of the Convention in this respect. The Convention just would not re-open the question of the Constitution, or do more than adopt one or two of Jefferson's ideas. The members were tired of the question. Wythe had simply arrived too late. For the most part, Wythe's work in the Convention was concerned with trivia. That great revolutionary, Patrick Henry, showed the basic conservatism motivating the Convention when he wrote to Richard Henry Lee:

> ". . . I fear too great a Byass to Aristocracy prevails among the opulent. . . . Vigor, animation, and all the powers of mind and body, must now be summon'd and collected together in one grand effort. . . . And to see those who have so fatally advised us, still guiding, or at least sharing our . . . counsels, alarms me."[18]

What Wythe and Jefferson wanted was a document which would over-turn society itself. The Anglican Church must be shorn of its power, slavery itself must be whittled away—if not immediately destroyed, then it must be gradually ameliorated until it shrivelled up, dead. The "Byass to Aristocracy" must be overcome with the franchise widened, and public education made a reality. Since records are lacking, we do not know what arguments were used. But Wythe surely spoke with a firm, clear voice on what needed to be done. For, many years later, Edmund Randolph, who was Wythe's alternate, wrote that in this Convention

". . . the members who filled the most space in the public eye, were Edmund Pendleton . . Patrick Henry, George Mason, James Mercer, Robert Carter Nicholas, James Madison of Orange, Richard Bland, Thomas Ludwell Lee, Richard Henry Lee, Thomas Nelson, George Wythe and John Blair." [19]

It was Randolph likewise who later said of this Constitution:

". . . the qualification of electors . . . restricted to free holders . . . was submitted to without a murmur, and even without a proposition to the contrary . . ."

Since we have no evidence that this was not so, we have to accept it. Nonetheless it seems strange that Wythe should have "submitted" to this without a murmur. At any rate, the subject was not closed, for in his letter of 27 July, Wythe told Jefferson that he, Jefferson, was the one to change the system. This he should start to do when he returned from Philadelphia in October on his rotation leave, and by that time, Wythe himself would be back at his desk in the Congress.

The first official mention of George Wythe at the Convention that we pick up is on 28 June, 1776, where Wythe together with Curle, Dandridge, and Madison, was appointed to a committee to examine the ballot box during the governor's election. Patrick Henry was elected. That same day, George Mason, Richard Henry Lee, Robert Carter Nicholas, and Wythe were ordered to prepare a form for the oath of office to be taken by the Governor and his Privy Council. Thus Patrick Henry became the successor of Gooch, Dinwiddie, Fauquier, Botetourt, and Dunmore. Into the Governor's Palace he moved and there reigned in impotence amidst the tawdry refurbishings.

During the time the Convention had been so hard at work, great excitement had prevailed throughout the lower tidewater area. For at last the old fox, Dunmore, was cornered. After his defeat at Great Bridge, he had hovered about the mouth of the Chesapeake Bay for some months, receiving reinforcements from Gage. Finally in June, 1776, he sailed away from the Norfolk area forever, retreating to Gwynn's Island, some 30 miles north of Yorktown in the Chesapeake Bay. This island was some 2000 acres small, and was swampy to boot. Dunmore fortified it, but it lacked good water and was malarial. It is at the mouth of the Rappahannock River and is in fact just a few miles from Wythe's Chesterville. There the mighty Scotsman stayed for about the next six weeks.

The fight on Gwynn's Island, when it came on 12 July 1776 a week after formal independence was declared, was mercifully brief. And once again Dunmore lost the battle, being forced to sail to New York in complete defeat. So completely was he hated, that even the gentle Wythe, on this occasion, wrote:

27 July, 1776
"Williamsburg.
Thomas Jefferson:
     Lord Dunmore, driven from Gwins, retreated to St. George's Island in Potownack, a station we hear he found no less unquiet than that he left, so that he hath gone up that river, distressed, it is imagined for want of water. Ought the precept, "if thine enemy thirst give him drink," to be observed towards such a fiend, and in such a war? Our countrymen will probably decide in the negative; and perhaps such casuists as you and I shall not blame them. . . ."[20]

Even Richard Henry Lee rejoiced in his letter to Jefferson:

Chantilly   21 July, 1776
". . . I congratulate you on the great success . . . we have no reason to be sorry for the disgrace of our African Hero at Gwins Island. . . . Our friend Mr. Wythe proposes to me by letter that I meet him at Hooes ferry the 3d of September and I have agreed to do so, unless some pressing call takes me to Congress sooner. Can you have patience so long? . . ."[21]

     The really important business of the Convention completed, the oligarchy gave to a committee composed of Richard Henry Lee, George Mason, Robert Carter Nicholas and George Wythe the task of designing a seal for the Commonwealth. There has been much argument over who actually designed the seal which was adopted on the last day of the Convention's sitting, 5 July 1776. Rowland, in her biography of George Mason, pointing out that the great seal was made a specific provision of the Constitution, argues that Mason actually designed the thing.
     The design, however, is typical of Wythe's thinking. All the other colonies, when they came to design a seal, employed English heraldic forms, setting up a sort of medieval coat of arms. Thus, unconsciously, they mirrored their English origin. The Virginians did no such thing. True to Wythe's classical background, nothing feudal at all was used, but rather a Roman figure of Virtue, standing as an Amazon, one of the fighting women of ancient legend. In one hand she held a spear symbolizing victory, and in the other the sword of authority. The motto which circled the whole was "Sic Sempter Tyrannis," thus echoing the words of ancient and republican Rome. A couple of years later, a sword presented to George Rogers Clarke by a grateful Virginia had the same words engraved on it.
     In trying to concert political action, the Virginia radicals were hampered by the fact that the work had to be carried on in two places at once, both equally important. The one place was Philadelphia, where the radicals must not let the conservatives take over the control of the delegation. The other was Williamsburg, where the conservatives were already in control and must be broken. Jefferson as ever was impatient to return home, for he wrote to John Page on 30 July 1776:

". . . I propose to leave this place the 11th of August, . . . I hope to see Colo. Lee and Mr.

Wythe here, tho' the stay of the latter will I hope be short, as he must not be spared from the important department of the law." [22]

The plan of the radicals was that Lee and Jefferson, apparently, should concert the attack on Pendleton's machine in the Virginia assembly, while Wythe, for the moment, went to Congress:

". . . For news, I refer you to your brother . . . I shall return to Virginia after the 11th of August. I wish my successor may be certain to come before that time: in that case, I shall hope to see you, and Wythe, in Convention, that the business of Government, which is of everlasting concern, may receive your aid." [23]

Richard Henry Lee, having been in Virginia for about ten weeks, returned to Congress by 3 September. George Wythe, however, did not arrive for another week, until about 14 September, at which time he subscribed his name to the Independence parchment in great, bold and flowing letters, which may still be clearly seen on the document, the ink faded a little, under the glass in the Library of Congress.

On the 22d of August, the British landed on Long Island and began their investment of New York City. They had waited this long for the arrival of the mercenaries, the companies of which swelled the British army to some 35,000 men. This was a frightening menace for Washington to face, and behind him, the Congress. In the previous Spring, on 21 May, the Congress had received the news that George III, from whom they had not yet declared their freedom, had hired the German soldiers. The Congress set up a committee to address these hirelings, and the report in Wythe's writing still exists. Wythe declared the Hessians to be

". . . unprovoked enemies. We have not invaded your country, slaughtered wounded or captivated your parents children or kinsfolk, burned plundered or desolated your towns and villages, wasted your farms and cottages, spoiled you of your goods. . . . We have not aided ambitious princes . . . in subjugating you. We . . . glory in being instrumental in the deliverance of mankind from bondage and oppression. What then induced you to join in this quarrel with our foes, strangers to you . . . ? Were you compelled by your sovereigns to undertake the bloody work of butchering your unoffending fellow-creatures? Disdain the inhuman office, disgraceful to the soldier . . . Were you tempted by the prospect of exchanging the land you left for happier regions,—for a land of plenty and abhorrent of despotism? We wish this may be your motive; because we have the means . . . to gratify your desires . . . ." [24]

Treachery was indeed in the air for the very officer who was employed by Washington to translate these words to the Germans, Lt. Colonel Zedtwitz, offered to become a spy for Governor Tryon. Fortunately, he was caught and court-martialed.

At the very moment when the enormous weight of the British army was pressing upon him, Washington realized that his army was falling apart. He appealed to Congress for help and his appeal was handed over to Wythe's committee on the army. This was Washington's famous and desperate letter of 24 September:

> "From the hours allotted to Sleep, I will borrow a few moments to convey my thoughts . . . to Congress."

The General flatly and candidly informed the Congress that:

> "We are now . . . upon the eve of another dissolution of our Army . . . unless some speedy, and effectual measures are adopted by Congress, our cause will be lost."

The bounties in land offered by Congress were simply too skimpy. Men would not engage to fight and die for such pittances.

> "Something is due to the Man who puts his life in his hands, hazards his health, and forsakes the Sweets of domestic enjoyments."

Not only was the pay too low, not only was the militia cowardly, but the whole army was in a "confused and disordered state"—and would continue to be until proper rules of war were adopted. Without such, Washington could not govern the army.

> ". . . For the most attrocious offences . . . a Man receives no more than 39 lashes; and these perhaps . . . are given in such a manner as to become rather a matter of sport than punishment. . . . This . . . is inadequate to many Crimes it is assigned to, as a proof of it, thirty and forty Soldiers will desert at a time . . . Of late, practice prevails . . . of plundering . . . No man is secure in his effects . . . for in order to get at them, we have several Instances of People being frightened out of their Houses under pretence of those Houses being ordered to be burnt, and this is done with a view of siezing the Goods . . . .
> I have . . . used my utmost endeavors to stop this horrid practice, but . . . I might . . . as well atempt to remove Mount Atlas . . . ."[25]

Congress, however, had already been considering the matter of new Articles of War, and placed them in open debate in September. These rules should have taken case of the cause of Washington's complaints, for Article 5 proved that any soldier who should disobey any lawful command of his superior officer should suffer death.

Yet all was not self-seeking and plundering in the American army, for on 22 September—only two days before Washington, beside himself with anxiety for the safety of his army, wrote the letter to Congress complaining of his soldiers,—there died in New York City where he had been sent to spy, one Nathan Hale, who regretted that he had but one life to give for his country. It was on 22 September that that immortal patriot departed this life, hanged from a tree at Howe's orders.

On the same day as Washington wrote his letter, and before Congress had, of course, received it, Wythe was caught up with preparing additional instructions to those who were to be sent to France to seek Louis XVI's aid. The plan of a treaty had already been set up, so there was no argument about that. What was now considered was the instruction the agents were to follow. In order to induce Louis to join firmly in support of the United States, the agents were told to inform the King that the United States would never submit again to the British King. In addition to this, the agents were to assure the French that America would not terminate the war against the British until some six months after notifying the French of America's intention to do so. This part of the instructions is in the handwriting of George Wythe, and so it is probable that he had the major hand in framing them. Of course, only a prophet could have foretold the immense amount of trouble and double-dealing which was to arise at the end of the war because of this stipulation. But Wythe, as an honest lawyer, undoubtedly believed in providing an orderly finish to a contract, and this was his way of doing it.[26] But how Franklin must have rued this part of the alliance treaty, when he came to the business of making the peace in 1782!

Since Wythe was on the "Cloathing Committee," it was quite natural that he should be given the task of reporting on Washington's letters of the 24th and 25th. The letter imploring action in the matter of discipline we have already considered, but the next day, the General informed Congress that the

> ". . . Army is in want of almost every necessity: Tents, Camp Kettles, Blanketts and Clothes of all kinds . . . I confess that I do not know how they are to be got."

Thus Wythe, Francis Hopkinson, Edward Rutledge, John Adams, and Thomas Stone were given the task of finding the answer to Washington's problems. It was not until 8 October that the Congress could find the time to consider the reports of the Committee, so busy was it with other matters.

One would have thought that clothing and feeding the fighting men would have come first, but it didn't, for now the Congress found it necessary to argue over whom to send to France. The three men it chose were Benjamin Franklin, Thomas Jefferson, and Silas Deane. However, Jefferson, on fire with the need to reform Virginia's government, was in no mood to be sent to France, there to cool his heels in the antechambers of royalty's palaces. Besides, his wife was ill and he couldn't leave her. Jefferson therefore chose Virginia's welfare over that of the Continent and informed Hancock, the President of Congress, that he wasn't going. Arthur Lee, brother of Richard Henry, was chosen in Jefferson's stead. On 26 September, Wythe, Robert Morris, Richard Henry Lee, and John Adams had been chosen a committee to draft letters of credence for the commissioners, and also to find ways and means to support them on their mission abroad. Secrecy was enjoined on all in this matter, but so little was it observed that Richard Henry Lee, the very next day, had rushed off a letter to Jefferson to inform him he had been chosen. On 28 September, the letter of credence had been prepared, and was agreed to by Congress. It was further resolved that:

> ". . . the Commissioners should live in such a stile and manner at the court of France . . . to support the dignity of their public character . . . besides the actual expences . . . a handsome allowance be made to each of them as a compensation for their time, trouble, risque

and services. . . . That the Secretary of the Embassy be allowed a Salary of £1000 p.a., plus expences of his passage out and home."[27]

To pay for this, the Secret Committee was to export produce and goods from America until the sum of £10,000 sterling had been accumulated in France.

But after all was said and done, it was probably Wythe who decided that more might very well be accomplished in the matter of foreign aid. Richard Henry Lee had, in his letter to Jefferson, given some idea of the state of mind of the Congress when he wrote:

". . . What will be our situation the next campaign, when the present force shall be increased by the addition of 20 or 30 thousand Russians with a large body of British and Irish troops?"[28]

Remember, the Congress had just heard from Washington of the imminent dissolution of the American army. The important thing was to get aid from abroad and get it fast. That took precedence over new-modeling the army. But, bethought Wythe to the Congress, if the Commissioners are to go to France, why should they not also try to entice other Courts into an alliance? And so, in Wythe's handwriting there were prepared "Additional instructions to B.F., S.D., and T.J., commissioners from the United States of America to the King of France."[29] Wythe pointed out that while at the French Court, they would meet the ambassadors of other powers. Would it not be convenient to conclude treaties of recognition and peace with such powers as these ambassadors represented? To the sanguine Wythe, who knew intimately the provincial court of little Williamsburg, and the intrigues of the somewhat greater Congressional court of Philadelphia, it seemed indeed opportune to kill two birds with one stone. Since he never travelled abroad, he, for all his learning, never really understood the cruel and necessitous diplomacy of the European world. But even if the agents could not obtain treaties of alliance from other powers, at least they might, thought Wythe, prevent these nations from helping Britain. So the three Americans were:

". . . to the utmost of your power, prevent their taking part with Great Britain in the war which his britannic majesty prosecutes against us. . . ."

Again, during all this time, Wythe was given many jobs on small committees, many of which had to do with the disposition of prizes of war taken on the sea, as well as the review of all the regulations of Congress in the matter of such prizes. But in all his business in the Congress, Wythe must still have had a pleasant life in the bustling little city on the Schuylkill, for Mrs. Wythe was with him and they lodged together happily in an apartment opposite Mrs. Yard's. Since the house in Williamsburg was empty, Wythe wrote to Jefferson who, with his still-ailing wife, was now attending the House of Delegates:

"Make use of the house and furniture. I shall be happy if any thing of mine can contribute to make your and Mrs. Jefferson's residence in Williamsburg comfortable. Adieu."[30]

Wythe's letters to Jefferson were almost invariably short and to the point. A prolific letter-writer he certainly was not. The Jeffersons occupied the Wythe house during the Fall, moving out 4 December into new quarters.

In addition to his other assignments, Wythe was appointed, together with John Adams and others, to prepare and bring in a plan of a military academy for the army. The results of this were almost nil, but it is worthwhile noting that Congress was taking note of Washington's insistence that the army have good officers. Not only this, but on 15 October, Wythe was added to the Treasury committee.

But it was not only money or the lack of it, that engaged the attention of Wythe and his colleagues, it was the selfishness of many of their fellow-citizens. On 28 October Congress set up a committee of three, Wythe, Elbridge Gerry and Edward Rutledge, to inquire into the matter of certain persons who were striving to monopolize the food and supplies which were needed for the army, with a view to increasing the price thereof and the consequent profit to themselves. This was a perenial problem, but it did no good to fulminate (as Wythe's committee did) against the practice. It did even less good to recommend (as Wythe's committee also did) that the various states enact laws against engrossment and monopoly. This simply did not work. What was needed was effective taxation which would give a firm financial basis to Congress. And what was further needed was a halt to the everlasting printing of paper money. The country was rich, at least in food and fiber. And yet the army starved. It starved because the people were not willing to endure taxation. And even more, it starved because Congress would not set up a proper system of administration, giving over the care of the army to a really responsible Board of War. Incompetent and stupid officials, worse management, and too much paper money were not to be cured by Congressional resolutions. The inflation at this time was very bad: $100 would buy a pair of shoes. An equal sum would pay for a hundred pounds of flour. In such a situation, the poor suffered terribly. But even more, the army suffered as well, despite the efforts by Wythe and others to get supplies of "cloathing" and food to it.

But now Wythe's attention was engaged by a question from home. His erstwhile pupil, Jefferson, was deep in his attempt to revolutionize Virginia. Basic to such a revolution was a complete overturn of the laws of the country (i.e., Virginia). What person could better set up a new law code than George Wythe, in conjunction, of course, with Thomas Jefferson? And so the plan was broached. It met with immediate agreement from Wythe, who answered Jefferson on 18 November:

> "Whenever you and the speaker think I should return to Virginia to engage in the part which shall be assigned to me in revising the laws, I shall attend you. As to the time and place of meeting and my share in this work, I can accommodate myself to the appointment, and be content with the allotment my colleagues shall make. In the meantime, I purpose to abide here, if the enemy do not drive me away; an event some think not improbable."[31]

But however much Wythe was involved in the events which called to him from his homeland, his immediate work lay with the Congress in Philadelphia. And that work encompassed innumerable tasks: hearing cases of appeals from Admiralty Courts; receiving and deciding on petitions from soldiers for advancement and rewards; ascertaining the nature and punishment of treasons; inquiring into the need for and arranging for the maintenance of sutlers in the army; and so forth.

Notes to Chapter VII

1. Washington. *The Writings of*—. Ford ed, Vol. 3, p. 420.
2. *American Archives*—. Fourth Series, Vol. 4, Col. 1001.
3. John Adams. *Autobiography,* in, *The Writings of*—. Charles *Francis Adams,* ed., Vol. 3, p. 36.
4. *Letters of Members . . . of the Continental Congress.* Burnett, ed., Vol. 1, p. 386.
5. *Ibidem.* Vol. 1, p. 405–6.
6. John Adams. *The Works of*—. Charles F. Adams, ed., Vol. 10, p. 94.
7. *American Archives*—. Fourth Series, Vol. 4, Col. 1136.
8. John Adams. *Autobiography,* in, *The Works of*—. Charles F. Adams, ed., Vol. 3, p. 43.
9. *American Archives*—. Fourth Series, Vol. 5, Col. 1234.
10. Richard Henry Lee. *The Writings of*—. Ballagh, ed., Vol. 1, p. 176.
11. Second Continental Congress. *Journals,* Vol. 5, p. 405.
12. *Ibidem.* Vol. 4, p. 401.
13. Washington to the President of Congress, 8 June 1776, New York, in, *The Writings of*—. Ford ed., Vol. 4, p. 116.
14. Manuscript Collection. Massachusetts Historical Society, Boston, Mass.
15. *American Archives*—. Fourth Series, Vol. 6, Col. 834.
16. Moncure D. Conway. *Omitted Chapters of History, disclosed in the Life and Papers of Edmund Randolph.* (New York, G. P. Putnam's Sons, 1888). p. 29.
17. William Wirt Henry. *Patrick Henry*—. Vol. 1, p. 441.
18. Southern Literary Messenger. Vol. 8, p. 260.
19. Edmund Randolph. *Manuscript History*—. p. 51.
20. Jefferson. *The Papers of*—. Boyd ed., Vol. 1, p. 476.
21. *Ibidem.* p. 471.
22. *Ibidem.* p. 483. Thus this early the radicals planned to put Wythe to work in the great reformation of Virginia law which was to crown the work of revolutionizing Virginia.
23. Jefferson to Richard Henry Lee, 8 July 1776, Philadelphia, in, *Letters of the . . . Members of the Continental Congress,* Burnett, ed., Vol. 2, p. 2.
24. Second Continental Congress. *Journals,* Vol. 5, p. 708.
25. Washington. *Writings*—. Ford ed., Vol. 4, p. 438 et sequor.
26. Second Continental Congress. *Journals,* Vol. 5, p. 815.
27. *Ibidem.* Vol. 6, p. 897.
28. Jefferson. *The Papers of*—. Boyd ed., Vol. 1, p. 522.
29. Second Continental Congress. *Journals.* Vol. 6, p. 884.
30. 28 October 1776, in, Jefferson. *The Papers of*—. Boyd ed., Vol. 1, p. 585.
31. *Ibidem.* p. 603.

CHAPTER VIII

Wythe becomes Speaker of the House of Delegates.

But on the greater stage of the war, matters were coming to a violent head. Washington's weak army was being pushed around by the mighty force under the Howe brothers in New York City. The British had long since taken possession of the town, and had forced Washington to retreat up the Hudson Valley. He had been able only to hang on the flanks of the British, wounding them from time to time as his troops and equipment permitted. Now the enraged British came pushing out of New York City, and during the subsequent month of December they sent Washington's little army, becoming ever smaller by the constant desertion of the troops, reeling and stumbling across the flat plains of the Jerseys. It behooved all true patriots at this time to do all they could to aid the General and his army. One defeat after another pushed Washington backwards to the Capital. It this should continue, and it was entirely probable that it would, Philadelphia itself would fall to the enemy.

But even at this point, events of the least importance kept intruding. A group of Indians came to visit, and even though the hearts of the Congressmen were pounding with anxiety, no fear must show else the Indians would become aware that all was not going well. Wythe's Indian Affairs Committee had to entertain them, receive them in the State House and give them a present during their week-long visit. It was Benjamin Rush who gave us the picture of the Indians' reception in Congress:

". . . I had the pleasure of being present at an interview between some chiefs of the Six Nations and Congress in their hall in the State House. After a pause of about ten minutes one of the chiefs rose from his seat, and pointing to the Sun said "The business of this day will end well. Yonder Sun rose clear this morning. The great spirit is propitious to us. Brothers, we received the commissioners you sent us at the little council fire at Pittsburgh. We wiped the sweat from their bodies. We cleaned the dust from their legs. We pulled the thorns from their feet. We took their staffs from their hands, and placed them against the tree of peace. We took their belts from their waists, and after conducted them to the seats of peace."[1]

This oratory took place on the 9th of December.

How heartily the Congressmen must have wished their guests gone! Yet the Indians stayed around for several more days, witnessing the near panic which hit the city of Philadelphia at this time. The Congress was now receiving letters from Washington who had arrived at Trenton. One, dated 5 December, gave an indication of his plans:

". . . I shall . . . face about with such Troops as are here fit for Service and march back to Princeton and there govern myself by Circumstances and the movements of General Lee. . . . a fatal supineness and insensibility of danger . . . have been the causes of our late disgraces. . . ."[2]

But for the Commander-in-Chief to govern himself by the actions of General Lee was supreme foolishness, for that silly general was in but a scant nine days taken prisoner by the British, on 13 December. The Indians, still hanging around Philadelphia, seeing the general fear, may very well have felt, despite the braggadocio of Congress, that the American cause was sinking. For on the ninth, the Congress resolved that if it should "be under the necessity of removing from Philadelphia, it shall be adjourned to Baltimore." Be under the necessity indeed! On the 12th of December, the Congressmen ordered that the apothecary pack up "immediately" all the medicines belonging to the Continent and remove them from the city.

Now the Congress, spurred on by emergency and fear, really moved. There was little necessity for debating endlessly now. One directive after another went forth. Frigates were prepared for the defense of the city. A fast ship was sent to Cape Henlopen at the entrance of Delaware Bay to warn off all in-coming American ships not to proceed to Philadelphia. They might arrive to find the British in possession of the city. (That was thoughtful of Congress!) Another thoughtful thing the Congress now did was to order all its prisoners to be sent to Baltimore, under guard, of course.

But Congress was solicitous not only of its prisoners, but also of itself. It did not want the appearance of running away, and so called a conference with Generals Putnam and Mifflin, who were in the city and were charged with its defense by Washington. These two advised the Congress that it should retire (after all, what good would a Congress captured by the enemy do the country?). Accordingly, James Wilson was sent to tell the Assembly and Committee of Safety of Pennsylvania that it was leaving town. But, of course, both of these would follow suit shortly, anyway. And so on 12 December, the Congress resolved to meet again on the 20th in the safety of Baltimore town. But one last act before it went. The delegates now, at long last, gave a plentitude of power to Washington to act and direct all things as he thought best. At last he was free to direct the war for a few months at least without the interference of Congress. In the affairs of the army, he was now almost a dictator. But Congress was determined to have the last word. It published an address to the people urging continued resistance. Written on 10 December, its words ring out with false and silly assurance:

> "Even a short resistance will probably be effectual, as General Lee is advancing with a strong reinforcement, and his troops in high spirits. . . ."[3]

High spirits indeed! In three days time, the highly-touted General Lee, renegade Englishman, was languishing in a British prison camp. The address, of course, was put forth mostly to the people of Pennsylvania and the city of Philadelphia in particular. A further address was prepared for a rather more august audience. On the 11th, the Congress proclaimed a day of fasting and humiliation:

> "*Resolved,* That it be recommended to all the United States, as soon as possible, to appoint a day of solemn fasting and humiliation; to implore of Almighty God the forgiveness of the many sins prevailing among all ranks, and to beg the countenance and assistance of His Providence in the prosecution of the present just and necessary war . . . ."[4]

The next day the Congress removed to Baltimore.

And where was Wythe in all this? One doesn't know, but it is probable that he had removed himself and Mrs. Wythe from the city with the rest of Congress. He had, certainly, business elsewhere. For on the 4th of December, back in Williamsburg, the Virginia Assembly had appointed Mann Page to succeed Wythe in the Congress, the latter being needed at home to help prepare the revisal of the laws of his native country. Since it took about ten days for the news to arrive in Philadelphia, it is probable that the notification of his successor's election reached him just as Congress was evacuating the city. Wythe's term did not automatically end then for Page would not arrive in Congress for quite some time, and Wythe was empowered to continue to act in Congress until the said Page actually took his seat therein.

It was left, not to Congress, but to that wicked old sinner and reprobate, Tom Paine, to produce the words which would ring down the centuries in defiance of the English at this time. When Philadelphia, the national capital, was in imminent danger of being taken by the enemy and the national assembly fled away, Tom Paine uttered the words which even today inspire by their bravery and nobility. Flinging defiance at the gods of war and fate, Paine burst out on 19 December:

> "These are the times that try men's souls. The summer soldier and the sunshine patriot will, in this crisis, shrink from the service of his country; but he that stands it now, deserves the love and thanks of man and woman. Tyranny, like hell, is not easily conquered."[5]

Of summer soldiers and sunshine patriots there were plenty. It was at this time that Galloway and the Allens (Andrew, John, and William) slunk away from Philadelphia to the British lines,—now Tories. By the hundreds, erstwhile patriots in the Jerseys took the oaths of loyalty prescribed by General Lord Howe. And as for faith in the future of the Revolution! John Dickinson wrote a letter to his brother General Philemon Dickinson which says more plainly than anything else can what he thought of it:

> "Receive no more Continental money on your bonds and mortgages. The British troops having conquered the Jerseys and your being in camp, are sufficient reasons. Be sure you remember this. It will end better for you."[6]

The servant who carried the letter was apprehended and the missive was laid before Washington who sent it on to the Pennsylvania Committee of Safety.

Robert Morris, being left by the Congress in Philadelphia, reported to the Commissioners who had by now sailed to France:

> "The city was . . . the greatest scene of distress that you could conceive: everybody but the quakers were removing their families and effects, and now it looks dismal and melancholy. The quakers and the sick soldiers alone remained. . . . You may be sure I have my full share of trouble . . . but having got my family and books removed to a place of safety, my mind is more at ease. . . ."[7]

On the 20th of December, the Congress opened for business in Baltimore, to the unending distaste of the delegates. Benjamin Harrison unburdened his soul to Robert Morris back in Philadelphia:

> "I wish Congress may remove back with all my heart for I am most horridly vexed with this Place, indeed I had like to have been with Philadelphia; nothing but the little circle of acquaintance I had there prevented it, but this tryal of Baltimore will make me . . . set a much greater value on them, but on the Town most certainly however I am told the Yankeys are gainst it, if so we *go not,* they Rule as absolutely as the Grand Turk *dos* in his own Dominions. . . ."[8]

This was written on 8 January, 1777. On Christmas Day, he had written his friend Morris: ". . . if you desire to keep out of the Damdest Hole in the World come not here."[9]

The evening before, Washington and his men were extricating the nation from the damndest hole in the world by crossing the Delaware and falling upon the Hessians at Trenton. His great and famous victory there restored the credit and strength of the nation, as he chased the British back across the Jerseys the way they had come. By his daring and bravery, he had saved the Congress, which was now somewhat shame-faced:

> "As things turn'd out I am very sorry we remov'd at all and indeed I think we were full hasty enough, it damp'd people much, but your continuance there and Conducting business there will give a Spring, and join'd to the influence of our successes will make up for the Flight of Congress . . ."[10]

Thus John Hancock to Robert Morris on 14 January 1777.

In Baltimore, the Congress met in an old tavern. It was situated at the west end of Market Street, on the south side of the street. A most unprepossessing building, it had merely a very long central room, with two fireplaces, two large closets and two doors. But however rough the accommodations, it was sufficient for what work Congress had to do. Having situated themselves as best they could, the delegates set to debating. Seemingly their greatest worry was, as always, Ticonderoga. Wythe wrote the report which the committee which had visited the Northern Army finally submitted. They were concerned that the soldiers be supplied with vegetables and ordered that "effectual measures" be taken that "they be well supplied with vinegar." But more to the point, the Congress was afraid that as soon as Lake Champlain was frozen over and capable of bearing horses, Carleton might come down from the Canadian border and attack Ticonderoga. They had asked the New England states to send posthaste reinforcements to the great fortress. In addition, a fort was to be constructed on Mount Independence: caissons were to be sunk in the water near the fort to bar naval passage, and Fort Stanwix (where now stands the modern city of Rome) was to be strengthened. Other fortifications were to be erected on the Mohawk River. All this activity was to secure the northern frontier. One might suppose indeed that there were no English closer than Lake Champlain. The report is in Wythe's handwriting, and the submitting of it was probably the last activity of his in the Continental Congress.

For the law revisal was in the offing, and he must leave Congress (at this crucial point!) to go home to rewrite the laws of his beloved Virginia. Although Mann Page did not take his seat until 30 January 1777, we know that Wythe had left Baltimore at least by that time. We can, however, pinpoint his departure from the Maryland city even closer. For the Congressional committee to which he had been appointed to consider the hearing of the appeal against the sentence on the libel "John Craig *vs.* the Brig Richmond, etc." on 27 November met 4 January without him. As the laconic Journals have it:

". . . Mr. . . . Ellery be added to the said committee, in the room of Mr. George . . . Wythe. . . ."[11]

As we know, the great plan of the law revisal had been in the air for some time. Jefferson and Pendleton (and probably Wythe too, although such letters as might bear witness are lost) discussed the need for a law change all during the summer of 1776. It was Jefferson who began the work by entering the bill in the October, 1776 session of the Virginia legislature. The very fact that these men began to change the fundamental basis on which their lives were legally founded shows that they firmly believed the revolution (i.e., the military one) would succeed. The political and legal revolution they carried out all during the time Washington, in his lonely struggle, was fighting the English. If Washington had failed, all that these men were trying to do would have failed too.

The astute politician that Jefferson had become succeeded in getting the bill passed by the Assembly. But those in charge had known that that would happen: in fact, before the bill became law Pendleton wrote to Wythe to ask when he could return to begin the work. Wythe answered confidently:

> ". . . I am in Receipt of your letter of the 22nd. It is the part of my countrymen to say when I shall return to assist in revising the laws; it is mine to obey. With most profound respect, I am, Sir your humble servant.
>
> G. Wythe"[12]

To this committee the Virginia Assembly named five men: Jefferson himself, Wythe, Pendleton, George Mason and Thomas Lightfoot Lee. These were great men, but the fact must be noted that all this was primarily the work of Jefferson. They had been given full power to do the work as they should decide, and while this seems *carte blanche,* it was really no such thing, for the Assembly was to pass finally on everything they did. If the Assembly didn't approve, then their work would go for nothing. It appears that the first meeting (although there is some doubt about this) took place in Annapolis in Maryland. The five there decided that the laws should be revised, not written anew. The positions they took are somewhat surprising. For the radicals (Wythe, Jefferson, and Mason) wanted merely to revise—that would be task enough. However, the most conservative member of the group (Pendleton) apparently wanted to frame the entire legal structure of Virginia anew. The three radicals, however, were able to convince him that this was too great a work, that the complications would be insurmountable. And reluctantly, Pendleton agreed. After the Annapolis meeting, the revisors met again, this time in Fredericksburg (one of the towns familiar to Wythe from his youth). And there they came to a further decision. George Mason was not a lawyer. He felt strongly out of place and therefore decided to resign. Thomas Ludwell Lee, ill and tired, soon died. Thus the group was now reduced to three. The Assembly had foreseen that this might happen and had granted the committee the right to fill up vacancies as they wished. However, they had by now decided on a plan of work, and if they brought in new members, the plan might be disrupted. And so the three went to work without increasing their number.

The plan which had been originally decided upon for the law revisal while Mason and Lee were still members was substantially that the Common Law was not to be changed, save where a different wording might clarify the intent, or where archaic expressions could be expunged. The statutary laws (the legislative enactments) were to be changed as needed, always with the view in mind that the British connection was now severed. The enactments were to be syncopated and the diction modernized. In all, as few changes as possible were really to be introduced. To rewrite the entire code of laws from the beginning would be a work of enormous proportions, far beyond the ability of five or, as it turned out, three men, however skilled in the law they might be.

Each of the revisors took a part of the work: Jefferson took the Common Law and the statutes to the year 1607 (which was when Virginia was established, four years after the accession of James I to England's throne). To Wythe was assigned the task of re-framing the British statutes passed by the Parliament in England from 1607 to the Revolution. And to Pendleton was given the work of revising the laws passed by the Virginia Assembly (the House of Burgesses and the Council) for the same period.

For the next two and a half years the revisors worked. Not continuously, of course, for they all had other things to do during those years. But as they found the time, they reworked the laws, consulting by letter and otherwise with each other as the need came about. Wythe, of course, was an old hand at this work, for he had helped in the previous revision of 1769. But never before had there been such a radical and far-reaching change in the laws as this was to be. A good deal of their work is law for Virginia right down to the present day. And, of course, a good deal is not, for much of what they did was simply too radical and far-reaching (as, for example, Jefferson's attempt to establish a system of public education) for the men of that day. Even after the revisors had submitted in 1779 their work to the legislature, only about one-half of the laws were passed, and in these there were many changes made.

After the scramble of the centuries which have passed since then, it is virtually impossible to discover exactly which of the bills Wythe worked on. Of course, we can make out some of them. Jefferson left a memorandum of such bills as were to drafted and we see that, for example, the oath of fidelity to be taken by all officers was written by Jefferson, as was the law for the maintenance of public roads, and the government of slaves. George Wythe, however, drew up the bills for Appeals and that for the establishment of the Admiralty Court.

For the next months, then, Wythe at his beautiful home in Williamsburg rested from the alarms and excursions of both war and Congress, enjoyed the company of his wife and friends, and worked on the new law code. But he was not to remain at peace long. The winter over, the spring came and with it, new political life. His fellow citizens of Williamsburg unanimously chose Wythe to represent them in the General Assembly on 7 April 1777, and so Wythe was once again in a legislature.

And now came a tragedy. For Pendleton, tall and strong, was struck down by an accident. Hitherto, he had been, as Speaker of the House of Delegates, the leader of the conservatives and one of the most powerful men in Virginia. This, of course, he continued to be, but in his illness, he was unable to be Speaker. Jefferson, alert as always to the exigencies of fate and fortune, saw the opportunity and used it. He knew well that Wythe's prestige was enormous. Why not with one bold stroke take control of the House and put Wythe in as Speaker? And so the thing was done. This action put the progressive group, with Jefferson as leader, firmly in control. There had been three candidates for the Speakership—Wythe himself, Benjamin Harrison, now returned from Congress, and Wythe's old friend and associate, Robert Carter Nicholas. When the votes were counted, Wythe had a lead of five votes and so won. At long last, he had reached the Speakership.

Pendleton, ill at home in Caroline County, wrote to his friend General William Woodford, on 15 May, that Wythe, assuming his new office, had declared that he held it *vicariously* only—that he was fully determined to resign the position as soon as Pendleton returned. However that may be, certain it is that Wythe did no such thing. For Pendleton did not return to the Assembly until the October session, and when he did so, Wythe certainly continued to hold the Speakership. According to Pendleton, Wythe's securing the job was not a particularly great coup:

> "Our Assembly after waiting 4 days for members, made a bare House & chose Mr. Wythe Speaker by a Majority of 5."[13]

Sour grapes or not, this victory clearly gave the progressives control of the machinery of government.

It did not, however, result in easy passage of the laws Jefferson had in mind. This was clearly not Wythe's fault, as Jefferson himself testified:

> "Mr. Wythe, while speaker in the two sessions of 1777, between his return from Congress and his appointment to the Chancery, was an able and constant Associate in whatever was before a Committee of the Whole. His pure integrity, judgment and reasoning powers gave him great weight. . . ."[14]

It was Jefferson also who declared that George Wythe and George Mason, with James Madison (the future president) as a third, aided the most in passing those laws which Jefferson brought into effect the great revolution in Virginia.

But politics went on as usual. The conservatives certainly were out to destroy Lee. At a time when Virginia should have been straining to win the war, the delegates made their House a theater for the most infamously partisan and personal vendettas.

Lee was well aware of the attack directed at him. He forthwith demanded an inquiry by the House of his public conduct, and this inquiry was granted. The actual substance of the attack revolved around an attempt by the latter to have his tenants pay him rents in produce rather than in money. In effect, this meant that Lee would not be subject to the inflation which was then making money meaningless in Virginia. But it also gave his enemies a weapon with which to attack him. For it make Lee appear in the same light as John Dickinson in his letter to his brother, Philemon. In short, insinuated Lee's enemies, the famous Richard Henry was unpatriotic, refusing to receive good Virginia money. He was, perhaps, a secret Tory . . . ?

This was the calumny into which Lee demanded a public inquiry by the House. It must have been quite a scene. George Wythe presided in the House. The Senate had been invited to sit in as an audience, and the Senators all came.

Lee was one of the finest orators in a day of fine orators, and he was defending himself and his good name. Although none of his self-defense survives, he must have been very eloquent indeed, for the House completely vindicated him. Indeed, it ordered the Speaker to exculpate Lee publicly:

> ". . . the Senate withdrew; and the House came to the resolution, in consequence of which, the speaker, the venerable George Wythe, addressed Mr. Lee in the following words: 'Sir—it is with peculiar pleasure that I obey this command of the House, because it gives me an opportunity, whilst I am performing an act of duty to them, to perform an act of justice to yourself. Serving with you in Congress, and attentively observing your conduct there, I thought that you manifested in the American cause, a zeal truly patriotic; and, as far as I could judge, exerted the abilities for which you are confessedly distinguished, to promote the good and prosperity of your own country . . . The House have come to this resolution: '*Resolved*. That the thanks of this House be given by the Speaker, to Richard Henry Lee . . .' "[15]

So Lee was exonerated. But Speaker Wythe was busy with other things at this time. As Speaker, he had necessarily to direct the business of the House, and one task concerned Lee. Or rather, George Mason. For on 14 June, Wythe's erstwhile colleague in Congress resigned. When wasn't George Mason resigning from something? He had had the small-pox, and so had to resign from the national Congress. The Assembly thought to make up the differences to Lee by appointing him in Mason's room. And so it was Mason's seat in Philadelphia that Lee got.

As Speaker, Wythe had to advise Governor Henry on Western lands, how to deal with the Cherokees, Tories and lukewarm patriots, the setting up of iron works, the calling out of the militia, etc. But finally the Assembly went home, and gave Speaker Wythe a rest. All during that summer, he worked on the law revisal, and prepared for the legislative program to be enacted the following autumn. When October finally came, so thin was the attendance in the House that it was some time before Wythe was able to assemble a quorum. Pendleton himself got there almost a month late. There were three most important pieces of legislation awaiting the delegates: how to find soldiers; how to find money, and how to set up a judicial system.

The only way of putting an army together, it finally appeared to the delegates in the House, was by draft. The fight over this was long and angry, for many were opposed to such a thing. Finally, however, the law was passed.

The second of the works of that Assembly was the finding of some means of raising a revenue. Again, there could be no popularity for such an act. It is surprising in this modern age to discover that one expedient thought of (but not very highly) was an income tax, seemingly a modern device. This was, however, turned down, with the Assembly finally establishing a direct tax on property. The really important measure, however, was the setting up of courts. This was one of Jefferson's great enactments. He had tried to get the courts opened exactly one year earlier, but the Assembly would have none of it. The members all owed a great deal of money, and if the courts were opened, they could be sued. So they turned down the measure of 1776. It is no accident that within a mere three months, Jefferson introduced (14 January, 1778) an "Act to open the courts of justice" and another at the very same session to "Sequester British Property, enabling debts owed to British subjects to be paid into a loan office established by the State."

Since the planters were protected by this bill from seizure of their lands by creditors, the Jeffersonians could now move to set up the judicial system. Jefferson submitted the bills he had written the previous fall. They consisted of a Chancery Court, and a General Court. There was not too much opposition in this session when Jefferson's bills were voted on. The delegates set up a General Court on which there were some five judges, having jurisdiction in both criminal and common law cases. The High Court of Chancery was made the supreme court of Virginia, and it continued as such until the Court of Appeals was finally set up. This Chancery Court had three judges and obtained original and appellate jurisdiction in all cases of equity. For the General Court there were to be two sessions a year, each of 24 days, the Spring session to begin on 1 March, and the Fall session to start on 10 October.

Since the Chancery Court was the supreme court of the state (at least temporarily) its session had necessarily to be after those of the General Court, so that appeals could be made to the Chancellors from the lower bench. Therefore its sessions began on 5 April for the Spring, and 5 September for the Autumn, term. When it came time to fill up the places on the Chancery Court, there was no contest at all over who the men should be: the House of Delegates chose on 13 January, 1778 only three men, Pendleton, Wythe, and Robert Carter Nicholas. On the following day, 14 January, the Senate confirmed this choice without even the formality of a ballot. And so for the rest of their lives, these three men were through with active politics. From now on, the Bench alone would receive their energies.

But before Wythe formally entered on the Bench, there took place a matter of the greatest importance for both Virginia and Wythe. It will be remembered that Wythe, together with Jefferson, had been concerned with the efforts of the Indiana Company to get control of the wilderness region of the West. While they were Congressmen, both Wythe and Jefferson had worked to prevent this, and to make sure that Virginia's rights, which existed from the original charter, were unimpaired.

The Henderson company was powerfully connected in Virginia, and so had continued to press such claims as it had in the very Assembly of Virginia itself. There were, however, others who opposed the attempt by the Henderson interests to seize the West, and among them was a young pioneer named George Rogers Clark. A Kentuckian, he was elected by his fellows to the Virginia Assembly as the Delegate of the County of West Fincastle. The pioneers had set up this county and sent Clark himself and his companion, Captain John Gabriel

Jones, to Williamsburg, but the session was over when they got there in that revolutionary year of 1776. As Clark's *Memoir* gives it:

"Mr. Henry, the governor, lay sick at his seat in Hanover, where I waited on him . . ."[16]

Almost a year and a half went by. And now the frontier was aflame, for the Americans had lost in Canada, and the British were able not only to activate the frontier posts along the Great Lakes (Detroit, etc.) but also to stir up the savages to attack the settlers on the Western Waters. Hideous Indian warfare now flared along the settlements, with all its attendant barbarities. On 10 December, 1777, Clark again visited Williamsburg. He had a definite scheme in mind—nothing less than a daring attack on the British positions in the Western wilderness in Illinois country. By counter-attacking there, Clark could, if given men and money and support, save the settlers on the frontier and give the English a staggering blow. If he won, it would hurt the English all the more since they had just been given the bitter defeat of Saratoga, with Burgoyne being taken prisoner with all his men. Again, Clark is our witness:

". . . I communicated my views to Governor Henry. At first, he seemed to be fond of it; but to detatch a party at so great a distance . . . appeared daring and hazardous, as nothing but secrecy could give success to the enterprise. To lay the matter before the Assembly, then sitting, would be dangerous, as it would soon be known throughout the frontiers. . . . He had several councils, composed of select gentlemen. After making every inquiry into my proposed plans of operation (and particularly retreat, in case of misfortune, across the Mississippi into Spanish territory) the expedition was resolved upon. . . ."[17]

The "select gentlemen" with whom Patrick Henry had the "several councils" were Wythe, Jefferson, and Mason. Henry, as Governor, had really very little power. He was realistic enough to go where the power was, and that was with the Speaker, Wythe, and with Jefferson the head of the Progressives, and with Mason, his efficient coadjutor. (It is significant that he did not call Pendleton.) Above all the men concerned were aware that no expedition could succeed unless some reward was given, or at least promised, to the men who were to do the fighting. Since the plan could not be broached to the legislature, then the men who did the promising had to be men able to deliver on their promise. The only thing Virginia had to give at this time was land, and so the land it promised to the soldiers of Clark's expedition was land these men were themselves to conquer.

Accordingly, the promise was duly spelled out in a letter written by the three men:

"Williamsburg   January 3, 1778
Sir, As some Indian Tribes to the westward of the Mississippi have lately without any provocation massacred many of the Inhabitants of the Frontiers of this Commonwealth in the most cruel and barbarous Manner and it is intended to revenge the Injury and punish the Aggressors by carrying the War into their own Country. We congratulate you upon your Appointment to conduct so important an Enterprise in which we most heartily wish you

Success and we have no Doubt but some further Reward in Lands in the Country will be given to the Volunteers who shall engage in this Service in addition to the usual Pay if they are so fortunate to Succeed. We think it just and reasonable that each Volunteer entering as a common Soldier in this Expedition, should be allowed Three hundred Acres of Land and the Officers in the usual Proportion, out of the Lands which may be conquered in the Country now in the Possession of the said Indians, so as not to interfere with the Claims of any friendly Indians, or of any People willing to become Subjects of this Commonwealth; and for this we think you may safely confide in the Justice and Generosity of the Virginia Assembly. We are Sir Your most Humble Servants G. Wythe, G. Mason, Thomas Jefferson. To George Rogers Clarke, Esq."[18]

It is needless to add that Clark's expedition was highly successful. Virginians were exceedingly pleased that their claim to the vast wilderness was now made good by actual conquest, obtained by Clark and his men. The promises of Wythe, Mason and Jefferson were fully carried out by a grateful Virginia.

This was the autumn of Ticonderoga's fall, and of the victory both of Oriskany and Saratoga, as well as that of Bennington. And yet while these victories in the North brought rejoicing to Washington, yet other concerns overwhelmed the Commander-in-chief. He knew full well that the war ahead was going to be long and hard, and that the years of fighting were as yet far from over. Of the things a nation newly born needed in its fight for life, an army was one. But a competent and intelligent legislature was certainly another. Washington could build the army, train it, lead it. This might take years, but it could be done. But he couldn't create a Congress. Only the States could do that, and they were not doing it, for the States sent their poorest and least able men to staff the great national council. And these took off all the time they could, absenteeism being as usual the plague of the Congress. Washington mourned this situation in a letter to Benjamin Harrison:

"Middle Brook   December 18, 1778
. . . That Speculation, peculation, and an insatiable thirst for riches seems to have got the better of every other consideration. That party disputes and personal quarrels are the great business of the day whilst the momentous concerns of an empire, a great and accumulated debt; ruined finances, depreciated money . . . are but secondary considerations and postponed from day to day . . . . I have no resentments . . . I have every attention paid me by Congress that I stand well in their estimation but in the present situation . . . I cannot help asking; Where is Mason, Wythe, Jefferson, Nicholas, Pendleton, Nelson and another I could name; and why, if you are sufficiently impressed with your danger, do you not . . . send an extra Member or two for at least a certain limited time. . . ."[19]

Thus, Washington cried for help from those who had led him into the awful situation in which he and his army found themselves. For the victory of Saratoga found Washington in Winter Quarters at Valley Forge—where the soldiers starved. The great ones, the skilled and able ones preferred, evidently, to make their careers at home where their comforts lay, rather than to hazard things in the national Congress. Jefferson and Wythe, Pendleton and Harrison preferred to fight it out in Virginia.

In the next session of the House, Benjamin Harrison was chosen Speaker, since Wythe had vacated the position by entering the High Court of Chancery. It was on the 6th of April, 1778, that Wythe, Pendleton, and Nicholas stood before the council of State and the Governor, Patrick Henry tendering the required oath to the three men.

For the time being, the three judges had really little work to do for there was during this war-time period very little litigation. First of all, many of the lawyers were either in the army or in the legislature. Secondly, many of the natural litigants, namely the British merchants, were incapacitated from suing by the war. So for the time being, the duties of the courts were light. This was not to be the case when the war ended, however. For then the lawsuits started up in earnest, and continued with enthusiastic determination. There were few things a Virginian enjoyed more than a case in court.

During these war years, then, Wythe and Pendleton had time to work on the law revisal, as did Jefferson also. The latter had less time, of course, for he was still the political leader, as he was also the supreme theoretician. Nowhere was he more so than when explaining the basis and nature of his law reforms. It was his belief that witnesses and their testimony should be presented in Chancery Court cases, and that trial by jury should likewise prevail therein also. And so it was at first. But as the years wore on, and it became more and more apparent that the system didn't work, the juries were thrown out of Chancery Court. It is Jefferson likewise who gives a most succinct explanation of what Chancery Courts are in his letter to Philip Mazzei.

It appears that there are two systems of law, in both the United States (i.e., Virginia) and England: The common law and the chancery law. Common law was historically that written law which was common to all England, and the courts of the common law guided themselves by the strict letter of that written law. This produced legality, but it did not necessarily produce justice or what is called equity. In the course of history, it became apparent that strict legalism did not cover all possible cases which might occur, and therefore injustice might result from following only the letter of the law. One who felt himself so injured could appeal to the king for relief, and the king gave (usually) the case over to an official called the Chancellor. Thus the origins of the Chancery. It was this official's duty to redress such injustices as the common law courts had worked. Since the Chancellor was usually an ecclesiastic (in, at least, pre-Reformation England) and since he was usually therefore trained in Roman (or Canon) law, Chancery decisions came to based upon and to have a distinctly Roman law flavor. Jefferson gives three areas in which the Court is potent to relieve:

1. In cases where there is no remedy at the Common Law.

2. In cases where the Common Law renders an imperfect or flawed decision.

3. In cases which were not intended to be comprehended in the original framing of the Common Law.[20]

Since the Chancery could override the ordinary Common Law Courts, there must be some hedge against the legal absolutism of the Chancery Court. In

England this was found in the House of Lords. And in Virginia, it was found in the Court of Appeals (as set up in 1779) of which, together with the General Court and the Court of Admiralty, the Judges of the Chancery were members.

It was during the summer of 1778 when, the Chancery Court being as yet uncluttered with work and the new Chancellor Wythe missing the excitement and companionship of the great national Congress at Philadelphia, he wrote one of most touching of letters to his old colleague, Sam Adams:

> "Friend Adams, how d'ye? Are you disposed to devote a few minutes to conversation with an old acquaintance? Has governor Johnstone sent you no letters—offered you no guineas? While you are answering these questions, if they are worth answering, tell me what more you would say if we were eating a saturday's dinner at mrs. Yard's, smoking a pipe in the political club at the Indian queen—holding a tete a tete at my apartment opposite to Israel's gardens—or rambling towards Kensington. In a word, anything, news, or what you please will be gratefully received. Where is Ellery? I have not had a couplet from him since I left Philadelphia. You may show him the inclosed, but must not let any one know who so employs that time which he should spend better.   G. W. Williamsburg   1 August, 1778 My compliments to mr. Hancock, mr. Gerry, mr. Dana, and such of your colleagues, as I know."[21]

Although the Chancery truly was not pressed with a great deal of work, Wythe was nevertheless very diligently employed. It is true that he had his part of the law revisal, but there was even more than that. For it was now in a very little time that Wythe became Professor of Law and Police at William and Mary College. This chair was the first such in America and the second in the entire world. (Only the Vinerian Chair of Law at Oxford antedates that of William and Mary.)

At this juncture, the College was dominated by Tories. President Camm was notoriously affected to the Royal Government, and so had the professors also been. Indeed, no more staunch supporter of Lord Dunmore had lived in the colony than the President of the College. The student body had, of course, been staunchly rebel. So unwilling had the faculty been to go along with the Revolution, that in the early days of 1775-6, when James Innis raised a company of soldiers from among the students and young men of Williamsburg, the faculty roundly condemned him. By the spring of 1777, the Visitors of the College (of whom Wythe was one—he had been on the Board for many years) had had enough of this Toryism. Professor Gwatkin, the chaplain of Lady Dunmore and master of the Grammar School, had long since departed with the lady for whose spiritual welfare he was responsible. Emmanuel Jones, Master of the Indian School (the Brafferton) and Librarian, and the Reverend John Dixon, Professor of Divinity, both left—at the probable urging of the Visitors. The President refused to accept the authority of the Visitors in such matters, and was simply suspended. He retired to his country home, and sat out what remained of his life there, dying in a couple of years.

Since the old faculty was now almost completely gone, the Visitors appointed a most singular man to take over the College: the Reverend James Madison who, at the age of 28, became the President of William and Mary. He had been in 1773 appointed Professor of Natural Philosophy and Mathematics, after having won the Botetourt Medal in the previous year. His tenure in this chair was brief, for his wandering soul appears to have yearned after other professions—one being the law. He became then a student of George Wythe when that man had finished training St. George Tucker. Madison was actually admitted to practice law, and did take one case. But only one. What made him change his mind this time is not known, but he did not remain unattached for long, since he left for England in 1775. Not that he was a Tory—far from it. No more staunch Republican ever lived. Not for him any kowtowing to a king. But Madison wished to study again, this time for the ministry of the Church of England. And so it was. He was finally ordained in England and returned to America, passing through the British lines in New York. In the Spring of 1777, Camm having retired to his estate, the Visitors, probably at the urging of Wythe, who knew Madison's republican sympathies well, made the young man President.

It was after Jefferson was elected Governor in 1779 that Wythe's first pupil became *ex officio* a Visitor of the College. And now he prevailed upon his fellow board members to effect that revolution in the College which he had failed to bring about in the legislature. In the first place, William and Mary now became a university, the first such in the new nation. In the second place, the Visitors abolished the Grammar School and the Divinity School and replaced these with faculties of Modern Languages, to which Bellini (a friend and compatriot of Mazzei) was appointed; of Medicine, to which James McClurg (a future member of the Federal Constitutional Convention of 1787) was appointed, and of Law and Police, to which George Wythe was elected. President Madison himself occupied the chair of Natural Philosophy and Mathematics, while Robert Andrews was Professor of Moral Philosophy.

Of all the works and deeds of Wythe's life, it is probable that the greatest and, for him, the most productive of happiness was this teaching of the law (which he loved) to young men (who loved him). For the next dozen years the great lawyer was to give his time and his devotion to the task of preparing not only his country's lawyers, but also its statesmen. For Wythe's law school was the nursery in which most of the next generation of legislators were trained. As the war had displaced so many of the older generation (some of whom went the way of all mortals, and others of whom became Tories, etc.) and as the normal training which the apprentice system might have provided to young men was disrupted by the need to serve in the army, it was obvious that something was necessary if the country was to have leaders, and what is more, trained leaders. This is what Wythe's school accomplished.

From the very first, the Law School was a success, as Jefferson noted:

Our new institution at the college has had a success which has gained it universal applause. Wythe's school is numerous. They hold weekly courts and assemblies in the capitol. The professors join in it; and the young men dispute with elegance, method and learning. This single school by throwing from time to time new hands well principled and well informed into the legislature will be of infinite value.[22]

On the 8th of January, 1780, the President and professors of William and Mary had decreed that henceforth the elective system was to prevail. The School year was to begin on 17 January, with the fees for attendance on any two professors being 1000 lbs of tobacco. How far Wythe acquiesced in the elective system it is impossible to say. Certain it is that the dropping of Latin and Greek saddened him, for he later came to offer to teach the ancient languages to such students as did not possess them.

An intimate view of college life is afforded us by the letters of one John Brown, who, having been a student at Princeton until the British occupied that place, removed to Williamsburg to continue his education, where he came under Wythe's tutilage in the law. In one of his letters, Brown declared that he was indeed reduced to straits, for he had had to give up the study of fencing:

". . . I am very sinsible that the knowledge of the sword is a very important accomplishment; but money is so very scarce I am apprehensive the expence of my Board and attendance upon Mr. Wythes Lectures will be oppressive . . . I have quit the French . . . for no other reason than that the Visitors raised the price of attendance on that Branch to a Hd of tobacco. . . . I apply closely to the Study of the Law and find it to be a more difficult Science than I expected, though I hope with Mr. Wythes assistance to make some proficiency in it; those who finish this Study in a few months either have strong natural parts or else they know little about it."[23]

In yet another letter the student Brown gives evidence that his cousin John Breckinridge studied at William and Mary. That remarkable person was elected by his fellow citizens to the legislature when he was only nineteen. So young indeed was he that the lawmakers refused to seat him. It took two subsequent elections before he was able to take his place therein. Breckinridge later removed to Kentucky, became Senator therefrom in the national government and eventually Attorney General in Thomas Jefferson's cabinet. As so many others of Wythe's pupils, he became celebrated in the fields of law and government. The Browns and the Breckinridges were closely related also to the Prestons, for which family Wythe had often in the past been an attorney in the courts.

Brown gave a concrete instance of the way in which Wythe taught his students:

". . . Mr. Wythe ever attentive to the improvement of his Pupils, founded two Institutions for that purpose, the first is a Moot Court, held monthly or oftener in the place formerly occupied by the Genl Court in the Capitol. Mr. Wythe & the other professors sit as Judges, Our Audience consists of the most respectable of the Citizens, before whom we plead Causes given out by Mr. Wythe Lawyer like I assure you. He has form'd us into a Legislative Body, consisting of about 40 members Mr. Wythe is speaker to the House, & takes all possible pains to instruct us in the Rules of Parliament. We meet every Saturday and take

under our consideration those Bills drawn up by the Committee appointed to revise the laws,
then we debate & alter (I will not say amend) with the greatest freedom . . ."[24]

But the peaceful life of the college and the student was interrupted often now
by the alarums of war. Having failed so signally to conquer the North, the British were determined to destroy the South. After the defeat at Saratoga and the
subsequent imprisonment of Burgoyne's troops, Cornwallis and his fellow
generals made ever more frequent interruptions into the South. Their target
was often the great state of Virginia, which was at that time the empire state of
the Confederation government. Because of this precarious situation, keeping the
College and the Law School open was pretty much a touch-and-go operation.
One student Wythe didn't have at this time was the future President, James
Monroe. This young man had served in the North under Washington and had
now returned to his native country to take part in the battles there. While waiting for an active assignment, he became again a student at William and Mary,
and attended classes, though not in Wythe's school. The young soldier was in a
quandary, and asked his uncle Joseph Jones: Should he study under Wythe, or
should he rather become a pupil of Jefferson? The harassed governor, despite
his official duties, was still taking students, William Short and Archibald Stuart
among them. The canny Jones replied:

> ". . . If Mr. Wythe means to pursue Mr. Blackstone's method I think you ought to attend
> him. . . . I incline to think Mr. Wythe, under the present state of our laws, will be much
> embarrassed to deliver lectures with that perspicuity and precision which might be expected
> from him under a more established and settled state. . . . I have no intimate acquaintance
> with Mr. Jefferson. . . . You do well to cultivate his friendship. . . ."[25]

This worldly-wise advice Monroe adopted and so when Jefferson moved the
Capital to Richmond, Williamsburg being too exposed to the enemy, Monroe
followed him. (This was, of course, the reason that Wythe was able to use the
old Capitol as his classroom, since the legislators no longer occupied it.)

It was at this time, too, that William Cabell, Jr. studied under Wythe. He
was the treasurer of Phi Beta Kappa, that debating society which was the earliest and most prestigious of the nation's honor societies. At Leslie's invasion, in
October and November of 1780, Cabell went off to fight the British, as did most
of the students. John Brown would have gone too, but as he wrote his uncle, he
was simply too sick:

> ". . . my Illness . . . two months tomorrow since I was taken with a most violent Billious
> Fever . . . strangers, bad attendants & the worst weather all these conspire to sink my Spir-
> its & have reduc'd me to a mere Skelliton. . . ."[26]

And again:

> ". . . my great uneasiness of mind occasioned by the Invasion of the English who have been
> expected daily in this Town, Mr. Cocke with whom I board moves away tomorrow with his
> Family, Mr. Madison is gone, the Town almost deserted . . ."[27]

Leslie's invasion, however, was nothing to that which Phillips and the new traitor Benedict Arnold undertook. They showed up on 27 March 1781, and then came an incident which gave George Wythe, now well past middle age, a chance to strike a blow himself against the enemy. Arnold had had no more staunch supporter while Wythe was in Congress and the gallant and brave Benedict was fighting his country's battles in Quebec and Upstate New York. But now the General had sold out to the British and made his name an everlasting symbol for betrayal and shame.

It is Pendleton who describes in rather derogatory terms the invasion by Phillips and Arnold.

> "To James Madison   23 April, 1781
> Since my last . . . the fleet up Potowmack proved a . . . mere plundering party. . . . I am just now told they are in possession of Williamsburg. . . . Should they mean to take a Post there, they will command the whole Neck down to Hampton. . . . I fear our crops, of corn particularly, will be much Injured by the large Number of Militia already in Service. . . . Yr brother left me this Morning . . . Mr. Wythe having advertised his lectures to commence the 1st of May. I expect yr brother will hear of the Enemy's possession . . . , and return. . . ."[28]

To be noted is the sentence: "Your brother left me this Morning . . . Mr. Wythe having advertised his lectures to commence the 1st of May." And so while Wythe apparently stayed on in Williamsburg, the same was not true of Pendleton. For that worthy put as much distance between himself and the British as he could, leaving his home in Caroline County to cross over beyond the Blue Ridge. It was especially brave of Wythe to stay, for the British would dearly have loved to get their hands on a Signer. But Wythe did more than remain in the Tidewater area, refusing to allow the dastardly English to chase him away. It is William Tatham, writing many years later to William Armistead Burwell who recalled the events of that exciting time.

The British fleet was hovering about the lower James River, the commanders apparently undecided whether to proceed up the river to seize Richmond (which they ultimately did), or to attack Williamsburg. Baron Steuben and General Nelson were waiting in the offing to try to drive the English away, but it was Wythe and some of his friends who started the action. The old Chancellor and his fellows, out hunting at the mouth of Archer's Hope Creek, which empties into the James, saw the British put out their boats preparing to land on the shore. Undoubtedly the old patriots were out partridge shooting, trying to fill their depleted cupboards at home. Without hesitating, the old men, seeing the invaders, "took a pop at them" and gave them such a hot time of it that they scuttled back to their ships and safety. The Fates must have laughed indeed to see Wythe's lead peppering the Arnold forces, remembering how Wythe had worked in Congress to keep Arnold, in other years and other places, well supplied with—lead.[29]

However, the actual occupation of Williamsburg by Cornwallis did what threats of war could not do. For Cornwallis seized the town in June, 1781, and made the President's home his headquarters. Now, the school stopped completely, and this was the first time it did so, for when the lower York peninsula saw that actual marching back and forth of huge armies and the awful battle of Yorktown, the students all became soldiers. Exactly where Wythe went at this point is not known. Surely he did not take himself and his wife to the Back River plantation—that was too exposed to plunder by the British. Nor was it safe for a Signer to stay in town, for even if the English did not harm him, they would at least have forced him to sign a parole. And that surely the brave and resolute Wythe would not do.

Notes to Chapter VIII

1. Benjamin Rush. *Autobiography.* p. 121.
2. Washington. *The Writings of—.* Fitzpatrick ed., Vol. 6, p. 331.
3. Second Continental Congress. *Journals,* Vol. 6, p. 1020.
4. *Ibidem.* p. 1022.
5. *American Archives—.* Fifth Series, Vol. 3, Col. 1290.
6. *Ibidem.* Col. 1255.
7. *Ibidem.* Col. 1334.
8. *New York State Historical Society Collections.* 1878, p. 407
9. *Letters of the Members . . . of the Continental Congress.* Burnett, ed., Vol. 2, p. 183.
10. *Ibidem.* p. 215.
11. Second Continental Congress. *Journals.* Vol. 7, p. 13.
12. 18 November 1776, Manuscript Collection, New York Public Library.
13. Manuscript Collection, University of North Carolina Library.
14. Jefferson. *Autobiography,* in, *The Writings of—.* Washington ed., Vol. 1, p. 41.
15. Virginia. State. General Assembly. *Journals of the House of Delegates and Senate.* 1776—. (Richmond, 1827), p. 84.
16. William H. English. *Earliest Virginian Conquest of the River Ohio 1778–1783—.* (Indianapolis, Indiana & Kansas City, Missouri, 1898), p. 461.
17. *Ibidem.* p. 468.
18. *Ibidem.* p. 102–3.
19. Washington. *The Writings of—.* Fitzpatrick ed., Vol. 13, p. 467.
20. Jefferson to Philip Mazzei, Nov. 1785, Paris, in, Jefferson, *The Papers of—.* Boyd ed., Vol. 9, p. 67.
21. Manuscript Collection, New York Public Library.
22. Jefferson to James Madison, 26 July 1780, Richmond. in, Jefferson. *The Papers of—.* Boyd ed., Vol. 3, p. 507.
23. To Col. Wm. Preston, 15 Feb 1780, Williamsburg, in., William and Mary—. First Series, Vol. 9, p. 76.
24. *Ibidem,* 6 July 1780.
25. Daniel C. Gilman. *James Monroe.* (Boston & New York, Houghton Mifflin, 1898), p. 13–15.
26. To. Col. Wm Preston, 16 Oct. 1780, in, William and Mary—, First Series, Vol. 9, p. 82.
27. 27 October 1780. *Ibidem,* p. 83.
28. James Madison. *The Papers of—.* Ed. by Hutcheson and Rachel, Vol. 3, p. 80.
29. 13 June 1805, Georgetown, Columbia, in, Thomas Jefferson, *The Papers of—.* Boyd ed., Vol. 7, p. 273.

CHAPTER IX

Wythe, Chancellor and Teacher.

Although Cornwallis treated the College contumaciously, the turn of the English was coming, the gods of war having prepared reverses for the invaders. With a splendid coordination, the French fleet moved down the coastline from Rhode Island and blockaded Cornwallis on the seaward. And down the continent by land came Washington's army, moving through the Jerseys, Pennsylvania, Maryland and eventually into the home state of Virginia. When the land army and the sea fleet met in a pincers, they had Cornwallis between them. And the Battle of Yorktown was the outcome.

It is St. George Tucker, Wythe's former student, who relates to us the events of the day on which Washington entered Williamsburg, Cornwallis now being backed into his narrow trap.

15 September 1781
Williamsburg

". . . General Washington . . .

About four o'clock in the afternoon his approach was announced. . . . He approached without any pomp or parade attended only by a few horsemen and his own servants. The Count de Rochambeau and Gen. Hand . . . were with him. . . . To my great surprise he recognized my Features and spoke to me . . . Gen. Nelson, the Marquis, etc. rode up immediately after. . . . The Marquis rode up . . . clasped the General in his arms. . . . The General, . . . rode through the French lines. . . . His quarters are at Mr. Wythe's house. Aunt Betty has the honor of Count de Rochambeau to lodge at her house. . . ."[1]

And so it was. Wythe had invited the Commander-in-Chief to make use of his house as the headquarters and Washington did so. Where Wythe lived while the fighting was going on is difficult to discover. Yorktown is directly between Williamsburg and Back River, so there was plenty of battling, and surely Wythe did not expose his wife to such danger.

But when the battle was over and the English were taken, things had some-how to be put back together again. At their surrender, the English had ordered their band to play the tune "The World Turned Upside Down." And indeed it was, but for others than the English. Williamsburg was in no shape for the College to resume sessions. For the rest of the year the French troops remained encamped in the vicinity, and there were also in the town some hundreds of English prisoners. These were unguarded, and acted with general lawlessness, stealing as much as they could. Runaway slaves roamed the countryside, also stealing what they could. Great old plantation houses, run-down by years of neglect, gave the aspect of depression to the area. Sickness, filth and flies, the inevitable attendants upon war, prevailed in the area.

The Capital had been removed to Richmond, so that revenue was gone. All that remained was the College, and that was so run-down that the Reverend James Madison even thought for the moment to give up his ministry. How was he to live?—His professorship gave him no income. Even the old Governor's Palace had burned to the ground, and was now a hopeless pile of bricks. The Capitol, where Wythe had held his sessions with his students, had likewise become a hospital, occupied by the French. This was true of the College build-ing also, where the President's house was accidentally burned to the ground. Of course, recompense was forthcoming and the building was later re-erected (but not until 1785). It was Wythe's great worry that something similar would happen to the College, and he wrote Washington to ask that the General intercede with the French to use care.

> "Sir: The professors of William and Mary are separated by various avocations so that it will perhaps be difficult to suddenly convene them. The answer therefore . . . may be inclosed in a letter directed to me. . . . There are . . . a costly library . . . a valuable apparatus for making philosophical experiments. I beg your Excellency to signify to the Count de Rocham-beau that you will take it kindly if the officers . . . be desired to prevent any injury to those articles and the place in which they are deposited. . . ."[2]

Washington's reply to this letter was certainly non-committal, to say the least.

All that winter of 1781–82, the French army remained in Williamsburg. Washington having returned to his beloved Mount Vernon for the time being, Rochambeau took up his quarters in the now-vacated Wythe house. One is left to suppose that Wythe and his lady must have stayed with friends in town, when they were not at Chesterville.

When the College finally re-opened, the professors were buried with work. This was especially true of Wythe, as Mazzei noted. Now that the Revolution was practically over, the law courts were fully open and the Virginians were as litigious as ever. All the law suits for years back could now be tried, and so Judge Wythe was fully occupied. But he had teaching to do as well. Not only did the Professors have to work hard for what they got, but the College itself was almost impoverished. Before the Revolution, the revenues were some £5–6000 a year. After the Revolution, these revenues were almost totally gone, and the College could count only on the income from some 22,000 acres of land, an income which amounted to very little in the Virginia of that time.

The British were as niggardly as possible where William and Mary was concerned. The celebrated Boyle fund (otherwise known as the Brafferton) was a sum of money, the interest of which had for long supported the College in some part. During the war, the money was of course tied up in England, but after the war the College expected as a matter of course that Boyle's bequest would continue to be honored. In 1783, the Faculty directed Wythe to confer with Judge Blair on the legal status of the Fund, and subsequently the College drew up a bill on the agent in London for the money in his hands which arose from rents and interest from the Brafferton. After this, the Bishop of London, Belby Porteus, brought suit in the English courts to prevent the payments, and the money was accordingly diverted to the West Indies. Thus far the generosity of the British to a victorious enemy.

The French, however, helped as much as they could. The Chevalier de Chastellux, for example, gave the College Library an "elegant edition of the work *De la publique*," of which he was the author. Books were always welcome, and the faculty resolved that a letter of thanks should go to the French knight. There was much friendliness between the College and the French troops. Chastellux was especially taken with the school and its faculty:

> "The beauty of the building is surpassed by the richness of its library, and still farther by the distinguished merit of . . . its professors, such as the Doctors Madison, Wythe, Bellini . . . who may be regarded as living Books . . . they have already formed many distinguished characters, ready to serve their country in the various departments of government."[3]

Not to be outdone, the College bestowed an honorary degree on the noble Frenchman. Indeed, the College gave out degrees with a diplomatic hand. But if diplomas, honorary or otherwise, could be diplomatic, they could also be comforters. It was probably Wythe who had the idea of conferring an honorary degree on Jefferson, who had fallen pretty much into political oblivion. The investigation which the Assembly had given him had exonerated him of all blame for the debacle of Arnold's invasion, but Jefferson's political star did not rise thereby. To assuage the wound in his former pupil's heart, and to give him perhaps some added prestige, Wythe pushed the College into making the former Governor a Doctor of the Civil Law, *causa honoris*. Wythe well knew how to phrase the citation:

> ". . . the high opinion we hold of Thomas Jefferson, . . . who having been educated in the bosom of our alma mater . . . most skilled both in private and public law; of exceptional love for his country; illustrious . . . in championing American liberty . . . he seeks his reward not from popular acclaim but from the deed itself. . . ."[4]

Well, this was one instance in which the College sought to inspire popular acclaim.

It was Wythe likewise who framed the diploma conferring an honorary degree on James Madison, the future President of the United States:

". . . I have the pleasure, sir, to forward to you the testimony, herewith enclosed, of our University. Distinctions of this kind will I am persuaded be not unacceptable, whilst we continue to bestow them on such men as Franklin, Jefferson, Rittenhouse, Edmund Randolph, John Page of Rosewell, etc., etc. *Caeteraque extra animum,* in the diploma, which may perhaps appear an obscure expression, is used by Tacitus, in the sense here intended, to signify those things which contribute not to the improvement of the mind. Permit me to subscribe myself Your friend, G. Wythe"[5]

The patronizing Rives cites this letter as an example of that "which sometimes wore the air of pedantry in its distinguished author."

But there is in existence a letter written by Wythe, some time earlier than that to Madison cited above, which cannot be cited as an example of pedantry. It is, in fact, a most remarkable letter indeed, showing as it does how little concerned Wythe was with the acquisition of money. Untainted by that greed which has so characterized so many of the legal profession, Wythe wrote to John Tabb on 22 September, 1782:

"Mrs. Wythe, Sir, informed me, that you civily wished me to send you an account of fees. In my book messrs Rumbold Walker and Tabb stands charged with fees . . . to £26.0.0. . . . Several of the suits, but which I do not recollect, were not finished, when I was taken from the bar; so that I am not intitled to, nor would I receive, the whole balance, altho I had almost as much trouble with them as if they had been finished; and I shall be content with half, or as much less as you think just, or even without any. I am, Sir, Your obedient humble servant. G. Wythe."[6]

This reluctance to pursue gain is all the more remarkable since it occurred at a time when Wythe must have been in considerable difficulty about money. For his plantation at Back River was now in an extremely tangled situation.

There had entered George Wythe's life, some time prior to 22 December 1773, a character with the wonderful name of Hamilton Usher St. George. Out of Wythe's traffic with this man came betrayal and near financial ruin, St. George being the man Wythe hired to manage his plantation, Chesterville. There is a letter of 22 December, 1773, from Wythe to an unknown person which, while not proof that Wythe had hired St. George by that date, at least proves that the two had dealings. One of the difficulties in the affair is that of the two, St. George's account is untrustworthy and Wythe's does not exist. In several important matters, St. George proves himself a liar. And if Wythe ever wrote anything about his dealings with his manager, such has not survived. One is therefore dependent entirely on what St. George said about things.

In the middle or early 1770's therefore, Wythe engaged St. George to act as his manager. St. George himself writes:

"I often was pressed by Mr. Wythe to join him in his farm before I agreed to do it, and what caused me to agree at all was his obliging himself to take upon him at his own expense the education of my son, to have him brought up to a knowledge of the law and languages. Indeed my agreement with him promised satisfaction and advantage of us both; for exclusive of half the new profitts of the Farm; I was to have everything necessary for the Supplying of my table, that the Dairy, garden and Foul-houses produced; without being accountable for the same in our Farm Account. . . ."[7]

Thus Hamilton Usher St. George gave the terms upon which Wythe engaged him. And it may very well have been so.

This St. George had been in the cattle business on Hog Island, a large flat island in the James River opposite Jamestown. He furnished people in Williamsburg with meat, and his farm served as a ferrying-place across the river for people bound for the little city. Travellers left their horses with St. George, and this gave the man an added profit. One cannot be sure, but it may be that he succeeded in selling this farm on Hog Island (he advertised it for sale in the Virginia Gazette) before he associated himself with Wythe. So far the story is one of simple contract, honestly begun.

But now came the difficulty. For the Revolution came on swiftly. And Wythe's overseer was no patriot. In fact, he was, as he blandly admits, an obdurate Tory, supporting Lord Dunmore and spying on the Americans. It is here that it is hard to believe St. George, for surely Wythe, a true patriot, would never have continued to tolerate a traitor and a Tory on his plantation. Nevertheless we have St. George's word that from the very beginning of the Revolution, he acted the part of an open Tory:

"Brothers could not be better disposed to serve each other than we were before the war. But my refusing to take the command of their first Regiment of Horse, or to accept the offers made me by the rebel General Lee; offended him [George Wythe] and made him my worst enemy, and brought many evils upon me and terminated in my ruine in America, without the benefit of the commission promised by Lord Dunmore. . . ."[8]

St. George, writing after the war was over to ask the Office of American Claims in London, a bureaucracy which adjusted the losses and claims of Loyalists, for compensation for his losses in America, secured the further depositions of both Dunmore and Cornwallis, as well as affidavits from Colonel John Hamilton, the Reverend John Agnew, Major John Grymes, Robert Steward and Bridger Goodrich. But on his own account, St. George spun a remarkable tale indeed. For he said that he stayed with Dunmore the night before that noble lord went on board ship in 1775. Dunmore told him, said St. George, to stay ashore and "mix freely with the enemy." As, apparently, a spy. And St. George, faithful to Dunmore, said he did so. Nor was this all, for St. George declared that Dunmore promised to pay him for such supplies as he should furnish the English troops. This payment was to be in gold and silver, and St. George was to have a "commission which would subject him to no man's command but his own." Accordingly, St. George delivered to Lord Dunmore, while that erstwhile warrior was sailing up and down the Virginian rivers and bays, both before and after the defeat at Norfolk and Gwynn's Island, many hundreds of bushels of potatoes, oats, wheat, and dozens of cattle and sheep.

Apparently, St. George delivered grain, grown on Wythe's plantation at Back River, to Dunmore also. Dunmore, in fact, wrote to the Office of American Claims, certifying that the debt was a just one. He even figured out the interest for 13 years at 5 percent—and the sum amounted to £4516/17/6. To the claim that some of this belonged by right to Wythe, St. George answered:

". . . it is observed . . . that in his former demand for losses . . . he only claimed for the oats & wheat now demanded, one moiety thereof, Mr. George Wythe being equally concerned therein."

St. George in reply explained that Mr. Wythe

". . . though concerned with him was much more in his [St. George's] debt than the whole amount of the oats and wheat. That he had collected them . . . for . . . the King's fleet . . . he conceives entitled to payment for the whole."[9]

This deposition was, of course, in London in 1789, when St. George was facing Debtor's prison. However much he may have wanted to exaggerate, he could not very well have done so for there were too many Loyalists in Britain who could give him the lie. (Indeed, on one occasion, at least, one such did so.) At any rate, so St. George's account goes, he collected the oats on Back River "stored in his own Granary." Supplies from Hog Island were delivered up to Bridger Goodrich, who was sent by Lord Dunmore up the river to get them. Dunmore, said St. George, had asked his help and he had given it. When Dunmore after Gwynn's Island had had to leave Virginia, St. George was left a prisoner with the rebels:

". . . arraigned at the bar, tried for my life, . . . Negroe men imprisoned, they took jail fever, 14 of them died, burned my house, offices and crops . . . suffer every hardship but that of my life."

Now said the Tory, he was 63 years old, sick and poor. He was also, according to Dunmore's affidavit, facing debtor's prison, there in cold, damp, friendless London in 1789.

This whole story is quite inexplicable, for surely George Wythe would never have allowed St. George, having shown himself a fervid supporter of the English, to have continued on as his overseer all during the war. Wythe was well aware of all that went on in that part of Virginia. Yet not once in any letter does Wythe mention St. George's treason towards Virginia or betrayal of himself. It is true, of course, there might have been letters which have not survived.

That St. George's respect for the truth was not too precious can be discerned from that fact that some of the deponents giving affidavits for him speak of the Back River plantation as belonging to St. George. For example, Colonel John Hamilton, in a letter of 12 March, 1789, declaring that he knew St. George from the year 1766, said he visited St. George's place on Back River. Declaring that the subject was a good farmer, Hamilton said that he often went there. This was, declared Hamilton, St. George's own plantation. Of course, we know it wasn't.

At any rate, St. George, despite his Tory sympathies, did apparently remain at Chesterville during the war years. And then this enemy of America compounded his wickedness by aiding the English in 1781. For Hamilton Usher St. George declared that he was the first to give Cornwallis, then backed into his peninsula at York, the news of the arrival of the French fleet. Lord Cornwallis himself testified that this was true. In fact, since this treasonous act made him a destitute fugitive, Cornwallis gave him money, money which St. George, evidently at that time (late September, 1783) in New York City as a refugee, sent to his wife and children by a Mr. Coleborn Barrell who promptly stole it (said St. George).

It is Mrs. St. George who gave her husband the lie outright: for in his affidavit the husband had declared that the Americans had confiscated his lands and Negroes. But this was not so, said Mrs. St. George. The lands were retained only, not confiscated. And so here was another lie on St. George's part. And this lie St. George admitted to the London examiners, as he had to in view of the forthrightness of his wife's testimony. This testimony had come in the form of a letter from Mrs. St. George of 10 July 1782, which was received (apparently) in New York City:

> "Immediately after the surrender of York Mr. Wythe took possession of *Chesterville,* where he has chiefly resided ever since; and obliged us to move off, at an unseasonable time of the year (for I could not possibly get away till the 20th of December) without any stock which he would allow no part of; without any kind of provision not even Bread for the people [the slaves]—he did indeed promise before my Brother Josiah, to let me have Corn & Pork, but he has since refused to let me have it."[10]

In her letter to the Board of Commissioners, Mrs. St. George flatly said that she had retained St. George's servants without being molested. Also that no part of his lands had been confiscated. And so St. George had the lie given him direct.

But what was Wythe's account of the affair? Extremely laconic. For what has survived is the merest hint in a letter to Jefferson:

> 31 December 1781
> "A few days after the reduction of York I returned to Williamsburg, and accompanying Mr. Madison, waited on general Washington, with an address of the university among other things, desiring him to give orders, that the college, which we found employed as a hospital, might be evacuated so soon as it could be done conveniently. He was very civil, and gave a kind answer; but for that business referred us to count de Rochambeau and general Nelson: from the latter of whom as we saw no prospect of redress, we made no application to the other. But some conversation, which I had with general Chastellux, and a letter, which he wrote to me, since, give me some hopes that the college will be restored, in two or three months. During that interval, I know not a place, at which my time would pass so happily as at Monticello, if my presence at Chesterville were not indispensably necessary to adjust my affairs left there in some confusion by the manager who hath lately eloped. I can therefore only thank you for your friendly invitation and offer. You must allow me to insist that you

send me but one horse, in exchange for him you had of me, without compensation for difference of value if any there be and even that one I desire not unless you can spare him conven-
iently. In our dealings, you, and not I, if either, ought to have the advantage, for more reasons than I can enumerate.   . . . Adieu."[11]

The manager who hath lately eloped! No more than that!

But perhaps Wythe was too busy to give explanations concerning his business
affairs. After all, the College had to be put to rights again, and that took much
time and energy. In addition, there was plenty of teaching to do. It had been in
that hectic, troubled period immediately before Yorktown that Wythe had
instructed in his classes one of the most remarkable of all his pupils. That was
that young soldier returned from the wars, John Marshall. The warrior had
come back to his native Virginia fresh from serving under General Washington.
The war was certainly not yet over, but just as James Monroe had returned to
Virginia to await a new command, so did John Marshall. His father in the
Spring of 1780 was commanding the forces in the soon-to-be-famous village of
Yorktown. Since young John had fallen in love and wanted to marry and so
needed a profession, the soldier came to attend Wythe's course in law at Wil-
liam and Mary.

It is shocking to note that the future Chief Justice stayed in law school only
six weeks, absorbing what he could in that short time. He couldn't really have
learned very much, although he may have known more law than what Wythe
taught him, for we know that from Marshall's childhood he had read Blackstone. The English lawyer's work had been put into his hands early in life, and
he read it thoroughly. Since Wythe used Blackstone as a text, Marshall was on
familiar ground. In addition, Marshall must have had a good deal of familiarity
with some forms of the law for he had served in Washington's army during that
terrible winter at Valley Forge, as Deputy Judge Advocate. This means that the
young man, lately promoted to captain, had charge of preparing and trying
delinquent soldiers in courts martial.

Wythe gave instruction in the form of lectures, as William Small had done,
and as is the modern method. Marshall took notes of what Wythe said, and his
notebook exists to this day. We know, therefore, just what was taught. As the
young soldier was in love, one can today find written the name of his
beloved—"Maria Ambler"—all over the pages of the notebook. So the great
teacher had competition for Marshall's attention as he held forth on such subjects as: Abatement (Marshall wrote three pages of notes on that), Annuity and
Rent Charge (two pages sufficed here), Bail in Criminal Causes (here Marshall
took some two and a half pages of notes), Estates in Fee Simple (this got only
one and a quarter pages of attention from Marshall) and so forth. After some six
weeks of this, the budding lawyer went to Richmond and got Jefferson, then
Governor, to sign his law license! Marshall then was admitted to the bar of
Fauquier County on 28 August 1780.[12]

The newly-made lawyer then returned to the army to do what fighting he could in response to traitor Arnold's invasion some four months later. He actually practiced law when peace once more broke out. With such a paucity of knowledge and training (not to say experience), one wonders how clients could have dared trust him with their litigation. However, within a few years and whatever the explanation, John Marshall was a rising lawyer and a success at the bar. What he became later in life, everybody knows. Even as a practising lawyer, he was elected to the House of Delegates. Since the courts and the legislature met in the same building in Richmond, Marshall and the other lawyers had no difficulty in being both legislators and lawyers at once. Indeed, Marshall could easily move from the downstairs room, in its plain republican simplicity where Chancellor Wythe and his colleagues held their court, to the legislative chamber upstairs, with its equally austere simplicity. And so the young Marshall, all through the 1780's, practised before the judge under whom he had studied, which means, in effect, that Wythe continued to be his teacher.

Another of Wythe's students at this time was William Branch Giles. This was indeed a redoubtable character. Like many another college youth, the war was a kind of vacation from College for Giles. In 1781 he received his degree from Princeton, and came to Williamsburg to study law under Wythe. Having graduated from Wythe's school, his rise was rapid for he was sent by Virginia to the National Congress in the 1790's and there he became friendly with Jefferson. In after years he was a member of the small group which ran Virginia as a sort of private political preserve. Indeed, at one time he was practically the ruler of Virginia and had enormous influence on national politics.

Another of Wythe's students in those early days was Spencer Roane. After receiving his law training from Wythe, he went on to become the most determined of the enemies of John Marshall. As the judge of the Virginia Court of Appeals, he was the greatest judicial opponent of Marshall's nationalism. Marrying a daughter of Patrick Henry, he became a judge in 1786 although he could have been out of law school only perhaps five years. As were most of Wythe's pupils, Roane was on the side of Jefferson in the latter's great struggle against the Federalists and on behalf of democratic principles.

Wythe's main work in this period was teaching, however much attention his judicial decisions might demand. He knew very well what he was doing—training for the future welfare of his state and his nation the best minds he could find. He wrote a letter to John Adams, his old colleague in Congress, pointing this out:

5 December 1783

"Often had I almost resolved to write to you, to supply, in some measure, by an epistolary correspondence, the want of that conversation which I had no other cause to regret than the interruption of it by the distance between us; and had more reasons than I can enumerate to covet. But uncertainty of communication and a doubt whether the merit of any thing I could say would be an apology for diverting your attention from affairs incomparably more momentous hitherto kept me reluctantly silent. Your letter, therefore, by mr. Mazzei, delivered to me this day, by which I learn your wish to receive a line from me, and that too wherever you be, was received with joy. I accept the invitation with a pleasure one feels in renewing an acquaintance with an old friend whose company was entertaining and improving. O were our habitations so neighboring, that.

Καί κε θαμ' ἐνθάδ ἐ ὄντες ἐμισγομεθ' οὐδέ κεν ἡμεας ἄλλο διεκρινεν φιλεοντε τέ τερπομένω τε πριν γ' ὅτε δὴ θανατοιο μελαν νεφος ἀμφεκαλυψεν.

A letter will meet with me in Williamsburg where I have again settled, assisting, as professor of law and police in the university there, to form such characters as may be fit to succede those which have been ornamental and useful in the national councils of America. Adieu."[14]

Among those future leaders of their country were the sons of the Lee family. On 28 February 1783 Richard Henry Lee wrote to Wythe that his son Ludwell Lee was again putting "himself under your patronage in his Law studies." Ludwell had been one of those forced, apparently, to interrupt his work under Wythe by the late unpleasantness on the part of Cornwallis. It is significant of the position Wythe was coming to occupy in the minds of his fellow countrymen that Lee should address him as "Much respected Worthy Sir."[15] Writing to George Washington at about the same time, Lee addressed him merely as "Dear Sir,"[16] and a letter to Governor Benjamin Harrison simply bore the greeting "Sir."[17] Thus the descending scale of prestige.

Another Lee was Thomas Lee Shippen, nephew to Richard Henry and son of Dr. William Shippen, Professor of Anatomy in the University of Pennsylvania. It is this Thomas Shippen who gives us a chance to see the day-to-day workings of Wythe's school. On 5 February 1784 he wrote to his father:

"Last Saturday was the day of my political birth . . . for . . . I delivered an oration for the first time in our grand and august Assembly. . . . very lately Mr. Wythe has a lofty presidential Seat erected, which adds very much to his dignity and may . . . be called his hobby horse. This *entre nous*. This throne has a greater effect in throwing a damp upon the spirits of the speaker, than you can imagine . . .

. . . the subject was the Impost recommended by Congress, the bill for which I attacked in all its parts with warmth and violence and was supported by Ludwell. . . . It is now committed and we mean in the Committee to make such alterations in the Bill, that the end will be destroyed. . . ."

Two weeks later, he again writes his father:

". . . before Breakfast, I generally read an hour and a half, some times two hours in Blackstone or else am employed in compositions, which by the advice of my instructors I pay a great deal of attention to. From breakfast to dinner, I read Blackstone, Hume or Montesquieu. After dinner If I dine at home . . . I play a piece of music on the violin, or read some entertaining book in French or . . . some favorite Roman author Horace, Virgil or Terrence . . . . At night . . . read . . . until 10, 11, or 12 o'clock. . . . But as Mr. Wythe lectures every Tuesday and Mr. Madison every Thursday and Saturday . . . I can read very little on those days between breakfast and Dinner, as we are at College from 10 to 12. . . ."

Shippen formed here a lifelong friendship with Wythe for he was often invited to the latter's home. While there he met Wythe's niece-by-marriage, Miss Nancy Taliaferro. Shippen was charmed by her, writing to Miss Anne Livingston, a Philadelphia friend, on 29 October 1783:

". . . I am sure Miss Nancy Tolliver would frown very severely upon me if she knew that when speaking of ye beauties of Wmburg I did not mention her first. I will now with sorrow for my neglect . . . delineate her character . . . . She lives with her uncle Mr. Wythe at whose house I have once dined with her. She is generally supposed to be the prettiest girl now in town, but there is a want of animation in her countenance, which prevents my giving her the preference. She has however fine eyes, good features and a charming complexion. She is extremely diffident, but very well bred. She it is who has counted our friend Ludwell among her slaves and prides herself . . . upon her conquests. . . ."[18]

Thus a young man of the 18th Century on the subject of women.

Another of Wythe's pupils was John Minor 3rd, who was the son of Major John Minor. Both father and son were in the American army and took part in the siege of Yorktown. The son, twenty years old at the time of Yorktown, was born at Topping Castle in Caroline County. As soon as the war was over, he began his studies under the great Wythe and when he had them completed, he went to Fredericksburg to live and practice. He became famous for his eloquence and skill at the bar, and while still a young man, he was sent to Virginia's legislature where, true to Wythe's teaching, he entered two bills into the House. The first of these provided for gradual emancipation and the second was concerned with transporting and colonizing the freedmen elsewhere. Jefferson approved of them, but they failed of passage, nonetheless.

Peter Carr, the son of Jefferson's dear and never-forgotten boyhood friend, Dabney Carr, was even more beloved by Jefferson since the boy was his nephew as well. Remembering with affection and gratitude his own training, Jefferson, now American minister to France, applied to Wythe that he might take young Peter's education in hand. No request from Jefferson could be refused, and Wythe was eager to teach anybody who applied, anyway. Peter therefore came to Williamsburg and enrolled in Wythe's classes at the College. He took part in the law training of Wythe's moot courts and the mock Assembly, but, in addition, Wythe poured out on him all the overflowing knowledge and love the boy was disposed to accept. There was a certain impatience on the boy's part, however, since like all young men, he was eager to get at the main business of life—action. As Wythe insisted that the men he trained should be—as far as he could make them—men of learning as well as men of law, he took the boy as a private pupil in the study of Latin and Greek. Carr read Herodotus, Sophocles, Cicero and Horace with him. Carr himself goes on to say interesting things about the *obiter dicta* which accompanied the instruction:

". . . he adds advice and lessons of morality, which are not only pleasing and instructive now, but will be (I hope) of real utility in future. He is said to be without religion, but to me he appears to possess the most rational part of it, and fulfills that great command, Do unto all men as thou wouldst they should do unto thee."[19]

Carr, however, was fearful. Wythe had given him Lucretius to read and the Latin poet's great work "De rerum natura" was the basis of a certain agnosticism. Carr applied to Jefferson (of all people) to advise him on the subject of religion. He added that men regard Lucretius as "dangerous" but "under so good a guide I fear not his [Lucretius'] opinions whatever they be . . . ." In this letter also, he added a certain criticism of Wythe's instruction, feeling that Wythe was giving him too much to study. His attention, he feared, was being directed to too many things, and he would perhaps ends up with an imperfect knowledge of his subjects.

In addition to teaching Peter Carr, Wythe was concerned about the attempt to re-found the nation on a new constitution. He wrote to ask Jefferson's opinion.

> 22 Decemb 1786
>
> "Lest a letter, which a few days ago, i wrote to you, should not come to your hands, i now write this, to entreat, that you will let us have your thoughts on the confederation of the american states, which is proposed to be revised in the summer following. I mentioned in that letter, that Peter Carr was attending the professors of natural and moral philosophy, and mathematics, learning the french and spanish languages, and with me reading Herodotus, Aeschylus, Cicero, and Horace; and that i wished to know if you approved of the course, or would recommend any other. Farewell"[20]

It had been to Peter Carr that Richard Randolph, the brother of John Randolph of Roanoke and the foster son of St. George Tucker, had written on 30 October 1786 from Matoax asking that he pay "Mr. Wythe" the money due him, "As I shall never again return to Williamsburg." Of Richard Randolph there is the saddest of all the stories of Wythe's pupils. His brother John was a most brilliant and able man, who came to be one of the most powerful politicians of the Jefferson era. His cruel wit, however, undid him, but even more so his eventual insanity. John was never Wythe's pupil, although he often practiced law in Wythe's court. But Richard had been.

So unlike his sardonic brother, Richard was gentle and rather retiring, but was caught up in early manhood in a dreadful scandal, which involved adultery and the birth of an illegitimate child. The infant subsequently died or was murdered in an attempt to conceal its birth and the resultant trial was a celebrated and heart-breaking affair. Richard Randolph himself died early, but not before he, true to the ideals he had learned from Wythe, had liberated his slaves. He made Wythe the executor of his estate, with the proviso that the slaves be given land which they might farm. This was done but the affair was a total failure. Unused to freedom, the former slaves hadn't the slightest idea of how to provide for themselves and their establishment became a rural slum.

In the early 1780's, there occurred one of the high points of Wythe's judicial career—a matter in which the stand he took even today affects the political life of Americans. Affairs in Virginia prior to 1782 had, as we have seen, been in a chaotic state. There had been the raid by the British general Phillips in 1781, and this was followed by that of Benedict Arnold. Now many who for the past several years had concealed their sympathies, being secret Tories, came out on the side of the British. The King's armies seemed, certainly, to be in control of the state. They could drive the legislature over the mountains, send the Governor fleeing from his hill-top home, sack the Capital, and do, apparently, as they pleased with the prostrate body of Virginia. And so the Tories rode high. But then came Yorktown and its aftermath. In the course of rounding up the Tories who had aided Cornwallis, the Americans captured three scoundrels—Joshua Hopkins, James Lamb, and John Caton. They were tried on a charge of treason at a Court of Oyer and Terminer in Richmond, being condemed to death by hanging.

The three appealed for mercy to the General Assembly, and the House of Delegates gave them a pardon. But, according to the Virginia Constitution, the whole Assembly, both House and Senate, must do the pardoning. And the Senate refused to concur. This puzzled the sheriff, for now which should he obey? He took the question to the Attorney General, Edmund Randolph, who told him to go ahead with the hanging, declaring the Delegates' pardon to be invalid. The case came to the Supreme Court of Virginia, the Court of Appeals. Sitting thereon were the Judges of the General Court, the Admiralty Court, and the Court of Chancery.

Excitement was intense. The attention of the public was fixed on the court. Andrew Ronald was defending the prisoners, and he was only 28 years old. Edmund Randolph, the prosecuting Attorney-General, was only 29. The case was thrown open to any lawyer who wished to make a statement, and many of them did. Samuel Hardy, for instance, one of Wythe's students, came and gave his opinions at some length. When the talking was finally over, a decision had to be given. There were really two decisions to be handed down, and the first one was—did the Court of Appeals really have the right to try this case, that is, did it have jurisdiction? Some judges said no, but the majority said yes. The next question concerned the action of the legislature itself.

And this becomes involved. First of all, it was the position of Jefferson that the Virginia constitution was not organic law. That is, it wasn't framed by the people of Virginia in Convention expressly called to frame a constitution. But whether organic law or not, the Constitution existed. And it declared that the Governor shall, with the advice of his State Council, grant reprieves or pardons, save only where the House of Delegates itself shall have carried on the prosecution. Where this had happened, only the House could grant a pardon.

In the course of time, the General Assembly, which had enacted this Constitution, further enacted that when a person was convicted of treason, his conviction being based on his own confession or the testimony of two witnesses, the Governor shall not have the power to grant pardons. He could, however, suspend the execution until the General Assembly should meet, when the two Houses might do as they pleased about the conviction. So here was an Act in direct contravention to the Constitution. Which should have precedence in law? If the Constitution was only an enactment of the legislature, then the legislature could repeal what it had enacted (the Constitution itself or any part of it). If it wasn't, but was organic law, then the legislature couldn't touch it. It was inviolable and could be changed only by the people of Virginia in Convention.

Pendleton was especially culpable in this matter, for he was, as his latest biographer admits, the President of the Convention which wrote the Constitution and also the Speaker of the House which passed the Act. He dodged the real issue by declaring that nothing had happened. The House had started an enactment—the pardon of the traitors—which hadn't ever been completed. And that was all. Consequently, the traitors should hang.

Justice Carrington didn't even see any conflict between the original Constitution and the Assembly enactment of a law taking from the Governor the pardoning power. Chancellor Blair declared that the pardons were invalid since the Senate hadn't concurred. Justice Lyons' opinion was that the pardons were void. But Dandridge said they were good, since, in his opinion, either of the two branches, alone or together, could pardon. Justice Mercer declared the pardons were good; that the House did have the right to grant them, and that the Act of the Assembly was unconstitutional. Disagreeing with him was George Wythe, who in a splendid call to justice, declared for the over-riding power of the Court to review the enactments of the legislature—a call which has come ringing down the years to our own time.

So emphatic was Wythe's exposition, that although it is *obiter dicta,* it is worth including here.

"I have heard of an English chancellor who said, and it was nobly said, that it was his duty to protect the rights of the subject against the encroachments of the crown; and that he would do it, at every hazard. But if it was his duty to protect a solitary individual against the rapacity of the sovereign, surely it is equally mine to protect one branch of the legislature . . . against the usurpations of the other . . . Whenever traitors shall be fairly convicted, by the verdict of their peers before the competent tribunal; if one branch of the legislature, without the concurrence of the other, shall attempt to rescue the offenders from the sentence of the law, I shall not hesitate, sitting in this place, to say to the general court, *Fiat justitia, ruat coelum;* and, to the usurping branch of the legislature, "You attempt worse than a vain thing; for, although you cannot succeed, you set an example which may convulse society to its centre." Nay more, if the whole legislature, an event to be depreciated, should attempt to overleap the bounds prescribed to them by the people, I, in administering the public justice of the country, will meet the united powers at my seat in this tribunal, and, pointing to the constitution, will say to them, "Here is the limit of your authority; and hither shall you go, but no further."[21]

With these stirring words, Wythe flatly indicted the legislature for usurping authority and in the process decreed, by implication, the organic nature of the Constitution and thus undid Jefferson's argument. But even more important, Wythe publicly announced the doctrine of judicial review—a doctrine which John Marshall, when that individual was years later leading the Supreme Court, would use again and again to strike down the enactments of both the Federal and the State governments. And this power the Supreme Court wields today with all the strength of Marshall's precedents. Thus the famous case of

Commonwealth vs. Caton, with the traitors being condemned to hang, as their sentence was upheld.

It was shortly after the Proclamation of Peace that Wythe was given another chore on behalf of his beloved little city. A scheme of high political consequence was under way and it involved much bargaining in the national Congress. The question which was before the country was—where shall be the national capital? The citizenry of Philadelphia cared so little that when a mob of unpaid soldiers set upon the Congress, the citizens let it be chased out of town rather than protect it. The Congress alighted in Princeton and did not sit again in Philadelphia until 1790.

Among the places proposed was Williamsburg, other cities being Trenton, Georgetown, even Chestertown in the Eastern Shore of Maryland. Few people were really serious about Williamsburg, however, for it was too distant and difficult to reach. Nonetheless, the proposal had to be considered since it had been made. Accordingly, Governor Benjamin Harrison wrote to the city's mayor, who replied by calling a meeting of the inhabitants for five miles about and George Wythe, with his parliamentary experience, was asked to chair this meeting. Wythe himself knew, and undoubtedly informed the various citizens at the meeting, how vague were the proposals of Congress. He no doubt understood, too, that the issue was really without much importance, for Williamsburg was being used as a sort of political catspaw. The citizens therefore did precisely what was expected of them—they agreed that their city could be made into a sort of federal district, and the area would yield to Congress whatever might be necessary. But what was really expected of them? That Congress should be sovereign over the city and its environs? No one knew. The meeting did the best it could with such vagueness and resolved that they were agreeable to

". . . submit to any such jurisdiction as may be comparable with their political influence, and worthy of generous minds either to demand or yield."[22]

To this the Governor remarked to the Virginia delegates in Congress that the Williamsburg people were "still jealous of our Liberty and are unwilling to give up any part of it even to Congress." This wasn't really quite fair of Harrison, in view of the lack of really clear proposals.

And now added to an already busy life came the need for a second law revisal. True, the previous or Revolutionary law revisal was still being put through the legislature by bits and pieces. But a new gathering of extant laws was now provided for, and the job was given to Wythe and his fellows. This provoked his friend Mazzei to write to William Short, now with Jefferson in Paris:

"I wish that . . . Jefferson would send over orders, expressed in clear terms, to prevent poor George being killed by hard labour in his old age. I would think myself guilty of cruel indiscretion, if, considering his noble and humane feelings, I was silent on that subject."[23]

There may very well have been a certain impatience on Wythe's part at this new task, although he agreed readily enough, as he informed the Governor:

". . . utterly regardless of any pecuniary satisfaction, I shall be ready to undertake my part of the business. . . ."

But he was very busy:

". . . But if, that I should supervise the impression, in order to correct any typographical errors, be meant by the note, from attending this duty, I must beg to be excused."[24]

But busy or not, the work was done by 1785 when it was printed at Richmond.

About the year 1785, there occurred a matter which must have brought back to Wythe his memories of the old Continental Congress. For the Congress was still trying to settle differences (and there were many) between the various states. The loose confederation yet prevailed, and, above all, harmony was needed. But there was as usual a long-standing quarrel over the possession of certain lands, and no quarrel was more interminable than that between New York and Massachusetts, the latter state claiming the larger part of the west of New York, including most of the area from Syracuse westward. New York, of course, resisted and the Congress at Annapolis suggested they submit their quarrel to a jury composed of Robert Hanson Harrison and Thomas Jefferson, John Rutledge, George Wythe, William Grayson, James Monroe, George Read, Isaac Smith and William Patterson. Both states agreed to accept these men. Wythe's old associates, Duane, Jay and Livingston, wrote to him asking that he be a part of the tribunal. Of course, where public service was concerned, he was willing But he was no longer young, his wife was ailing, his work both as Chancellor and as teacher was of great importance to him. As delicately as he could, he stipulated that the judges would have to meet in Williamsburg, since he could not travel. He informed Congress of this, and the Congress was agreeable. However, the other judges were not, and so four other places were proposed, none of which was acceptable to Wythe. With great regret the venerable statesman had then to decline the appointment:

Williamsburgh 23 Apr. 1785

". . . Indeed, gentlemen, that i am obliged to reject all the four places proposed by you; on several accounts eligible before Williamsburgh, so much distresses me, and that you should come to the last, to accommodate me . . . i should take so much shame to myself that, if you could know what i feel, you would believe me very much in earnest when i reiterate the request that my name be left out of the list.

With extreme solicitude that you should have so much trouble about me, i have the honour to be gentlemen, your most obedient servant. George Wythe."[25]

Thus he wrote to the agents of Massachusetts and New York. Wythe had at this time begun to use the peculiar style of lower case for his personal pronouns, believing that this indicated to the world his idea of equality among men. He yet according to the custom of the 18th Century continued to use the flowery valediction "Your most obedient servant." This addiction to the ideals of democracy was not unique with Wythe—Jefferson himself in imitation of his teacher gave up the use of capitals also, although he did not carry it to the extent Wythe did.

Notes to Chapter IX

1. St George Tucker to Mrs. Tucker, in, Mary Haldane Coleman, *St. George Tucker, Citizen of No Mean City*. (Richmond, Dietz Press, 1938), p. 70.
2. Manuscript Collection. Historical Society of Pennsylvania.
3. Chastellux, Francois Jean, Marquis de. *Travels in North America—*. Revised ed., (Chapel Hill, 1963), Vol. 2, p. 443.
4. Jefferson. *The Papers of—*. Boyd ed., Vol. 6, p. 221.
5. William C. Rives. *History of the Life and Times of James Madison*. (Boston, 1859–68), Vol. 2, p. 6.
6. Manuscript Collection, Haverford College, Pennsylvania.
7. PRO/AO SR 2830 M491, Public Record Office. London, England.
8. *Ibidem.*
9. Hamilton Usher St. George to the Office of American Claims. PRO/AO SR 2830 M483, p. 433. Public Record Office, London, England.
10. Mrs. Hamilton Usher St. George to the Office of American Claims. PRO/AO SR 2583 M491, p. 21.
11. Jefferson. *The Papers of—*. Boyd ed., Vol. 6, p. 144.
12. Albert J. Beveridge. *The Life of John Marshall* (Boston, Houghton Mifflin, 1916–19), Vol. 1, p. 174.
13. "And often we would be accustomed to converse together here. Nothing would have separated us—the one welcoming a guest and the other delighted until the black cloud of death enfolded us." Thus Menelaus spoke of his friendship with Odysseus, as given by Homer. Translation, kindness of William James McCoy, Georgetown University.
14. John Adams. *Works of—*. C. F. Adams, ed., Vol. 3, p. 384.
15. Richard Henry Lee. The Letters of—. Ballagh ed., Vol. 2, p. 279.
16. *Ibidem*, p. 291.
17. *Ibidem*, p. 275.
18. Manuscript Collection, Library of Congress.
19. To Thomas Jefferson, 18 April 1787, Williamsburg, in Jefferson. *The Papers of—*. Boyd ed., Vol. 11, p. 299.
20. *Ibidem*. Vol. 10, p. 622–3.
21. Tyler. "George Wythe" in *Great American Lawyers*. p. 76.
22. Philip Mazzei to William Short, 8 December 1784, Williamsburg, Va., in, Manuscript Collection, New York Public Library.
23. Jefferson. *The Papers of—*. Boyd ed., Vol. 7, p. 555.
24. Manuscript Collection. New York Public Library.
25. Manuscript Collection. New York Historical Society.

CHAPTER X

To Philadelphia again, and then to Richmond

There was in Williamsburg in those days a grammar school conducted in the chambers of the old Capitol building by the Reverend Walker Maury, where the children of the town were taught Latin and Greek. From time to time, Wythe and his fellow professors of the College were called upon to inspect the school, which took the place, in a private way, of the old College Grammar School Jefferson had abolished some years before. Eventually Maury closed his school and removed to Norfolk. The little town, now without even a grammar school, needed one badly.

Wythe, busy as he was, himself took on the job, advertising in the newspaper that he would accept children for instruction in Latin, Greek, Literature, and Mathematics. And this he continued to do from the middle 1780's until he finally left Williamsburg. Nor did he accept any pay for this work. It was at this time that he was able to repay his old friend, Ben Waller, for the guidance and teaching Wythe had received from him. Waller's daughter, Dorothy Elizabeth, had married Henry Tazewell and from the marriage had come a child born in 1774 who was given the remarkable name of Littleton Waller Tazewell. Because of family circumstances, the little one lived with his grandfather Ben Waller. During the wild period of 1780, the child was sent to Greenville County to the Wickham family estate to escape the invaders.

Here the little boy came under the guidance of a youth of sixteen, John Wickham. This Wickham ultimately became one of the foremost lawyers of Virginia. He was now, however, himself one of the victims of the war's confusions. The boy of sixteen and the child of six apparently got along famously, Littleton remembering all his life the kindness of the older one. After the war, the Wickham family was apparently proscribed, and the young man was sent to military school in Arras, France. But he wanted to be a lawyer and so came, in 1785, to Williamsburg. Here he studied under Littleton's father, Henry Tazewell. In addition, he became Wythe's pupil, attending the moot courts in the old Capitol and the make-believe sessions of the legislature.

There came, in 1786, that very sad time when Ben Waller, now old and tired, died. Knowing that he was going, he called in Mr. Wythe, his old friend, and entrusted to him the care of his grandson Littleton, then twelve years old. For approximately the next five years the child lived in the home of Mr. and Mrs. Wythe, even after Mrs. Wythe died. The child had attended Walker Maury's school, but now that was closed, Wythe himself took on the boy's education. Wythe had first become aware of Littleton's existence when he, with the other Professors, was examining Maury's school. Being called on to recite, Littleton did so well that Wythe was impressed. The child had translated from Cornelius Nepos' life of Sumenes, and it excited Wythe's surprise and amazement that a child could do so well. The elderly lawyer and chancellor had become almost a recluse, avoiding all public life, spending his time in his library. As Tazewell himself put it:

> ". . . my grandfather never went out and Mr. Wythe rarely, yet he made it a point to call to see my grandfather once or twice a year, and to spend an afternoon with him."

In their relationship, Wythe treated the older man with the greatest veneration, never calling him anything but Mr. Waller, while the latter used the first name of George to Wythe. On one of those visits, Wythe made the child again recite, and told the older man

> ". . . Mr. Waller, this is a very clever boy, and when he has advanced a little further, you must let me have him." To this the old man replied . . . "George . . . this boy is the sole comfort of my old age . . . , I cannot part with him while I live, but when I die, if you will take him under your charge, I will consider it as the greatest . . . favor you can confer on each of us."[1]

Shortly after this, Wythe called on the father, Henry Tazewell and asked that the child be sent to Wythe's home each day for instruction. Beginning in the fall of 1786, therefore, Littleton went every day to Wythe's home. He was the youngest child Wythe had ever taught, and while the elderly patriot was truly a great teacher, some of his methods were fitted more for adolescents and adults than for children. As usual, for his work Wythe took no pay. The child came every morning—so early that he was at the Wythe home (just down the street from his own home) by sunrise (yet he found the teacher waiting for him). The instruction took place in Wythe's library, from the shelves of which Wythe would take at random a book in the Greek language. He would tell the child to recite whatever passage might come to Wythe's attention. In this, the boy was not allowed to use a dictionary or even a grammar. Whenever he stumbled Wythe took the occasion to explain the difficulty, holding forth on the varied nature of the ancient Greek dialects.

At the same time he would remark on the different circumstances of Greek history, in regard to their customs and laws.

> ". . . he asked me to explain the allusion, and when I failed to do so satisfactorily (as was often the case) he immediately gave a full clear and complete account . . . having done so, I was bidden to remind him of it next day, in order that we might learn from some better source whether his explanation was correct or not; and the difficulties I met with on one day, generally produced the subject of the lesson of the next."

The two studied together until the time for breakfast came, when the child returned home. He came back again at noontime, when the two took up some Latin author. At about two o'clock they separated, the boy again going home, while the old man gave himself to his legal work. Two hours later the child returned and they studied mathematics until dark. In this they used French texts, probably purchased by Jefferson in Paris for Wythe. Littleton was thus given a chance to learn mathematics—in which Wythe delighted—and French (at least to some extent) at the same time. The child apparently did learn a great deal by this method, since when he finally entered College he was placed in the foremost of his mathematics class at William and Mary.

In the evening the old man and the boy studied English literature, for Wythe employed the child in reading to him passages from the English authors of past time and the periodical literature of the day. As the reading went on, Wythe would relate some anecdote which a particular passage might have suggested to him. As Wythe had taken part in a mighty effort of history—the American Revolution—his anecdotes would have been of great value if Littleton had only set them down on paper.

Littleton did not get as much profit from all this as he might have had he been older, since Wythe's methods were better suited to an adult. The child was clever and knew how to sidetrack Wythe into some aspect which would cover up Littleton's lack of preparation. After a year of this life, the child's father bought the estate of Kingsmill and was to move there, but Wythe had become so fond of the boy that he asked Henry Tazewell to let the child live with him. This was agreed to, and for the next three years, Littleton lived in the Wythe house. There was room there now, since Miss Taliaferro had married.

> "To enumerate marriages would be endless . . . I will add . . . a brother of Gen. Nelson with the Miss Taliaferro whom you knew a very small girl at Mr. Wythe's. . . . we are no longer young. Those whom we knew as children have now their children and are pressing us towards a door out of which they must follow us . . ."[2]

It must have been quite a life, for all visitors to Williamsburg, famous politicians and writers passing through the town, invariably came to call on the famous old man. So proud of the child was he that Wythe always showed him off to the visitors, having the boy read from some Latin or Greek author. And an added delight was the philosophical apparatus which Wythe imported at this time. This was an electrical machine, coupled with an air pump. Now the leisure moments of the child and the old man were spent in making this instrument work.

This must have been a very happy time in Wythe's life. He was corresponding now rather more frequently than usual with Jefferson in Paris, and his letters give us a chance to see his many and varied interests. Wythe, ever alive to history, was intensely concerned to discover the origin of the name of the family into which he had married. He was very fond of his nephew by marriage, Major Richard Taliaferro, and wanted to make him a present. He therefore on 10 January 1786 asked Jefferson to help him get the armorial design of the Taliaferro family, and have it made into a bookplate. In order to do this correctly, Jefferson, thorough as always, would have to inquire of the Italian Taliaferro family for information—which he did.

Wythe at this time was waiting for Jefferson to send him the latter's famous work, *Notes on Virginia*. This work had been undertaken when the French minister in America asked Jefferson, then Governor, to describe his native state and answer a set of questions the French government had posed. Jefferson's reply was made into a book which became famous almost at once. He was reluctant to have it published, however, for it contained severe criticism of negro slavery in America, but when the book was pirated by a European bookseller, the author decided to publish it himself. Wythe had seen an early copy but wished for the complete edition. It was not until 13 August 1786 that Jefferson replied, assuring Wythe in a beautiful tribute that he indeed would send his former teacher a copy of the *Notes*.

"Your wishes, which are laws to me, will justify my destining a copy for you, otherwise, I should as soon have thought of sending you a horn-book; for there is no truth in it which is not familiar to you, and its errors I should hardly have proposed to treat you with."[3]

James Madison was still trying to get the Law Revisal (or parts of it) through the Virginia Assembly. He was, for example, still attempting to have the education part of the Code (which would have provided a beginning of free public education) adopted as law. This, to Jefferson, was the most important thing that the code contained—

"No other sure foundation can be devised, for the preservation of freedom and happiness."

And the 18th Century rationalist spoke to his old teacher—

"If any body thinks, that kings, nobles or priests are good conservators of the public happiness, send him here. It is the best school in the universe to cure him of that folly. . . . Preach, my Dear Sir, a crusade against ignorance; establish and improve the law for educating the common people."

No one needed, however, to urge Wythe to continue his work in education for he was forever devising ways to improve his teaching, as his letter to Jefferson of 23 December 1787 shows:

"Would not the figures to which one must advert in studying geometry, formed of wood, metal, or ivory, be more instructive than those, which are delineated on paper? If you think so, and if such figures can be procured where you are, i wish to know the cost of them, that i may remit money to pay for them, when i will beg the favor of you to send them to me."[4]

It was about this time, too, that Wythe, feeling sympathy for Jefferson's fear that pro-slavery elements might make capital out of his anti-slavery remarks in the *Notes,* suggested that the professors be given sundry copies to hand out to those students who were advanced enough in their thinking to benefit by the work. In other words, there was no point in distributing them indiscriminately. This suggestion was apparently adopted.

There was coming quickly now one of the most momentous of the achievements of Wythe's whole life. For some time past it had been apparent that the old Articles of Confederation, with the loose union they provided, were unsatisfactory. There were so many problems the nation faced—problems with the English, with a domestic depression, with commerce, with the western territories, that the weak confederal government simply could not handle with the power given it by the Articles. For a long time many in Virginia, Wythe among them, had worked carefully for a stronger national government. Among these had been Mazzei, who had founded in his scattered way a Constitutional Society to discuss what sort of foundation the government might need. With great satisfaction, Mazzei noted in his *Memoirs* that John Blair of Williamsburg was elected president of this Society.[5] Wythe must surely have attended closely upon this movement, which held its meetings at Blair's Williamsburg home. This society, founded in 1784, was in a sense, part of the widespread belief of a deistically-inclined society which thought it could apply the laws of science to government. It had its counterpart in a political society in Richmond, which was in existence down to the time of the writing of the new Constitution itself—indeed, it continued until the convention of Virginia ratified the Constitution in 1788.

The idea of changing the confederal government met with fierce opposition. We have seen how even in Wythe's school (for he allowed the students, apparently, complete freedom) the law students had rejected in their mock legislature under Shippen's leadership the 5% impost on all goods. This was to have been the revenue of the Congress and would have strengthened the national government to some extent. But even the law students opposed it.

As early as 16 April 1781, Joseph Jones, James Monroe's uncle, had written to four "Gentlemen of respectable abilities" about the need to strengthen Congress—especially in its ability to coerce the states to give it the means to fight the war (which was then, of course, still on). The Articles of Confederation had just been ratified (finally) by Maryland, the last of the states to give assent. The four "Gentlemen" whose advice Jones asked were Madison, Wythe, Jefferson and Pendleton.[6] These last three had worked on the great law revisal and so Jones especially valued their opinion. Jefferson, of course, was then still Governor of Virginia. The need to give power to Congress was apparent to Jones at least, for

". . . without it we shall be a rope of sand and the Union be dissolved."

Jones even wanted the Confederal government to have the power to force recalcitrant states to obey it by placing their ports under embargo. This was a very dangerous proposal as anyone who remembered the Boston Port Bill could testify.

James Madison too had been concerned to change the national government and approached Wythe to give him some ideas, especially as to how the Confederation had been originally proposed. However, Wythe hadn't any of his notes on the Confederation or even copies of his proposed amendments thereto. He had lost his notes, seemingly, somewhere along the years. Yet another of those who wanted change was St. George Tucker, who wrote a pamphlet urging that better accommodation be made for the furtherance of American trade. Finally the Annapolis Convention was proposed—not, admittedly, to change the basis of government. But there it was proposed that a convention be called to do just that. The three Virginia delegates to Annapolis were St. George Tucker, James Madison and Edmund Randolph. The larger meeting they proposed was to find ways of regulating the commerce of the entire United States.

And so it was to be. The new Convention was to be held at Philadelphia and would in no way compete with the Second Continental Congress which held forth then in New York City. Of all the states, Virginia was the first to select her representatives—for on 4 December 1786, the Assembly chose Washington, who received a unanimous vote. Patrick Henry was next in size of vote followed by Edmund Randolph (who was soon to be the Governor), then John Blair, James Madison, George Mason and then George Wythe, who was given the fewest votes of all. After all, Wythe was no politician, came to Richmond only for the Chancery Court sessions, and hated to leave his comfortable home and his students. There were others put into nomination: Thomas Nelson, Jr., Benjamin Harrison and even John Page. These, however, were defeated. Despite his election, Patrick Henry "smelled a rat" and refused to go.

The Assembly had a hard time filling Henry's place. At first they appointed General Nelson when the great Patrick refused, but he likewise declined. Eventually James McClurg was chosen. He had earlier been Wythe's colleague at William and Mary, being Professor of Medicine.

Since the roads to Philadelphia were abominable, the delegates couldn't go by coach—it would be springtime when they would travel and the roads would be rivers of mud. Nor could either Wythe or Blair go by horseback, for they were by now simply too old to ride hundreds of miles. The Assembly therefore provided that a vessel should wait upon them as close to Williamsburg as possible and carry them up Delaware Bay. Therefore, these two old men sailed in some style to the Philadelphia meeting.

Now, once again, Wythe returned to the scene of his labors of some ten years before. Richard Henry Lee, his old comrade, wasn't there, of course, and neither was Edmund Pendleton, nor Thomas Jefferson, nor John Adams. But this was nonetheless (in Jefferson's words)—"an assembly of demigods," so celebrated and able were the men who were present. As the delegates from the various states straggled in, Wythe must have found pleasure in greeting old friends—Benjamin Franklin not the least of them. The venerable old scientist-diplomat-legislator was now the President of Pennsylvania. Dickinson, whom Wythe had fought so ably over the question of independence, was present also. There was Rutledge of South Carolina as well as James Wilson of Pennsylvania—another old opponent. In all there were eight Signers of the Declaration of Independence. Morris, and Livingston, Pinckney, Gerry and Sherman—all of these had come. They were resolute men, strong-minded men, able politicians all, some of them good thinkers, others merely men of action. But all of them had long years of experience, either in the Senate-house, or on the battle field. And leading them all was the mighty Washington.

Wythe and Blair sailed from Yorktown on 7 May 1787 and reached Philadelphia by 14 May. Thus these two old men had outpaced all the other members of the Virginian delegation. According to Washington's *Diary*, the representatives of only two states (Virginia and Pennsylvania) had reached Philadelphia by 14 May.[7] Since Governor Randolph got there on 15 May, and Dr. McClurg arrived on the 16th, and George Mason completed the delegation by getting there on the evening of 17 May, it follows that the two old men were the ones who had made it by the 14th. Since the Convention did not open until 25 May, the delegates must have had a fine old time, gossiping and visiting with each other,—old friends not seen for many long years.

George Mason wrote a revealing letter to his son George about their situation in the old city.

20 May, 1787

"We found travelling very expensive—from eight to nine dollars per day. In this city the living is cheap. We are at the old *Indian Queen* in Fourth Street, where we are well accommodated, have a good room to ourselves, and are charged only 25$ Pennsylvania currency per day, including our servants and horses, exclusive of . . . liquors and extra charges; so that I hope I shall be able to defray my expenses with my public allowance, and more than that I do not Wish."[8]

Since all the Virginia delegates had reached the city by 20 May, they decided to meet each day at three o'clock to discuss their plans and the tactics they should use. By 25 May, the delegates of seven states had arrived, and a quorum was thereby set up at the Convention. When the meeting opened, Washington was the unanimous choice of the Convention as Presiding Officer. The great man was now at the height of his popularity and his fellow citizens loved him. When he had arrived in the city, on Sunday, 13 May, he had been met at Chester by Generals Mifflin, Knox and Varnum, as well as other military men. The City

Light Horse, commanded by Colonel Miles, had met him at Gray's ferry. So, escorted into the city, the bells of the churches began to boom out their message that Washington had come. The people pressed in crowds into the streets, while Benjamin Franklin gave him the official greeting of the State. The General was carried by Mr. and Mrs. Robert Morris to their house where he lived during the Convention.

At last, 25 May came and with it the quorum. The delegates met in the Pennsylvania State House and proceeded to organize themselves. A Major William Jackson was chosen Secretary. Doorkeepers were also appointed but before this a committee was set up, consisting of Wythe, Hamilton and Charles Pinckney. Their task was to prepare the parliamentary rules by which the Convention was to govern itself. Wythe with his vast experience, was the head of the committee, since Hamilton had military experience but as yet little real practice in a political assembly. Until this committee should report, the members were at leisure to continue their own pursuits, and so the first meeting ended.

But before it did so, Washington, who was not quick of wit or glib of tongue, nor a profound thinker or a mighty orator, somehow found the words to dedicate these men to their purpose:

> "It is too probable that no plan we propose will be adopted. Perhaps another dreadful conflict is to be sustained. If, to please the people, we offer what we ourselves disapprove, how can we afterward defend our work? Let us raise a standard to which the wise and honest can repair; the event is in the hands of God."[9]

At 10 o'clock on the morning of 27 May, Monday, the Convention met again. Wythe made the report of his rules committee, and the Assembly considered it until 2 o'clock in the afternoon. The leisurely pace the convention had set by now gave a foretaste that they would be at their work all summer. In the preceding two weeks, the Virginia delegation had met each day and decided on the strategy to be followed. The Convention argued over Wythe's rules of order the next day, and on Wednesday, Edmund Randolph set forth the Virginia plan. And over it the greatest debate of the Convention revolved. While we do not know what part Wythe took in the discussion, we do know that he did participate. On the fourth of June, the delegates discussed the "Question for a single Executive"—that is, whether or not the Executive of the nation should be one man or several.

With the experience of Virginia in the governorship and council, and knowing how inadequate the office of governor had been (especially to his friend Jefferson), Wythe would have supported the single executive motion. However, by this time word had come to him that his wife was very ill. And so anxious was he to be with her that he left the Convention and returned home. So we have only the laconic observation in Madison's Notes—

> "On the question for a single Executive, it was agreed to,—Mass. Conn., Penn., V. (Mr. Randolph and Mr. Blair, No; Dr. McClurg, Mr. Madison and General Washington, aye; Colonel Mason being no, but not in the House, Mr. Wythe, aye, but gone home) . . ."[10]

Wythe's letter to Edmund Randolph, governor of Virginia and head of the state's delegation still in Philadelphia, breathes his concern for his wife:

> "Mrs. W's state of health is so low, and she is so emaciated, that my apprehensions are not a little afflicting, and, if the worst should not befall, she must linger, i fear, a long time. In no other circumstances would i withdraw from the employment to which i had the honour to be appointed. But, as probably i shall not return to Philadelphia, if, sir, to appoint one in my room be judged advisable, i hereby authorise you to consider this letter as a resignation, no less valid than a solemn act for that express purpose. my best wishes attend you and the other most respectable personages with whom i was thought worthy to be associated. Williamsburg, 16 of June, 1787."[11]

Mrs. Wythe had been ill much earlier, as we know from a letter to Jefferson from John Blair of 28 March, 1787:

> ". . . Mr. Wythe seems to have much uneasiness on account of his lady's ill state of health. Yet this is not likely to hinder his going to Philadelphia, in May, in order to attend the convention . . . ."[12]

By the early part of June, her illness was so advanced that Wythe was beside himself with worry and so had left the great business of constitution-making. It was typical of him that before he did so, he distributed what remained of the money assigned him by the Virginia Assembly to his colleagues.[13] On 21 June, Governor Randolph wrote to Beverly Randolph, the Lieutenant-Governor of Virginia,

> ". . . Mr. Wythe before he left us requested that the Executive might, if they thought proper appoint a successor to him I informed him that I doubted whether at this advanced stage of the business, they would be so inclined—especially, too, as there was hope of his return; but that I would mention the matter to you."[14]

By 16 July, it was apparent that Wythe could not go back to the Convention. In a letter to the Lieutenant-Governor, he made it clear that his earlier departure must be considered final. Having hurried home to be with his wife, Wythe spent the summer in Williamsburg caring for her. But the end was not very long in doubt, for on 18 August, the lady died. Wythe found it very hard to accept this second loss. When he was younger and his first wife had died, he had had the resiliency of youth to help him over the sorrow. Now his youth was gone and he was once again left alone. However, it was at this time that the little boy Littleton Waller Tazewell came to live in the old man's home and the child's presence may have taken Wythe's mind off his sorrow. Despite this, the loss was hard to bear. It was probably Wythe himself who penned the obituary:

> "On Saturday the 18th instant, departed this life, in the 48th year of her age, Mrs. ELIZABETH WYTHE, spouse of the Hon. George WYTHE, Esq., of the city of Williamsburg, after a very long and lingering illness, which she bore with the patience of a true Christian.—Amiable in her disposition, engaging in her manners, and possessed of every virtue which could render her beloved . . . The voice of reason . . . steals but in whispers upon the care of affliction and both fortitude and philosophy are too weak to struggle against

nature and affection. The husband and the friend must feel for a loss like this, nor can stoicism itself censure their sorrows.

For sure, when love and friendship, hand in hand,
O'er the cold grave, attending mourners stand;
The firmest heart dissolves to softness there,
And piety applauds the falling tear."[15]

Thus not all Wythe's stern stoicism was proof against the tears of things. It is from this time that Wythe seemed to turn again to the religion of his youth, abandoning the cold philosophy of Deism, this stoicism which failed to censure sorrow. An account by Nathaniel Beverly Tucker gives a picture of Wythe's melancholy.

"As he descended into the vale of years, childless, and almost without a kinsman in the world, a morbid sadness came over him, which disqualified him for social enjoyment. He was not gloomy nor morose, but silent and grave; his whole air and manner betokening a gentle sadness, which commanded the sympathy of those who knew nothing of its cause. And this sympathy was not misplaced; for though he moved through the world as if unconscious of all that passed around, yet there was that about him which showed that he had a heart to sympathize with others. The writer remembers once . . . when a child . . . the feeling of awe, mingled with pleased surprise, when accosted by the venerable, attenuated, ascetic old man, with his thin, pale face, and his clear, mild eyes, and his sad smile; and how he held out his long, lean finger to the little urchin, and led him into his house, and up stairs, and into his bed-chamber, and held him up in his feeble arms to the window to show him the working of the bees, in a hive attached to one of the panes . . . . It was but a manifestation of that kindly sympathy with all things human that lay locked in his breast, and only did not diffuse itself on every side, because a mysterious something which seemed to come between him and the objects around him, shutting them from his ken, and leaving him unconscious of their existence."[16]

After the death of his wife, Wythe could now return to the melancholy serenity of Williamsburg and his teaching. And there was certainly plenty of that for him to do. Peter Carr could grumble to Jefferson of the way Wythe's other affairs kept interfering with his teaching, but from now on, Wythe would be free. There came to him about this time a long letter from Jefferson. Just as Wythe had called his teacher "Mr. Waller," so Jefferson called his, "Mr. Wythe." And so "Mr. Wythe" learned from his great pupil that he had gone on a long journey of exploration to southern France and Northern Italy. He sent the documents about the Taliaferro family which he had gotten from a Mr. Febroni. And he also sent a copy of Polybius "the best edition." He gave the news that the European world was on the verge of war—but that was hardly news. His gifts to Wythe on this occasion were interesting as a selection of books. A three-volume Polybius in Greek and Latin, *Coluthi raptus Helenae*, *Fabulae Homericae de Ulixe*, Savary *Sur l'Egypte* in three volumes, as well as Volney *Sur l'Egypte* in two. And finally a *Code de l'Humanite* in thirteen volumes. Here was a fine autumn's reading.

It was shortly before the death of Mrs. Wythe that her husband had advertised in the Virginia Gazette (July, 1787):

"I propose in October, when the next course of lectures in law and police will commence, to open a school for reading some of the higher Latin and Greek Classics and of the approved English poets and prose writers, and also for exercises in Arithmetic. George Wythe"

And so it was. With the death of his wife, the celebrated lawyer and teacher became busier than ever. He continued to apply himself to the training of the younger generation, taking several of his pupils into his home with him, as we know from Littleton Waller Tazewell. This, however, did not work out well, for Wythe was advanced in years and had become a man of settled habits. The constant interruptions which a household of young men would entail simply proved too much for the old man. As Littleton, writing many years later, stated:

"The experience . . . taught Mr. Wythe, as ought almost any other man than himself to have foreseen that this time of life in his situation, and with habits the presence of a numerous family about him just occasioned much more trouble than he could sustain. The necessary domestic duties occupied so much of his time . . . He was irritated and vexed by a thousand little occurrences he had never forseen . . . ."[17]

The moment of truth arrived to the old man that the generations simply could not mix happily together, and so he broke up his establishment. Keeping the boy Littleton with him, he found lodgings elsewhere for the more boisterous of the young men. He continued to keep his school, only now the young men came to his home for instruction from their own boarding houses. This did not finish Wythe in the matter of taking individual pupils to live with him, however, for we know that he accepted William Munford as a pupil to live with him somewhat later. It was shortly after this time that he also took, not as boarders but as day scholars, both Charles Turnbull and John Thompson. The old man was always searching for young men of promise, and in the latter he found one. Sadly, the young John Thompson died in the fullness of his promise, but Wythe taught him as best he could, and while still in his early manhood Thompson wrote the famous "Letters of Curtius" which circulated widely in the Virginia of the day. He would have been one of the ablest of Virginia's scholars and lawyers had he lived.

Save for his judgeship, Wythe had thought he was finished with public life. But on the contrary, one of the greatest services was yet to be performed. The Constitution had now been submitted to the states for ratification. Virginia had enacted that a convention should meet in Richmond in early May, 1788, to pass on the new instrument. Seats therein were hotly contested for, and the elections were now beginning. The machinery of party was already started, the pro-Constitutionalists setting up their candidates in every district. They knew they were about to have a hard fight, so adverse were the people to the new Constitution. Washington himself, although he did not attend this Convention, was confident that the pro-Constitutionalists would win. As he wrote to Lafayette:

". . . as Pendleton, Wythe, Blair, Madison . . . and many others of our first characters will be advocates for its adoption, you may suppose the weight of abilities will rest on that side."[18]

But there were others who were not so confident, especially as Richard Henry Lee, Patrick Henry and George Mason were on the other side.

When the elections took place, a totally unexpected thing happened. The elections were, of course, public. The two candidates from each county stood publicly receiving the votes of the freeholders who called out their choice. General Nelson and Mr. Prentis were the two candidates standing for election and the former was against the Constitution. During the voting, a certain Charles Lewis stood up and declared that while he had always heretofore voted for General Nelson, he felt that he should this time give his vote for one who had not, as far as he knew, made up his mind on the new instrument. Lewis therefore declared his votes would go to George Wythe and John Blair. How he felt these two would be impartial isn't stated, but apparently he did so believe. The idea caught on and both Wythe and Blair were unanimously elected although neither of them was a candidate.

> "Scarcely were these words uttered by Lewis, when General Nelson . . . seizing him by the hand, thanked him . . . for what he had said and done. Adding that though Mr. Lewis had got the start of him in the support of Mr. Wythe and Mr. Blair, whose merit none knew better than himself . . . General Nelson placed himself at the head of his fellow-citizens, and they moved in procession to Williamsburg . . . they ranged themselves . . . in front of Mr. Wythe's house, Nelson as spokesman . . . .
>
> When General Nelson entered . . . , I was reciting a Greek lesson to Mr. Wythe. Nelson's address was short and rapid, for his utterance was always quick. He remarked to Mr. Wythe that the people were their own best governors . . . ."[19]

When Wythe realized the import of their message, he went outside the house, and with tears in his eyes thanked his fellow citizens for the trust they put in him. Although the work of public life was now distasteful to him, he accepted the decision. So the child Littleton remembered the incident.

That winter of 1787–88 was a time of much political activity. All over the state, the two sides worked to send their men to the Convention. Those in favor of the Constitution had great advantages. They had the immense prestige of Washington, for example. This faction planned their strategy well, and they used their heaviest guns. Some of the greatest men in Virginia were on their side, and they used them to the fullest. Such men as George Nicholas, John Marshall, James Madison, James Innes,—these were the men they tried to elect.

Nor did the anti-Constitutional faction lack organization, although it was not as well-planned or as thorough-going, apparently, as that of their opponents. At their head was the mighty Patrick Henry. Aiding him was the always-retiring George Mason. William Grayson, Theodorick Bland, John Tyler and Benjamin Harrison were also of Henry's mind. Richard Henry Lee, who might have been a stalwart assistant on Henry's side, did not stand for election and so was not present. This was a severe blow, for Lee was a splendid orator. The ultimate outcome was so close that the Henry faction would need every single vote they could get.

On the second day of June, 1788, the Convention met in a rather small, ugly building which had been built (of wood) as the main classroom of the Chevalier de Quesnay's Academy of Sciences. So it was here on the hills of the city, at Broad and Marshall Streets, that the fate of Virginia was decided, and by it the fate of the United States of America. The moment was crucial, for Virginia was then the greatest state in the Confederation, stretching from the Atlantic to the Mississippi. Virginia's stand would count for much where the other states were concerned.

The convention was a sizeable one (170 members) since each county and city had two delegates (save Williamsburg and Norfolk, which had only one each). There can be little doubt that most of Virginia's people were against the new form of government. And New York's people as well were opposed, its governor, George Clinton, being a most determined and able enemy. When the Virginia Assembly had passed the act to submit the Constitution to a Convention, Governor Edmund Randolph, as directed, sent a notification to all the states, including New York. Delayed in the mails, it reached Governor Clinton too late to be presented to the New York legislature. One provision of Virginia's Act had been that it wished to confer with the other states on the advisability of calling yet another Convention to frame anew the Constitution. By the first week of May, Governor Clinton wrote Governor Randolph that the New York Convention was meeting to vote on the new Constitution on 17 June, and that it would gladly confer with Virginia on holding a new federal convention. However, Governor Randolph suppressed this letter, which would have given much ammunition to the Henry and Mason forces. Randolph had not signed the Philadelphia Constitution, and so many supposed him against the work. However, secretly he was not. For the Virginia Governor, when the Convention began, came out openly for the new form of government. He came to be regarded as a traitor by the anti-Constitution men.[20]

Virginia's vote, then, was crucial, for at this time eight states had already ratified the new scheme, New Hampshire being in process of acting on it. And within two weeks New York was also to begin its consideration of the measure. Virginia's assent would mean nine states for it, and this was enough to put it into operation. However, if Virginia refused, New Hampshire and the rest might very well refuse also, the anti-Constitutionalists being emboldened enough in their respective states to overcome the opposition.

As soon as the Convention opened on the morning of 2 June, Judge Paul Carrington (his license to practice Wythe had signed way back in 1755) nominated Edmund Pendleton to be the Convention president.[21] The old patriot was now on crutches and discovered that simply being present at the Convention was a great difficulty. The anti-Constitutional forces knew they would suffer a defeat if they opposed Pendleton as president, and they did not want to start the Convention by losing. So they also voted for Pendleton, and he was elected unanimously. The Henry forces couldn't very well have done anything else, but the fact that the pro-Constitutionalists now held the machinery of the Convention in their hands told heavily in the latter's favor. Not only did the Federalists win on this election, but they won the next one too. For at once George Wythe was nominated as Chairman of the Committee of the Whole. And he too won unanimously. Both Pendleton and Wythe were simply too popular to have been voted down. The strategy of the Federalists was clear. Pendleton was to preside when necessary, but, as he was a good speaker and Wythe was not, let Wythe preside in the Committee of the Whole, and let Pendleton be thus free to operate on the floor. Within three days, the Convention was in such a committee, and stayed in it almost continuously, so Wythe really guided the working of the Convention in a parliamentary sense.

On the third day of the Convention, Wythe was put in the presiding chair, the session being one of a Committee of the Whole. This was on 4 June, a year lacking a day since Wythe had left Philadelphia to return to his ailing wife. The mighty Henry at once moved that the Act setting up the Constitutional Convention (that of Philadelphia) be read. This would show at once that the Philadelphia Convention had exceeded its powers, since it was supposed merely to revise the Articles of Confederation. This would have put the argument immediately where the Henry and Mason forces wanted it—to show that the Federalists were from the beginning in the wrong. But Wythe was too fast for Henry. Ignoring the former Governor, he gave the floor at once to Pendleton, who, leaning on his crutches, defended the Constitution:

> "We are not to consider . . . whether the Federal Convention exceeded their power . . . .
> Even if the framers of the Constitution had acted without authority, Virginia's legislature
> . . . had referred it to the people who had elected the present Convention to pass upon it."[22]

Thus Pendleton took Henry's ground from beneath his feet. The Federalists had done their planning well—they had, from an intimate knowledge of Henry's mind, apparently understood what the strategy would be, and the Chancellor, Wythe,

> ". . . a brisk, erect little figure—clad in single-breasted coat and vest, standing collar and
> white cravat, bald, except on the back of the head, from which unqueued and unribboned
> gray hair fell and curled up from the neck . . . ."[23]

as Grigsby describes him, had coordinated his actions with those of the other Federalists. This was to be the mode all through the Convention—the Henry forces were simply out-schemed and out-maneuvered. Neither Henry nor Mason were good parliamentarians, and they were also rather lazy. They simply hadn't done the long, hard committee-work which good planning and effective control of a body of men requires. The Federalists had, and so they outwitted their opponents but it was a battle of giants. One may very well say that Henry almost alone carried the burden of the battle, some of his speeches lasting for hours—for example, his "We, the people" speech was three hours long. And he spoke some two or three times a day. Nor was he boring. We know for a fact that the various delegates wandered in and out when the other orators held forth, but when Henry rose to speak, all came crowding back, breath bated to listen to the Demosthenes of Virginia. He stood there, taunting his opponents, his wig in his hand, often twirling it on his finger when carried away by the storm of his own oratory. According to Judge Spencer Roane, his son-in-law, he was:

> ". . . a man of middling stature. . . . rather stoop-shouldered . . . no superfluous flesh; his features were distinctly marked, and his complexion rather dark. He was somewhat bald, and always wore a wig in public. . . . not a handsome man, but his countenance was agreeable and full of intelligence and interest. He had a fine blue eye, and an excellent set of teeth . . . . His voice was strong, harmonious and clear . . . ."[24]

During the entire length of the Convention (some twenty-two days) not a day passed but Henry spoke, and sometimes several times a day. Without him, the opposition to the Constitution would have collapsed.

The Richmond Jockey Club races had begun only two days before, but the Convention nonetheless was full, so intense was the excitement that not even the Virginians' favorite sport could keep them from listening to the debates. So that even though the races were on, the delegates yet attended the Convention and heard Governor Randolph when he spoke contemptuously of the people as "The Herd." The Western element, which was the most strongly democratic and had come to revere "The People" as a sort of god, must be won over if the measure were to pass. The votes of the West simply could not be lost. Randolph's slip was therefore unfortunate for the Constitutionalists.

It was on this occasion that Governor Randolph publicly gave his support to the Constitution. This was a stunning blow to Henry's forces, for the popular Governor hadn't signed the Constitution and its enemies had therefore every reason to think that Randolph was against it. Randolph had opened his speech with a graceful allusion to the Chairman, Wythe—

> "Pardon me, Sir, if I am particularly sanquine in my expectations from the chair; it well knows *what is order,* how to command obedience . . . ."[25]

And then in the body of his speech proceeded to stun the opposition by the news of his defection from their ranks (only Washington had heretofore known of his intention). The anti-Constitutionalist were taken aback, for undoubtedly Randolph's action was a deciding factor, and from now on they attacked him with bitter rancor. Henry so angered Randolph that the Governor answered—

> ". . . if our friendship must fall, let it fall like Lucifer, never to rise again."[26]

Almost, it would seem, the delegates were on the point of a duel. There were times when tempers ran high, and it seemed as if personal insult might rule the House. Wythe had his hands full to keep order.

The anti-Constitutionalists had to take the offensive after Randolph's betrayal, and Henry did it on 5 June with his mighty "We, the People" speech. Here the orator held forth that the people by no means were creating the instrument, as the Preamble to the Constitution words it. On the contrary, the thing was done by the states. And Henry was right. For if the Preamble had been written as "We the States," truly a confederation would have been the result. The agreement would have been a contract between states, and this would have meant a confederal, not a unitary, centralized government springing directly from the popular will. Such an effect did this speech make that the next day the Constitutionalists set up their most effective speakers in rebuttal. Randolph, Madison, and George Nicholas followed each other in quick succession in an attack on Henry's position, allowing, apparently, little time for rebuttal. Madison was no orator, in fact, he spoke so quietly that often he couldn't be heard. He was so short that he stood on tiptoe to be seen. But he was pre-eminently a man of reason. And after all, Henry's oratory was magnificent, but who remembered it? A few hours after it was over, who could tell what he had said? This was Jefferson's impression and it must have been a correct one, for today only the slightest fragments of his speeches survive. Madison, however, was a tenacious and reasoning debater, who spoke slowly and gave careful study to his words. When he was finished, George Nicholas, large and grossly fat, took the floor. He was blunt, unpolished, bold. Moving him would be like trying to move a boulder. And when he was through, Henry Lee "Light Horse Harry," a great Virginian war hero, six feet tall and wonderfully handsome, took the floor to assail Henry's ideas.

And so it went. The arguments raged back and forth for some twenty-two days. Finally, the Constitutionalists realized that they must bring the matter—for good or ill—to a close. For the Assembly was to come into session in Richmond, and it would not do for the Convention to go on sitting at the same time. Many men were members of both, and if the Convention sat too long, the delegates might get impatient and throw the whole thing back to the Assembly. So they had to get a decision as soon as possible. The strategy came to a point of amendments. The pro-Constitutionalists didn't want them, but they realized that the Constitution as it stood couldn't pass without them. The question then was—should there be amendments made to the instrument *before* ratification or *after*? If after, then they could be disregarded, for the thing would have been ratified. If before, then the amendments couldn't be ignored for they would be *part* of Virginia's ratification. This whole affair smacks of a certain insincerity, not to use a stronger word. That Wythe could have allowed himself to be mixed up in what was essentially a parliamentary trick shows not that he was himself dishonest, but that he was terribly anxious to have the Constitution made the law of the land.

The Constitutionalists had taken a poll and the results proved to them that the instrument couldn't pass without amendments. Very well, the delegates wanted amendments—the delegates would have amendments. The strategy was carefully prepared. On 24 June, it being a Tuesday morning, Edmund Pendleton presided. The Convention went into a committee of the whole, but instead of Wythe taking the chair, Pendleton called Thomas Matthews to preside. This man was staunchly in favor of the new measure. Scarcely had Matthews taken the chair than he recognized Wythe. For it was the venerable old patriot who was given the task of presenting the amendments. The work had to be done quickly for Henry was about to offer his own. Wythe, no orator, was extremely tired and so nervous that he could not be understood when he first began. However, he conquered his agitation, and finished by making a speech which, according to Grigsby, made a strong impression on the delegates.

As soon as he had finished, Henry demanded the floor. He was in a livid fury, and delivered a point-blank attack on Wythe. He had been out-maneuvered, and he knew it. He made what was on this occasion one of the greatest speeches of his life. Beginning with sarcasm, Henry was

"... sure the gentleman meant nothing but to amuse the Committee. I know his candor,"

went on Henry,

"... His proposal is an idea dreadful to me . . ."[27]

Overcome by the storm of his own words, Henry went on and on, as the assembled delegates stilled themselves to hear him. As he rose to a great peroration, outside the building a storm arose, darkness came when the clouds covered the sun, the lightning punctured the stacatto rumbling of the thunder with its brightness, while within Henry went on and on. Finally, as the storm subsided to silence, Henry did too.

The impression he made was tremendous. But cold water followed with the reply of George Nicholas, stolid and imperturbable. He flatly moved that the question be put at the opening of the session of the next day. And the next day, immediately the business began, the chair gave Nicholas the floor. A great deal of debating went on, but the Constitutionalists were determined on a verdict, and so a vote was taken. Wythe's resolution was the question. Not the Constitution itself, but whether or not amendments should be—and the key word was there—"recommended" to Congress. And now victory was theirs, for by only a ten vote majority did the Constitutionalists win. And then the Convention went on to vote for the Constitution itself. And here too they won, again by the thinnest of majorities. But win they did, and the Federal Constitution was in operation.

This work was one of the high points of Wythe's life. For he was a key member of the group which put through the new instrument of government. Madison, who was floor manager and the general strategist of the Constitutionalists, put Wythe among the five most important delegates—Pendleton, Wythe, Blair, Innes and Marshall. But surely Madison was wrong. For there were seven of these—Madison himself, and Randolph. The latter's name would from now on be Benedict Arnold for those who had opposed the Constitution. But Wythe's wouldn't. Many of the men who were delegates had been his students at one time or another, and to them he was always the venerated and beloved teacher.

Notes to Chapter X

1. Lyttleton Waller Tazewell. *An Account and History of the Tazewell Family.* p. 150 et sequor.
2. Thomas Jefferson to Samuel Hanley, 27 November 1785, Paris, in, Jefferson. *The Papers of—.* Boyd ed., Vol. 9, p. 65.
3. *Ibidem.* Vol. 10, p. 243.
4. *Ibidem.* Vol. 11, p. 99.
5. Filippo Mazzei. *Memoirs of the Life and Peregrinations of the Florentine, Philip Mazzei, 1730–1816.* (New York, Columbia University Press, 1942), p. 285 footnote.
6. Jefferson. *The Papers of—.* Boyd ed., Vol. 5, p. 469 et seq.
7. Washington. *The Diaries of—.* Vol. 3, p. 215.
8. Kate Mason Rowland. *Life of George Mason, 1725–1792.* Vol. 2, p. 102.
9. Robert A. Brock. *Virginia and Virginians—.* (Richmond and Toledo, H. H. Hardisty, 1888). p. 281.
10. James Madison. *The Papers of—.* Gilpin ed., Vol. 2, p. 783.
11. Manuscript Collection. New York Public Library.
12. Jefferson. *The Papers of—.* Boyd ed., Vol. 11, p. 250.
13. "Mr. Wythe has left so much of his money to be distributed among such of his colleagues as should require it." Beverly Randolph was a former pupil of Wythe. Edmund Randolph to Beverly Randolph, 12 July 1787, Philadelphia, in, Virginia. *Calendar of Virginia State Papers.* Vol. 4, p. 315.
14. *Ibidem.* p. 298.
15. Virginia Independent Chronicle. 20 August 1787.
16. Southern Literary Messenger. Vol. 12, p. 446.
17. Lyttleton Waller Tazewell. *An Account—.* p. 163.
18. Washington. *The Writings of—.* Fitzpatrick ed., Vol. 29, p. 477.
19. Lyttleton Waller Tazewell. *An Account—.* p. 117 et sequor.
20. Hugh Blair Grigsby. *The History of the Virginia Federal Convention of 1788—.* (Richmond, Virginia Historical Society, 1890–91), Vol. 1, p. 84–5.
21. Grigsby thinks that Wythe had a good deal to do with the planning of this strategy which put Pendleton forward as the Chairman. Grigsby, *Opus citatum,* p. 64, note 75.
22. Jonathan Elliot, editor. *The Debates in the Several State Conventions—.* (Philadelphia, J. R. Lippincott, 1836–59), Vol. 3, p. 6.
23. Grigsby. *Opus citatum,* p. 87.
24. Adele Cooper Scott. "Patrick Henry" in, *Great American Lawyers—.* p. 142.
25. Grigsby. *Opus citatum,* p. 86.
26. *Ibidem.* p. 162.
27. Mays. *Edmund Pendleton—.* Vol. 2, p. 263.

CHAPTER XI

Wythe leaves Williamsburg for Richmond

On his return to Williamsburg from the Convention, Wythe resumed the pleasant, busy life of a William and Mary professor. More books came from Jefferson, sent with earnest kindness across the ocean. With this reading and with his other avocations Wythe could enjoy a splendid autumn. He was always interested in gardening and about this time he asked one of his pupils, John Wickham, who was visiting relatives in New York, to buy some fruit trees for him. Wickham was soon to return to Williamsburg, where, when Wythe finished with his work at the College, Wickham would take over Littleton's instruction.

While occupied thus, there came to Wythe the news that he had been chosen as the sole chancellor of Virginia. The Assembly of the State had, in this year 1788, re-organized the Chancery Court and established the Supreme Court of Appeals as a separate court. To this latter Pendleton was transferred, while Wythe remained in the Chancery. Now he was alone on his bench. His decisions would, however, be reviewed—occasionally to his annoyance—by the Appeals Court, where Pendleton and his colleagues sometimes reversed them. Therein was a very sore point indeed for Wythe, who took great care with his decisions, naturally felt that he was right—and to see Pendleton reversing them again and again rankled deeply.

Jefferson, having returned to Virginia by the latter part of 1789, wrote a most newsy letter to his friend, William Short, who had remained in Europe. In it he gave the news that Nancy Taliaferro had married "a Mr. Nicholas son of G. Nicholas Petersburg." Also that "Colo. Taliaferro near Williamsburg" had died. So there were two dear ones gone. One by marriage and the other by death. Jefferson also mentioned that

". . . Mr. Wythe has abandoned the college of William and Mary, disgusted with some of the conduct of the professors, and particularly of the ex-professor Bracken, and perhaps too with himself for having suffered himself to be too much irritated with that. The Visitors will try to condemn what gave him offence and press him to return; otherwise it is over with the college."[1]

Two of his students at this time (and whom he continued apparently to instruct on a private basis) were William Munford and John Coalter. The latter was a farm boy from the frontier, who was working as a tutor in the home of St. George Tucker teaching that man's children. He lived in the Tucker home in Williamsburg, and often visited at the Randolph plantation of Matoax, where he met people whom he would not otherwise have become acquainted with—judges, congressmen, colonels, etc. By this time, the University—for such it was now officially—of William and Mary had given Wythe an honorary degree: he was now to be styled Doctor. It is as such that Coalter, writing to his father Michael, on 30 January 1789, refers to him—

". . . I spend about three hours a day in my capacity of tutor of Tucker's children . . . shall attend Mr. Madison's lectures on philosophy, having received a very polite invitation from the gentleman himself to that purpose, and Dr. Wythe, as I mentioned above. Boarding is about 45£ per annum."[2]

The young man had an interesting living arrangement, for Tucker's house was too small for him to live there. He therefore slept next door at the house of John Wickham, who, now a lawyer himself, kept bachelor's hall. It was in the next autumn that Coalter first began to study law under Wythe, living in awe of his great teacher.

"The exalted character and tried abilities of that Gentleman promise the apt and diligent student a certain and noble source of instruction."

Thus he wrote his father on 24 November, 1789.

But it was not only students who wished to have the exalted character and tried abilities of Dr. Wythe at their service. The mighty Washington himself wanted them. For that gentleman had been elected the first President of the United States and was now trying to put together his government. So bitter had been the opposition that many people, among them men of wisdom and experience, thought he wouldn't succeed. And if he did, that the government he was trying to found wouldn't last long. Surely, under the stress of the many problems facing the country, the various states would fly apart again. In so tenuous a situation, Washington selected his officials with great caution—he wanted only those who could give to the new government that prestige it so needed. But he dared not risk too blunt a refusal, since that would be a loss of face. And so carefully and diplomatically, he sounded out the people he wanted. He had already asked Pendleton to be a Federal Judge, but he had refused. As Washington wrote to Edmund Randolph: "Mr. Pendleton declining to accept the appoint-

ment of District Judge has embarrassed me . . ." He had earlier asked Cyrus
Griffen to inquire about Wythe's willingness to work for the national government, and that gentleman had referred the matter to Edmund Randolph, who
was to approach both Wythe and Blair on the subject.

Randolph did so, but his answer was late in reaching Washington. Meanwhile Pendleton had refused, and the President was chagrined at the refusal. He
now had another problem—Pendleton had been asked first, and he had said no.
Since Wythe and Pendleton were lifelong rivals, would not Wythe be piqued at
being asked to take a position Pendleton had turned down? Not only this, but
Wythe's abilities were well known. Why, people were asking, had not a place
been given him in the new scheme of things? So Washington explained in his
letter—

> ". . . the character and abilities of Mr. Wythe did not escape me, . . . he had lately been
> appointed sole Chancellor . . . and engaged in other avocations which engrossed his atten-
> tions and appeared to afford him pleasure he would not exchange . . . for a federal appoint-
> ment. . . . the non-acceptance of Colo. Pendleton would be no inducement to him to come
> forward . . . . it would give me pain if Mr. Wythe or any of his friends should con-
> ceive that he has been passed by from improper motives . . . ."[3]

Edmund Randolph assured Washington that he need not fear that Wythe had
taken offense. On 15 December, he wrote to the President that he had conferred
with Wythe on the subject, and that the Chancellor wasn't interested. He
declared that Wythe

> ". . . sits in a kind of legal monarchy, which to him is the highest possible gratification."[5]

But Wythe was honored in other ways as well. The very names of the Virginian land bear testimony to Wythe's career, for on 1 December 1789, as a sort
of Christmas present, Virginia's Assembly named a county after Wythe. And
then followed a whole host of counties, named after his many pupils. And this,
of course, honors the teacher who helped to make them distinguished. There is
Hardy County, after that brilliant young man who went too soon to his death.
Jefferson County, formed and named in 1780, is as much a memorial to Wythe
as it is to Jefferson. Also there is Marshall County, formed in 1835, when that
Chief Justice was ending his long and tempestuous career. Again there is Nicholas County, named after Wythe's student Wilson Cary Nicholas, governor of
Virginia. Spencer Roane, Judge of the Supreme Court of Virginia and Mar-
shall's most redoubtable enemy, had a county named after him also. Nor should
Clay County be ignored, for the might Henry was Wythe's pupil too, as we
shall see.

In West Virginia a Tazewell County honors Littleton Waller Tazewell, who
became in the course of time governor of the state of Virginia. In Kentucky there
is a Breckinridge County, named for Wythe's pupil, John, who became Attorney General in Jefferson's Cabinet.

As long as these names would dot the land, the memory of Wythe as a teacher would remain.

But as Jefferson had mentioned, Wythe was no longer connected with William and Mary. Indeed, he soon would not even be living in Williamsburg, removing, in fact, to Richmand. It was about this time, however, that the artist John Trumbull, son of the patriot Governor of Connecticut, painted the picture "The Signing of the Declaration of Independence."[5] This now hangs in the rotunda of the Capitol in Washington. Trumbull was most concerned with accurate likenesses, and so journeyed about the country, painting the men who still survived. He had caught John Adams in London, and Jefferson in Paris. John Hancock and Samuel Adams were painted in Boston itself. And it was to Williamsburg in Virginia that Trumbull journeyed to paint Wythe's likeness. In the painting, Trumbull gave Wythe the position that is so symbolic of Wythe's entire life—for the retiring and modest Wythe is placed at the very edge of the painting, almost lost in the crowd of more forward Signers. He who had done so much to make the Declaration come about was thus placed at the very edge of the picture.

When the young John Trumbull was imprisoned in London in November 1780 and placed in jeopardy on suspicion of being a spy, the man who interceded for him was Benjamin West. The two artists became very friendly, and it was probably Trumbull who, making a pencil sketch of Wythe on 25 April 1791 in Williamsburg, suggested that Wythe get in touch with West for the design of a Chancery Seal. But this would be a work of some difficulty for which he would ask Jefferson's help. For the present, Wythe wrote to Jefferson on 10 July 1788, thanking him for the books the latter had sent but—

> ". . . my good sir, such presents are too costly. P. Carr still attends me daily. I think him well advanced in the greek and latin languages. . . ."

Now came the reason for the fewness of his letters:

> "To write is difficult, and sometimes a little painful; caused by a weakness in my right thumb. I should suppose it to be a gout, which i had slightly once in the foot, but that there is yet no swelling. This infirmity must apologize for the rarity and shortness of my letters. . . ."[6]

Now came the time when Wythe, his right hand so painfully afflicted, had to learn to write all over again—with his left hand. And eventually he did it, too. So persevering was he that at length his handwriting was once again as beautiful as before.

But for Wythe a decision had to be made, and not a judicial one either. Coupled with the act which had reduced the Chancery Court to one judge was the provision that Wythe's court hold its sessions four times a year in Richmond. In that case, he might just as well live there. So in effect the decision to leave Williamsburg was made for him. He would have to leave his beautiful house, but that probably didn't disturb him much. His wife's death, his niece's marriage, his annoyance at the College, all these things undoubtedly made him decide to move permanently to Richmond. He had by now withdrawn more and more from social life. He saw few people and even when among them, he was remote from them. He moved and lived isolated almost completely from human contact, withdrawn now into a world of books and the law. The following account is characteristic of his manner of life:

> "He sometimes politely bowed in persons calling on business, attended to it and then politely bowed them out of the house, without speaking a word. He was in the habit of going very early, rather in *dishabille,* to a neighboring bakery to buy his own bread; and for days successively put down his money and took his loaf without uttering a word. Judge Beverly Tucker communicated the following anecdotes: Mr. Wythe visited nobody but his relation, Mrs. Taliaferro, who lived four miles from Williamsburg; and being a great walker always went on foot, sometimes taking young Munford with him. One evening, as they set out together, Munford said on leaving the door, "A fine evening, Sir." To which as they entered Mrs. Taliaferro's house, the old man replied, "Yes, a very fine evening."—There was then a coffee-house in Williamsburg, next door to which my informant lived, and much of the gossip of which, of course, reached her. One evening, she says, Mr. Wythe was seen approaching the coffee-house. "Here comes Mr. Wythe," said one; "I wonder if he will talk this evening." Some said yes, some no. "I'll make him talk," said a saucy negro boy, who being always about the house had become a sort of licensed pet of the customers. The old man entered, walked in silence to the fire, and turning his back to it, stood with his hands behind him. The boy put the hot poker in his hand. "What did you do that for?" was all he said."[7]

Judge Beverly Tucker, the son of St. George Tucker, became—as his father before him—the occupant of Wythe's old Chair of Law at William and Mary College. Tucker was a child when Wythe was still in Williamsburg and must often have seen the old man in the course of his daily life.

As he became more and more immersed in a life of books, Wythe became ever more pedantic and obscure. At the same time, he sought out more and more the most esoteric of information, as the following letter to Jefferson, 22 April 1790 shows:

> "i have not been able, after long inquiry, to obtain the writings of Phlegon mentioned by Ferguson in his tables and tracts. Probably you can tell to whom and where application may be successfull. When you find convenient to give this information, add to the favour an etiquette, which may direct my London correspondent to whom, with it, i shall transmit a bill of exchange, in procuring some books from Strasburgh."[8]

Wythe had quoted from James Ferguson's *Tables and Tracts, relative to several arts and sciences,* London, 1771. p. 193-4:

> "Phlegon informs us that in the fourth year of the 202d olympiad (which was the 4746th year of the iulian period and the 33d year after the year of Christs birth) there was the greatest eclipse of the sun that ever was known: for the darkness lasted three hours in the middle of the day; which could be no other than the darkness of the crucifixion day; as the sun never was totally hid, above four minutes of time, from any part of the earth, by the interposition of the moon."

Jefferson was at this time in New York City, where he had become Washington's Secretary of State. As a confirmed and even virulent Deist, Jefferson had no truck with any nonsense (as he would regard it) concerning miracles on the day of the Lord's crucifixion. His letter in reply, for example, gives far more space to a new variety of rice than it does to Phlegon and his tales.

3 June, 1790

"Dear Sir: An indisposition of several weeks have prevented my sooner acknowledging the receipt of your favor of April 22. The bookseller whom I have employed at Strasburgh always is Armand Keonig. A Biographical dictionary to which I have been obliged to have recourse for information about Phlegon authorizes me to inform you of these circumstances relative to him. He was surnamed Trallion, from a city in Lydia, and a freedman of Adrian. There remains nothing of his at present but a treatise on those who have been long-lived and another on wonderful things. The best edition of these fragments of Phlegon is that given by Meursius at Leyden in 1622 in . . . . Greek and Latin with notes. He lived to the 156th year of the Christian era. The author adds "It is pretended that he spoke in the 13th and 14th books of his Olympiads of the darkness which happened at the death of our Saviour. Eusebius in his chronicle relates his words." I inclose a few seeds of highland rice which was gathered the last autumn in the East Indies. If well attended to, it may not be too late to sow and mature it after you shall receive it. I have sowed a few seeds in earthern pots. It is a most precious thing if we can save it. The house of representatives have voted to remove to Baltimore. It is doubted whether the Senate will concur. Perhaps it may end in a removal to Philadelphia. Adieu My Dear Sir, Yours affectionately."[9]

To replace Wythe, the Visitors of William and Mary College elected his former student, St. George Tucker to the chair of Law and Police, on 8 March 1790. It must have been a matter of great sorrow to Wythe to leave the lovely village where he had spent the majority of his years, and now in his old age forsake the company of the beloved friends of a lifetime. He settled his affairs by liberating many of his slaves. There are records yet existing of York County for 1787–88 which show that a certain Lydia (of whom we shall hear much in the future), and Polly and Charles were at this time given their freedom. Lydia, at any rate, elected to remain with Wythe and work for him. According to Richard Taliaferro's will, Wythe and his now-dead wife had life tenure in the home in Williamsburg. Wythe now abandoned his rights to Colonel Richard Taliaferro, Mrs. Wythe's nephew. The old man had dearly loved his nephew-by-marriage, and was very solicitous for him in his illness two years later in 1791. Dr. McClurg was in attendance, but for all his skill, Richard Taliaferro died, and by *his* will the house was sold, the proceeds therefrom being divided equally among his brothers and sisters.

But in his removal to Richmond, Wythe took with him one at least of his students. William Munford came of an old and prosperous Virginian family which had lost much of its money during the Revolution. Wythe recognized his abilities, especially his literary bent. The best the old Chancellor could do for him was to make him a lawyer that he might be able to earn some kind of a living. But Munford's real forte was, and always would be, literature. How-

ever, Wythe took him to live in his house while still in Williamsburg and later
when he went to Richmond, the young man went with him, Littleton Waller
Tazewell being given over to John Wickham, Wythe's neighbor, for continued
instruction. This was all right with Littleton, for the two were old friends and
got along well together. Munford had been especially eager for the association
with Wythe, knowing as he did that under such an arrangement his future was
assured.

> "Nothing could advance me faster in the world than the reputation of having been educated
> by Mr. Wythe, for such a man as he casts a light all around him."[10]

And so it was, for in April of 1791, he had

> ". . . settled as a student of law in the house of Chancellor Wythe . . . . I scarcely know a
> place more pleasing than Williamsburg, which may justly receive the title (which Homer
> gives Greece) of the 'land of lovely dames' . . . ."

William Munford was to be one of the greater lights of Wythe's teaching. His
joy at being received by Wythe as a student is almost naive.

> ". . . thru' the surprising friendship and generosity of Mr. Wythe, I live in his house and
> board at his table, at the same time enjoying his instructions, without paying a farthing. My
> esteem for this excellent man . . . increases every day. . . ."[11]

Wythe set Munford to making an epitome of Blackstone, as this was one of
the ways in which he instructed his students. Let them tear Blackstone apart,
and telescope him, and they would learn much thereby. Munford later on,
about 1804, spoke of how much he owed Wythe for his law training, saying that
Wythe always urged him:

> "Don't skim it; read deeply, and ponder what you read; they begin to make lawyers now
> without the *viginti annorum lucubrationes* of Lord Coke; they are mere skimmers of law and
> know little else."[12]

Before the removal to Richmond, Munford gave a touching instance of
Wythe's kindness. The young man had attended a supper-ball at the Travis
home in Williamsburg:

> "But my delight would not have been unmingled with sorrow if I had known the condition
> in which Mr. Wythe was . . . The poor old gentleman was . . . at the very moment in
> which I was hoping away with wonderful glee, stretched on his bed, sleepless and tormented
> by a terrible headache. He was taken with it the same day, early in the morning, but he
> smothered it so quietly, that nobody perceived his disorder, till it had increased to a violent
> height, and it has continued on him with very little abatement for near eight and forty
> hours. . . . When I returned from the ball (for I slept with Robin Carter and breakfasted
> at Mr. Madison's) I found a parcel of apples, peaches and plums on my table. . . . the old
> gentleman, not knowing of my absence, had sent them up to me . . . Would you believe it,
> . . . he has begun to teach Jimmy, his servant, to write?"[13]

This was not the only time Wythe taught a colored person—for his "sacred cause" of freedom for the slaves required that they be educated as well as freed. The selfish idea that the colored people were incapable of education was the child of the desire to keep them in subjection. And Wythe tried to prove that they were as capable of learning as any white person.

Wythe had gathered his goods together and taken a house in Richmond to live there until his death. The preparations for moving had been onerous, and in the middle of the work, Munford had been taken ill of the ague and fever. In spite of his student's illness, Wythe sent on his furniture to the ship which carried it up the river to the Capital. Munford came on somewhat—about a week—later and settled in with the Chancellor. The house, by no means grand or imposing, had once belonged to William Nelson, which may have been the reason Wythe bought it—for he and the Nelsons were related. It was on the very top of Shockhoe Hill, from which the inhabitants had a splendid view of the suburb of Manchester; the bridge across the river, and the rocks and islands which then encumbered the James.

Richmond at this time was becoming a bustling town, with trade expanding at a fast pace. Although tobacco was and continued to be the staple of Virginia, other commodities were also being produced, for at this time the great stands of timber in the Piedmont region were being cut down to be sent as lumber to the West Indies and other foreign parts. There was a great deal of wheat grown as well, and this was milled into flour before being shipped abroad. The James River was a great arrow pointed directly into the interior and old William Byrd II knew what he was doing when he built his town at the very point where the river ceased to be navigable.

But Richmond was a fact of beauty, too, for despite the jerry-built quality of much of the city, the forest still remained to some extent upon the hillsides, and standing on the top of the hills one could see, beyond the straggling city, the fields of wheat and corn shimmering in the summer's heat. The buildings of the Government—the Capitol and the Governor's Mansion stood adjacent, with a high wall of stone between them, which was supposed to stop up a ravine which split the hill, doing so, however, rather ineffectively. The Capitol was of brick and did not yet have its coat of stucco.

The important people lived, of course, on the high eminences. These included John Marshall, at first called General since he had served under President Washington to put down the Whiskey Rebellion. John Brockenbrough of the Bank of Virginia was likewise prominent in the society of the town, as were the Amblers. One of the finest mansions was that of Major Du Val, whose home was on the square directly to the west of Grace Street. Wythe, whose house stood as befitted so eminent a jurist on the very highest spot in the city, was his neighbor. Always fond of gardening, Wythe had planted a tulip poplar which bloomed before his home for many years. His house, a small, story-and-a-half wooden building, with a hip roof, stood on a square by itself, and had the usual outbuildings—sheds for horses, barns for hay and such-like.

Wythe was now an attenuated old man, living only for the law, and concerned with humanity only, as it were, as an afterthought. He lived in the body because one can't very well live on this earth without a body, but his material substance was the least of his concerns. Now that his beloved friends had gone before him in death, the only thing of any moment to him was the law, and of that he became the oracle. No human consideration concerned him when he entered his chambers—no human position, or human friendship, or even human compassion. Of the latter he had a great deal, for he was always one of the most compassionate of men. But in his judicial chambers, all that was put off, and only justice moved him. The story is told of him that he was appealed to by Bushrod Washington, of the family of the great General himself, that—

> "He called on the Chancellor with a bill of injuction in behalf of General—, to restrain the collection of a debt. The ground . . . was that the creditor had agreed to await the convenience of General—for the payment . . . and . . . it was not then convenient to pay it. The Chancellor . . . "Do you think, sir, that I ought to grant this injunction?" Mr. Washington blushed and observed, that he had presented the bill at the earnest instance of his client."[14]

Unpopularity likewise did not sway Wythe. Nowhere was this better displayed than in the British debt cases, and in the outcome of which cases he himself was to an extent concerned. His decision, when it ultimately came, did hurt to himself. But it came, nonetheless.

Some time before the Treaty of Peace with Britain in 1783, the Virginia Assembly had enacted a law that debts due British merchants could be paid by the Virginia debtors into the loan office, which then would be responsible for the payment of the debts. Many creditors gladly availed themselves of this office, and paid their debts by the use of depreciated currency. But the Peace Treaty stipulated that no state should put any impediment in the way of collecting *bona fide* debts. Which would come first, a Virginia law or a Confederation treaty? For the United States Constitution had carefully stated that treaties were the Supreme Law of the Land. This was so even though the Peace Treaty was pre-Constitutional.

The old Robinson estate now enters the story again. The two executors were Edmund Pendleton and Peter Lyons, and they wanted to get a settlement of the final debts of the estate. The estate had paid money due English creditors into the said loan office, but the loan office in turn had not paid the creditors. Naturally, it couldn't since there was a war on, but it hadn't anyway, since the state government had used the money to fight the war.[15] The British creditors sued Pendleton and Lyons as executors, and the case went to the Chancery Court. There Wythe pronounced judgement against the two executors (that is, against the Robinson estate, since neither Pendleton nor Lyons were personally liable). In May, 1793, the case of Page vs. Pendleton, Wythe boldly stated that the only way debts could be made void was by paying them. The Chancery Court was, he maintained, as it were a neutral country, and no amount of personal feeling towards the British could overcome the neutrality of his court.

"A judge should not be susceptible of national antipathy, more than of malice towards individuals;—whilst executing his office, he should be not more affected by the electric fluid in the circumjacent mass, whilst their communication is interrupted. What is just in this Hall is just in Westminister Hall, and in every other praetorium upon earth. Some Judges in the West Indian Islands have been execrated by citizens of the United American State, for several late sentences against the latter, in favor of British subjects, in certain maritime causes; justly execrated if fame hath not misreported their conduct. None of those citizens, surely can wish to see the tribunals of their own country so polluted."

So said Wythe. His decision was that the

". . . Treaty of Peace with Great Britain, if it be valid, abrogated the acts of every state in the union, tending to obstruct the recovery of British debts from the citizens of those states, . . ."[16]

Years later when delivering the oration at Wythe's funeral, William Munford stated that, to the honor of Virginians, Wythe's action did not diminish one bit his popularity. That was simply not so, for we know from several sources that Wythe was intensely unpopular in his native country after this case. The matter had brought about great excitement, for many Virginians were now liable once again for debts they had thought paid. Hundreds of thousands of dollars were in question, and added to this was the fact that Britain was even more unpopular itself for it had still not surrendered the Western posts, nor paid for the stolen slaves.

Washington, his ear carefully cocked for the temper of the people, sent Edmund Randolph around Virginia to sound out the popular attitude. Randolph replied that

"In this Place parties are strong; the friends to the general government are far inferior in *number* to its enemies . . . . The debtors . . . range themselves under the standard of Mr. Henry, whose ascendancy has risen to an immeasurable height. But . . . he grows rich every hour, and thus his motives to tranquility must be multiplying every day. Mr. Wythe, indeed, as chancellor, has determined against the British debtor; but his decree will, it is conjectured, be reversed in the Court of Appeals, unanimously."[17]

Whatever the Appeals Court would do, Wythe was ultimately sustained, for in Ware vs. Hylton (1797) the Supreme Court of the United States declared that the British could indeed recover the money due them from Virginians.

It must by no means be imagined that Wythe's political principles were involved here—only his judicial ones. For Wythe was not a Federalist, but rather a follower of Jeffersonian radicalism. His former pupil had no more staunch supporter than the old Chancellor, who believed strongly in the rights of the people as against the prerogatives of the rich and the well-born. No Federalist he.

During all this time, Wythe had been trying to have his seal for the Chancery Court made. His stern devotion to duty is well illustrated by the subject depicted on the seal. Designed by Benjamin West, it presented the legend of Sisamnes. Herodotus tells the story that King Cambyses had the unfortunate if dishonest

Sisamnes killed and skinned for the taking of a bribe. The skin, tanned and prepared, was cut into straps and used to upholster the seat of judges. Cambyses then made Sisamnes' son, Otannes, the judge and instructed him not to forget whereon he sat. This awful story was Wythe's choice for his seal, and gave all to understand that when they approached his tribunal they might expect the sternest justice. Wythe applied to Jefferson for help in having the seal made (the latter was then Secretary of State in New York City, being in Washington's Cabinet). The good old man desired his friend's approval—

> "When you can attend to trifles, tell me your opinion, in general, of the drawing . . . particularly should not parties appear before the judge? is not the skin of Sesamnes, whose story, you know, Herodotus relates added by mr West to the original design, an improvement?"[18]

It was in the next year (1794) that Wythe befriended a young man who seemed to him to have great promise. This was the as-yet unknown Henry Clay. At this time, Wythe's gout in his right hand continued to make writing an extremely painful thing. Still learning to write with his left hand, it was hard for him to prepare the long reports of his Court. There came to the Court at this time the young boy Henry Clay, about 16 years old. Clay's family was not as poverty-stricken as the "poor boy of the slashes" legend would make out, but they did have a hard time getting along. The boy was the son of a Baptist minister who had died in 1781, leaving Henry's mother a widow with seven children. The boy was sent to learn his letters in a log cabin school run by Peter Deacon, who was a hard drinker and an Englishman to boot. His mother married again, and accompanied her husband in 1792 to Kentucky, leaving the young Henry in the office of the Clerk of the Chancery Court, Peter Tinsley. Here his fine and regular penmanship recommended him to Chancellor Wythe, who, pleased with the bright child, took him under his care.

Wythe set out to give Henry a good education, while the boy at the same time acted as Wythe's secretary. Into the child's hands Wythe put Harris's *Homer,* Tooke's *Diversions of Purley,* Bishop Lowth's *Grammar,* Plutarch's *Lives,* and some books of law and of history. As always with his students, a large part of the boy's education consisted of verbal instruction from the old man, who had so much to give. Not this only, but Wythe introduced the boy, who had come to him still in his backwoods homespun pretty much a country boy, to the most prominent people in Richmond. During the time Clay spent in Richmond, he met Edmund Pendleton, Spencer Roane, John Marshall, John Wickham, Bushrod Washington, and finally, the then Attorney-General of Virginia and later Governor, Robert Brooke. This was important, since it was into Brooke's office that Clay went to study law.

Clay himself many years later gave testimony of how much he owed to Chancellor Wythe:

> ". . . he engaged me to act as his amanuensis and I attended him frequently, though not every day, to serve him . . . for several years. Upon his dictation, I wrote, I believe, all the

reports of cases which it is now proposed to republish. I remember that it cost me a great deal of labor, not understanding a single Greek character, to write some citations from Greek authors, which he wished inserted in copies of his reports sent to Mr. Jefferson, Mr. Samuel Adams, of Boston, and to one or two other persons . . . .

Mr. Wythe was one of the purest, best, and most learned men in classical lore that I ever knew. Although I did not understand Greek, I was often highly gratified in listening to his readings in Homer's *Illiad* and other Greek authors, so beautifully did he pronounce the language. No one ever doubted his perfect uprightness, or questioned his great ability as a Judge."

Even though some fifty years or more had passed over Henry Clay and he had in the interval met and fought with most of the great and famous of his day, his memories of the old man were still bright and clear in 1851.

"Mr. Wythe's personal appearance and his personal habits were plain, simple, and unostentatious. His countenance was full of blandness and benevolence, and I think he made, in his salutations of others, the most graceful bow that I ever witnessed. A little bent by age, he generally wore a grey coating, and when walking carried a cane. Even at this moment, after the lapse of more than half a century since I last saw him, his image is distinctly engraved on my mind. During my whole acquaintance with him he constantly abstained from the use of all animal food. . . ."[19]

In 1796, young Henry went to Robert Brooke's office to study the law. His stay there was a short one, but as we have seen, law training was often a short thing in those days. In November, 1797, the young man left Richmond to strike out for Kentucky and make his fortune, taking with him the ideals of Jeffersonian democracy which Wythe had increased in him, as well as the firm purpose to help wipe out slavery. However, this latter ideal did not last long. Henry wanted money and knew how to get it—by practicing criminal law. He became a great and much-sought-after defender of criminals. In addition, he wanted political power—and the way to that was through popularity. Thus, when he went to Kentucky, he found the strong politicians of that country already in control of the party organization *and* the issues. George Nicholas, John Breckinridge, John Brown—these were the powers in that state. The latter two had been Wythe's students also and they too had come to terms with political reality—the slave-owners were just not going to liberate their slaves, and abolition was a lost cause.

When he first arrived in Kentucky fresh from Wythe's hearth and teaching, he was full of the spirit of abolition. He wrote for the "Kentucky Gazette" a plan for gradually freeing the slaves and had this printed. This attempt to convert the Kentuckians did not, however, last long. Clay veered with the wind and Wythe's "sacred cause" went for nothing.

In the same year as that in which he took Clay under his guidance, Chancellor Wythe was again caught up in national politics. During this time, the French Revolution occupied the attention of the whole Western world. The ideals of that great and bloody affair—liberty, equality, fraternity—appealed to many in America and disgusted an equal number. These ideals turned swiftly into blood and then into general war. The French had to defend themselves from the attacks of the other European powers, among them Britain. And they called on the United States to honor the Treaty of Alliance which was still in force, dating from the American Revolution. Washington, of course, refused. The nation simply could not sustain a war with Britain and there was no overriding interest which would cause it to embark on a war to save France from the consequences of its own doctrinaire folly.

But the feeling ran very hot on the issue, for there were not a few who thought that America should help its old friend and ally. Among these Wythe was not numbered. Nor was Jefferson, who as Secretary of State, was very concerned with the antics of Citizen Genet—the latter was doing his very best to cause trouble between the United States and Britain. In fact, his activities were enough to bring America's very neutrality into question, since he was chartering ships and giving permission to Americans to privateer against British shipping. At this point, Washington issued his neutrality proclamation.

Something had to be done, if not to curb Genet, at least to dissociate him from the pro-French Republican Party of Jefferson and his followers. It was Madison, apparently, who had the idea of holding meetings about the country which would congratulate Washington on his neutrality proclamation and, being conducted by prominent Republicans, they would serve to emphasize the fact that they likewise disapproved of the French Minister's conduct. These meetings were accordingly held in various cities throughout the country. Pendleton, for example, supported the meeting held in Carolina County. It was Wythe who chaired the Richmond meeting, although Federalist John Marshall had a good deal to do with it. A great many Federalists attended, and although it may have been infiltrated by members of that party, it nonetheless served the purposes of both groups. On 17 August 1793, Wythe wrote to both Jefferson and Edmund Randolph asking that they submit the resolutions which the meeting had adopted to the President. These praised Washington

> ". . . our illustrious fellow citizen George Washington, to whose eminent services, great talents, and exalted virtues, all America pays so just a tribute, has given an additional proof of his watchful attention to his own duty and the welfare of his country by his Proclamation . . . ."[20]

They further went on to say, among other things, that

> ". . . any intriguing of a foreign minister with the political parties of this country . . . might . . . lead to the introduction of foreign gold and foreign armies, with their fatal consequences, dismemberment and partition."

This was signed by George Wythe, as President of the meeting. And with it went a rather florid letter

> ". . . When propitious Heaven had crowned with victory the efforts of your country and yourself . . . situated as this country is, no madness or folly cou'd ever be so supreme as to involve us again in European contests . . . ."

Thus was Washington congratulated on his decisive action. Not yet had that party spirit risen which would result in such vituperation of Washington as few presidents have had to suffer. The latter replied to Wythe and the meeting which he had chaired, sending, his ". . . affectionate acknowledgments."[21]

However much the party Jefferson was founding might turn and twist, of its ultimate objective there was no doubt nor was there any turning back. The determined Jefferson, doctrinaire to the core, expressed his true sentiments when he wrote to William Short in Paris

". . . My own affections have been deeply wounded by some of the martyrs to this cause, but rather than it should have failed, I would have seen half the earth desolated . . . ."[22]

To assist the pro-French movement and to overcome the influence of the Federalists, there was founded in Philadelphia a Democratic Society in May 1793. Soon these were springing up all over the country. That in Kentucky (Lexington) had Wythe's pupil John Breckinridge as president, with the objects in view of opening the Mississippi's navigation, helping the French, and denouncing Hamilton and all his works. There was a particularly active society in Richmond, the meetings of which the boy Henry Clay attended enthusiastically. Another came into existence in Norfolk as early as May, 1793. Since these all were organized in the Spring of that year, there is good basis for believing that Jefferson and his followers had a concerted plan in creating them. The Society in Wythe County was especially strong, while even Dumries had a Democratic-Republican Society.

The object, of course, was human amelioration, and the best way to bring that about was to take over the government. But education was yet another means to better society, and so these groups supported schools and colleges. In Virginia there was set up, among other schools founded at this time, Wythe Academy, with its home in Wytheville. In Kentucky, Transylvania Seminary was established, with John Breckinridge as President of its Trustees. Nor was this all. For these societies also pushed (to some extent, and at first) for the abolition of slavery. Or, if not the societies themselves, then the membership was often connected with other groups for the abolishing of slavery.

But the main object was to counteract the British influence. And these became especially prominent when the Jay Treaty was negotiated. Over this issue, all hell's fury was summoned up. John Jay, former Chief Justice, bought peace with Britain without getting in return one single important concession. Many Americans, Wythe among them, felt the Treaty was a betrayal of the country.

From all over the country protests poured in on Washington, asking that he refuse his signature. And equally powerful pressure came from the Hamiltonian faction that he should sign the Treaty. Among those protesting was George Wythe, who chaired another Richmond meeting—this time one indignantly asking that the President withold his approval of the pact. On 29 July 1795, the citizens of Richmond met at the Capitol, elected George Wythe to the presiding chair and framed a resolution.[23]

"The citizens of Richmond, awfully impressed with the momentous crisis of American affairs . . ."

As sternly as they could, they warned Washington that the proposed treaty was

". . . Insulting to the dignity, Injurious to the Interest, Dangerous to the security, and Repugnant to the Constitution of the United States . . . ."[24]

Washington's reaction to this was not happy. He took comfort from the account which reached him that the meeting wasn't well attended, with the most respectable people staying away. He wrote to Edmund Randolph, now the Secretary of State, referring to this Richmond meeting

". . . a meeting have been had there also, at which Mr. Wythe, it is said was seated as moderator; by chance more than design, it is added. A queer chance this for the Chancellor of a State."[25]

The President was sour on the petition, saying

". . . They have outdone all that has gone before them . . . ."

Truly, their language was strong, but it should have been since the Treaty demanded strong action. But Washington was unmoved, and the Treaty was signed.

It was in this same year of 1795 that Wythe put out the work he had been so long in preparing. He had dictated the most of it to Henry Clay, and now at last the work was done. It was his answer to the work of Pendleton who had in the Court of Appeals reversed so many of Wythe's decisions. It was natural that a man to whom the law meant so much should feel pain in finding that his ideas about justice were not accepted by his fellow judges. The only way he could justify himself was to publish his opinions with observations on the results as viewed by the higher court. The very title gives an instance of the kind of work it was—pedantic and filled with the most scholarly allusions: *Decisions of Cases in Virginia by the High Court of Chancery, with remarks upon Decrees, by the Court of Appeals, reversing some of those decisions. By George Wythe, Chancellor of Said Court.*

In his work, which caused embarrassment to many of the legal men of the day and, not least, to Edmund Pendleton at whom so many of his remarks were directed, Wythe brought forth all his arguments—many of which were taken from sources not usually cited by judges. He had no hesitation in going to the myths of antiquity to make his point. Nor did he eschew pedantry. In a sense, his work was a tremendous compliment to the lawyers—for it by no means used simple language, but rather, tacitly assumed their ability to understand Wythe and assumed likewise their possession of as great a background in learning and languages as he himself had. Of course, they had no such thing. When Henry

Clay could become a great lawyer (and a greater politician) with only one year
of legal training, when John Marshall could become Chief Justice with only six
weeks of the same, and Alexander Hamilton with less than six months, it is not
to be expected that lawyers would be scholars too.

The work was aimed particularly at Pendleton and while the learned Chancellor did make some caustic remarks about that judge, Pendleton thoroughly
deserved them. Wythe was, after all, an Eighteenth Century gentleman, with all
that that implies in the way of classical learning. But of knowledge of Greek and
Latin Pendleton had none. In the case of Eppes vs. Randolph, Pendleton in
reviewing Wythe's work spoke of "clashing jargon." True, his words might
have reference to the arguments of the lawyers, but also they might not. In any
case, Pendleton was less than gentlemanly. A further remark from the case may
be cited:

> "The term re-acknowledgement of a deed seems to have produced in the mind of the Chan-
> cellor mistaken ideas . . . A mistake which information from our clerk would correct."[26]

If ever a remark was uncalled for, this was one. To suggest that the clerk of a
court could teach Wythe law was not only ignorant, it was moreover rude. That
Wythe was extremely scrupulous in preparing his decisions, and in giving
ample time to counsel to prepare their cases is indicated by the following:

> 1797, Nominy Hall, June 18
> "Mr. Warden informed me that when the plaintiff's counsel in May in the Frying Pan land
> case pressed the reception of the reports, the Chancellor replied, "No, I can never be acces-
> sory to a rule of this court precluding this defendant from enjoying all the time his agent may
> wish, and was I to do otherwise it would be exhibiting to the world that the Court of Chan-
> cery was no longer a Court of Equity."[27]

There was nothing slap-dash about his court.

That Wythe's work, when it finally came out, hit the subject for which it was
intended is obvious from the fact that Pendleton turned over in his mind a similar project. Perhaps *he* should write a book in answer to Wythe? His friends,
however, dissuaded him from the project, saying that the old Chancellor's work
had really made little impression anyway. However painful the altercation
between the two old men may have been both to themselves and to their friends
and associates, the work did serve to put Wythe's opinions before the students of
the law. And if they read them they would certainly pick up, not only Virginian
law, but also a good deal of culture. For instance, in his decisions on the British
Debt cases, Wythe went to the basis of right and justice, declaring that no
human law could alter the law of God. The idea that Virginia by its own fiat
could do so was wrong. To confiscate the property of a man because he is the
subject of an enemy king was a wicked thing:

> ". . . in truth, acquirement by conquest is a relic of barbarism. Capture and detention of an
> enemys goods is just only where members of one community, injured by those of another,
> had not been able to obtain reparation otherwise than by reprisal. And there the reparation

ought to be commensurate to the injury. . . . those who are forced to make the reparation seldom or never happen to be those who had been perpetrators of the injury. . . ."

Wythe went back to the pagan Greeks to point out the nature of justice—

". . . the law of nature . . . the prohibitions to kill or wound our fellow men, to defame them, to invade their property, . . . are perceived intuitively . . . as Antigone says to Creon, in Sophocles, v. 463 . . .

      . . . unwritten laws divine,
   immutable, eternal, not like these of
   yesterday, but made e'er time began.

They are laws which men, who did not ordain them, have not power to abrogate."[28]

The Virginians didn't like this. Of course, they wouldn't like to be told that they were unjustly withholding money. But like it or not, Wythe bravely told them the truth. (And this was at a time when antagonism to Britain was at its height.)

Life went on serenely for Wythe, however, in these years of the 1790's. He was a householder in Richmond, with a comfortable home, he had his Chancery work, and in his spare hours he devoted himself to his laboratory experiments. His housekeeper was a former slave whom he had freed—Lydia Broadnax. A couple more of his freed servants remained with him. He went on his way, independent as ever. Henry Clay gives an instance of the way in which the old gentleman treated those who would buy his favor.

"A neighbor of his, Mr. —, who had the reputation of being a West India nabob, and who at the time had an important suit pending in the Court of Chancery, sent him a demijohn of old arrack, and an orange tree for his niece, Miss Nelson, then residing with him. When the articles were brought into Mr. Wythe's house, with the message from the donor, Mr. Wythe requested the servant to take them back . . . and to present . . . his respects, and thanks for . . . kind intentions, but to say that he long ceased to make any use of arrack, and that Miss Nelson had no conservatory in which she could protect the orange tree."[29]

It was in the year 1797 that Richard Randolph, Wythe's former pupil, died and left to him and others the task of settling his estate. It was to be especially difficult since Randolph was a true pupil of Wythe and accordingly manumitted his slaves, desiring that a settlement called Israel Hill be set up where the freedmen were to be provided with land and houses. Randolph had named as executors St. George Tucker, John Randolph of Roanoke, his brother Ryland Randolph,

". . . and the most virtuous and incorruptible of mankind, and next to my father-in-law my greatest benefactor, George Wythe, Chancellor of Virginia, the brightest ornament of human nature."

His will provided, for his own conscience's sake,

"To make retribution . . . to an unfortunate race of bondsmen, over whom my ancestors

have usurped and exercised the most lawless and monstrous tyranny and in whom my countrymen (by their iniquitous laws, in contradiction of their own declaration of Rights, and in
violation of every sacred law of nature . . .) have vested me with absolute property I
hereby declare that it is my will and desire . . . that my negroes, all of them be liberated
. . . ."[30]

In this action, Richard Randolph was squaring accounts with his own conscience (as formed by Wythe), but he was not alone in his detestation of negro
slavery. George Washington, Patrick Henry, Richard Henry Lee, St. George
Tucker, Thomas Jefferson—all of them wrote searing words on the subject of
the bondage which gave the lie to their words of liberty. The great cause of
human freedom could not permit the anacronism of slavery to grow like a cancer
within the economic and political body. But the opposition was so strong. By no
means did all Virginians share their viewpoint. Economic pressures grew
greater and stronger each year, and so much of the wealth of the South was
bound up in the fact of slavery that finally it came to be unthinkable to change
the situation. But of those who worked the hardest to prevent the Civil War,
Wythe was in the foremost rank.

Within the nation, political philosophies were rapidly coming to a head-on
clash. The southern Democratic-Republicans, planters though they might be
and also slave-owners, saw no contradiction in addressing each other with the
French Revolutionary title of Citizen. John Randolph of Roanoke, for example,
seriously addressed Abraham B. Venable, President of the Bank of Virginia, as
"Citizen" Venable! These people upheld the ideals of liberty, equality and fraternity in everything except in the matter of their slaves, with whom they by no
means pretended an equality. By now Jefferson had perfected the political structure with which he would take over the nation. No man in American history
ever had a more surprising turn of political fortune than Jefferson. He had been
a failure as Virginia's governor, had gone to France as America's minister and
had returned to rebuild his political career as the foremost exponent of French
radicalism, being hated and feared by the Hamiltonians, who espoused the
cause of the well-born as frankly as the Jeffersonians espoused the cause of the
people.

Jefferson was Vice-President, while John Adams, conservative as ever, was
President. Adams was puzzled as to why Wythe and Pendleton and his other
old comrades were opposed to him—

"While Wythe and Pendleton, and McKean, and Clinton, and Gates, and Osgood, and
many others I could name, were arrayed in political hostility against their old friend . . .
What is the reason that so many of our "old standbys" are infected with Jacobinism? The
principles of this infernal tribe were surely no part of our ancient political creed . . ."[31]

It was not until many years later that the bitterness wore off and John Adams
recalled the joy of knowing these men. In 1818 he wrote to William Wirt (who
had just finished his *Life of Patrick Henry*:

> "Your Sketches of the life of Mr. Henry have given me a rich Entertainment. I will not compare them to the Sybil conducting Eneas to the Regions below to see the Ghosts of departed Sages and Heroes: but to an Angel conveying me to the abodes of the blessed on high to converse with the Spirits of just Men made perfect. The names of Henry, Lee, Bland, Pendleton, Washington, Rutledge, Wythe . . . will ever thrill through my veigns with an agreeable Sensation . . . ."[32]

In the split between Hamilton and Adams (Adams being the Federalist candidate for President in 1800) the party was weakened. And so Jefferson, with his Vice-Presidential candidate Aaron Burr, won the election, with a majority of 73 electoral votes to 65. In Virginia, the Democratic-Republicans had chosen a very strong slate of men for the Electoral College. Among them were Edmund Pendleton, James Madison, John Page, William Branch Giles, Archibald Stuart, Creed Taylor, John Preston, William Cabell, and George Wythe, these men having been selected by their party on 21 January 1800.

The matter of selecting electors was carried on with great care, the Democratic-Republicans picking the most prestigious men they could find.[33] The leaders of the party knew that the common people simply would not vote against such men as Wythe, Giles, etc. When he informed Jefferson of the progress his group had been making, Philip Norborne Nicholas (Jefferson's party boss for Virginia) took particular care to tell him that Wythe had agreed to serve as a Republican Elector:

> ". . . it will give . . . great weight and dignity. And I cannot but augur well of a cause which calls out from their retirement such venerable patriots as Wythe and Pendleton."[34]

As yet the Electoral College was not a mere formality, for party discipline was not yet strong. The Electoral College, according to the Constitution, does the choosing of the President and theoretically, it can choose anybody it wants. That's the law, although it has not, for many decades past, been the custom.

After an election campaign of most unusual bitterness, the voters pronounced their choice. When the Virginia Electors met, in December 1800, they had been given orders by the party chieftains to vote equally for both Jefferson and Burr. Jefferson had arranged it so in order that he might not be blamed by Burr as having failed to support him. Jefferson himself candidly stated that he had arranged this, saying so in a note of some years later:

> ". . . the election of 1800 . . . that I considered it my duty to be merely passive, except in Virginia, I had taken some measures to procure for him the unanimous vote of that state, because I thought any failure there might be imputed to me."[35]

The New York politican was a strong, able and important man, and Jefferson did not want to offend him. As it was, the Republican Party won in New York only by a very small majority. But in the Virginia College of Electors, Wythe, who was so devoted to Jefferson, balked at throwing an equality of votes to Burr. He evidently had a very good idea of what might happen—as it very well did. Only when his fellow-Elector, James Madison, assured him that Burr's friends would in a different state throw votes to Jefferson, and thus unbalance the election, did Wythe go along with the scheme. As it was, Wythe was right and Madison was wrong, for the votes went equally in every state. So the election was thrown into the House of Representatives, and that was controlled by the Federalist Party. It was now a question of which man Hamilton hated the less. Hamilton was beside himself. Whichever one they chose, the next President of the United States would be a Democratic-Republican. The House of Representatives voted, and voted, and voted . . . Finally, they got tired of the nonsense and some Federalists simply abstained from voting. They gave a simply majority to Jefferson and he was accordingly elected. Wythe's pupil was now President of the United States.

Notes to Chapter XI

1. 14 September 1789, Eppington, in, Jefferson. *The Papers of*—. Boyd ed., Vol. 16, p. 25.
2. William and Mary—. First Series, Vol. 8, p. 153.
3. 30 November 1789, New York City, in, Washington. *The Writings of*—. Fitzpatrick ed., Vol. 30, p. 472-4.
4. Conway. *Omitted Chapters*—. p. 131.
5. John Trumbull. *Autobiography, Reminiscences & Letters of*—. (New York, Wiley & Putnam, 1841), p. 417.
6. Jefferson. *The Papers of*—. Boyd ed., Vol. 13, p. 329.
7. Benjamin Blake Minor, editor, in, "Memoir of the Author" in, Virginia. High Court of Chancery. *Decisions of the*—*with* remarks upon decrees by the Court of Appeals. 2d ed., (Richmond, J. W. Randolph, 1852), p. xxx, footnote.
8. Jefferson. *Opus citatum*, Vol. 16, p. 368.
9. *Ibidem.* p. 495.
10. William Munford to John Coalter, 23 April 1791, Williamsburg, in, William and Mary—. First Series, Vol. 8, p. 153.
11. William Munford to John Coalter, Manuscript Collection, Library, William and Mary College.
12. George Wythe Munford. *The Two Parsons*—. (Richmond, J. D. K. Sleight, 1884), p. 364.
13. William Munford to John Coalter, 22 July 1791, Manuscript Collection, Library, William and Mary College.
14. Henry Clay to Benjamin Blake Minor, 3 May 1851, Ashland, in, Virginia. High Court of Chancery. *Decisions of*—. Minor edition, p. 62.
15. Wythe himself had paid money into this load office (a small sum) and Jefferson also had done the same (a very substantial sum).
16. George Wythe, in, Benjamin Blake Minor, "Memoir of the Author," in, Virginia. High Court of Chancery. *Decisions of*—. Minor edition, p. xxi-xxii.
17. Edmund Randolph to George Washington, 23 December 1789, Richmond, in, Conway. *Omitted Chapters*—. p. 153.
18. George Wythe to Thomas Jefferson, 10 January 1791, Williamsburg, Manuscript Collection, Library of Congress. This makes it apparent that it was West, not Wythe, who selected this gruesome myth as the subject for the Seal.
19. Henry Clay to B. B. Minor, in, Minor. *Opus citatum*, p. xxii.
20. Virginia Gazette and General Advertiser, 21 August 1793, Richmond.

21. George Washington to the Inhabitants of Richmond, 28 August 1793, in, *Writings of*—. Fitzpatrick ed., Vol. 33, p. 72.

22. 3 January 1793. Jefferson. *The Writings of*—. Ford ed., Vol. 6, p. 154.

23. James Madison noted with especial satisfaction that Wythe was Chairman of this second Richmond meeting. "A circumstance which will not be without its weight, especially as he presided at the former meeting in favor of the Proclamation." Wythe's presidence over the meeting had precious little weight with Washington, however, who regarded the proceedings with a particularly sour light. James Madison to Robert R. Livingston, 10 August, 1795, in, *The Writings of*—, Hunt, ed., Vol. 6, p. 237.

24. Virginia Gazette and General Advertiser. 5 August 1795. Richmond.

25. 3 August 1795, Mount Vernon, in, Washington. *The Writings of*—. Ford ed., Vol. 13, p. 85.

26. Wythe had plenty of humility and did not hesitate to ask for information from others about the law when he needed to. An example is the following: "Gentlemen, desiring to know your opinion upon a point of law in a case depending before the high court of chancery, i have stated the question for that purpose, and directed the clerk of that court to wait on you with it. i am, with undissembled veneration, gentlemen, your obedient humble servant G. Wythe, june, 1789." Wythe to Hon. James Mercer, Chief Justice and other members of the General Court. Manuscript Collection. New York Public Library.

27. John James Maund to—. William and Mary—. First Series, Vol. 20, p. 278.

28. Virginia. High Court of Chancery. *Decisions of Cases in Virginia by the*—. Minor edition, p. 212, et sequor.

29. Henry Clay to B. Minor. 3 May 1851. Ashland, in, "Memoir of the Author" in, Virginia. High Court of Chancery. *Decisions of Cases in Virginia by the*—. Minor ed., p. xxiii.

30. Richard Randolph. Last will and Testament. Will Book of 1797, Clerk's Office, Prince Edward County, Virginia.

31. John Adams to Christopher Gadsden, 16 April 1801, in, *The Works of*—. C. F. Adams ed., Vol. 9, p. 584.

32. John Adams to William Wirt, 5 January 1818, Quincy, in, John P. Kennedy. *Memoirs of the life of William Wirt*—. (Philadelphia, Lee & Blanchard, 1850), Vol. 2, frontispiece.

33. Noble E. Cunningham, Jr. *The Jeffersonian Republicans.* (Chapel Hill, 1957), p. 151.

34. 2 February 1800. Manuscript Collection. Library of Congress.

35. Jefferson. *Anas.* in, *The Writings of*—. Ed. by H. A. Washington. (Washington, Taylor & Maury, 1854), Vol. 9, p. 205.

CHAPTER XII

Poison brings the end.

Going back to the middle of the American Revolution, Jefferson had tried to disestablish the Anglican Church in Virginia. In this he failed partially and succeeded partially. The public moneys which went to the support of that Church were suspended, and as time went on further attacks were made on its public nature by the Dissenters, the Baptist and Presbyterian groups in the state. Pendleton and Henry, aided from time to time by Richard Henry Lee, fought a valiant battle to save the old Church, but it was a losing fight. It had been brought about that in January of 1777, while Pendleton was Speaker of the House of Delegates, the Anglican Church was incorporated, and thereby it was maintained that its property, consisting of glebes, churches, rectories, church plate, and so forth, was legally secure. But this act was repealed some 10 years later almost to the day, the attacks of the Free Churches and Jeffersonians having continued.

The extent of the hostility to the Church, which by now by its act of adopting a new name in the Convention in Chestertown, Maryland, was now called the Episcopal Church (a convention over which the Reverend William Smith presided) is indicated by the following incident related by Bishop Meade:

> "Your uncle was the foremost and the most liberal in the effort at resuscitation. . . . He applied, for a contribution toward building a church, to a good Christian man in the neighborhood, who had been a soldier of the Revolution, to which the old Veteran replied, the fire of '76 flashing in his eye . . . 'No! I drew my sword once to put that church down; and, if necessary, I will draw it again to keep it down.' "[1]

The Church had been allied with the English government; its ruler was the Bishop of London and it received its new ministers from England for the most part. Often the Bishop unloaded rather unworthy men on the Virginian

Church. When the Revolution came, the connection was broken, and the Church entered on a decline from which only heroic labor could save it. When the Revolution began, there were some 91 ministers, who had 164 churches and chapels under their care. When it ended, there was a total of 28 ministers serving the Divine cause in the more settled parts of the state. Nor could the church very well expect new recruits to its ministry. The position of the clergy was so low that able and strong young men were deflected into more lucrative and pleasant callings. The Anglican Church, in short, was a broken thing.

The fight to strip it completely of its property lasted some 29 years, and ended with a total victory for the Dissenting groups, allied as they were with the Deists. In 1802, on 12 Jan., the Virginia Assembly passed an act that empowered the public officials to sell the glebe lands for the benefit of the poor of the community. Out of this act came the famous case of Turpin *et al* Vs. Locket *et al*. In the parish of Manchester, the public officials sold the lands of the church, and the Vestry and Church-wardens asked for a decree from Chancellor Wythe's court to enjoin against the sale. The lawyers the Church hired were celebrated for their ability—Bushrod Washington, Edmund Randolph and John Wickham. The argument of the overseers of the Poor (for these were the public officials involved) was that the Vestry could not produce a title to the lands by the Church, and they certainly were not the property of the Vestry. In addition, the law was obvious, the legislature had passed it, and so it was valid. Not this only, but the suit should not be tried in Chancery Court anyway, since that Court took only cases which did not have a complete and adequate remedy in other courts. With these arguments, Wythe agreed. And so the property of the Episcopal Church was stripped from it.

Of course, the Convention of the Episcopal Church in Virginia appealed, Bishop Madison, President of Wm. & Mary himself bringing the suit to the Supreme Court of Appeals. Now came one of the unfortunate happenings of the Church's history. For on the Court were Pendleton, a strong Churchman, Carrington, Lyons, Roane and Fleming. Fleming believed that he was too much involved personally, and so refused to sit on the bench while the case was being heard. Judges Carrington and Lyons both believed that the Assembly's Act of 1802 was unconstitutional. As did Pendleton. But so long did Pendleton delay, in his thinking over the decision, that death came to him the very night before he was to give it.[2] Had he lived, the decision would have been three to one, in favor of the Episcopal Church. But he died and in his place on the bench was put one of Wythe's pupils, St. George Tucker.

The main argument was over whether or not to sustain Wythe's decision that the question was not a proper one for the Chancery Court to decide. And the ultimate decision of the Appeals Court was that Wythe was right.

The Chancellor was now become a very old man. He lived what must have been a happy life, estranged from most society—certainly from the gay and luxurious social life of the monied people of Richmond. Staid in his simplicity, he continued, as old people are wont to do, to wear the clothing of his younger days—for in this he did not follow the French Revolution. The Virginians of that day aped the French egalitarians not only in their address of "Citizen" but in their clothing also—the most notable part of which were the pantaloons which now came into fashion. But Wythe continued to wear the short trousers which were gathered at the knee.

> "His dress was a single-breasted black broadcloth coat, with a stiff collar turned over slightly at the top, cut in front Quaker fashion; a long vest, with large pocket-flaps and straight collar, buttoned high on the breast, showing the ends of the white cravat that filled up the bosom. He wore shorts; silver knee and shoe buckles; was particularly neat in his appearance . . ."[3]

He continued his old habit of taking a cold shower, for both summer and winter he drew up the necessary buckets of cold water from the well in the yard and bathed himself in it. Being thus thoroughly awakened by his shower, he would return to the house and there read the newspaper, the Richmond Enquirer, having rung the bell for his breakfast.

Wythe's most cherished entertainment was, as always, his Chancery Court work. But he did have friends, two of them clergymen—Mr. Buchanan, a Scotsman, who was the Episcopal minister, and Mr. Blair, who was the Presbyterian. Since St. John's Church (as it came to be called) was on the far hill opposite, and a journey to it necessitated a hard walk down the ravine and up the other hill, services on Sundays were held in the legislative chamber of the Capitol. Each minister officiated on alternate Sundays in this hall, which had seen Patrick Henry declaim on the British Debt cases, and would in a short time hold the copious oratory of the lawyers engaged in trying Aaron Burr, when that gentleman was accused by a hostile Jefferson of plotting treason against the United States.

Another of Wythe's friends was Burwell Bassett, whom he had known from Revolutionary days. Wythe and he and the two clergymen used often in clement weather to sit in the yard of Wythe's house on Grace and Fifth Streets, and, enjoying the fine view, read the Greek and Latin poets—for they were all Classical scholars. Dr. James McClurg, an old friend and fellow laborer, lived not far away and used often to visit Wythe. Wythe's neighbor, Major William Duval, also gave the old man the benefit of his company. Now Wythe's old companion of Williamsburg days, John Page, was Governor of the State and so a resident of Richmond. Thus Wythe's declining years were very often enlivened by the friends of his earlier days.

Wythe, at this time, feeling that he was not too old to learn, studied Hebrew under Rabbi Isaac B. Seixas, the Rabbi of Congregation Beth Shalome. And he was able thereby to read the Bible in the original, spending many hours puzzling out the old Hebrew text, since he believed this was the only way to discover the true meaning.

As Wythe grew older he became ever more odd and withdrawn from the world of events. This was noticed by William Browne writing to Mr. Joseph Prentis, Jr., on 24 September 1804. Writing to Prentis in Williamsburg from his home in Richmond, Browne observed Wythe's habits:

> ". . . I have . . . marked great eccentricity in some of our public characters. The venerable Wythe is the one who has fallen more immediately under my Eye as he has been for some days engaged at the Capitol, he appears to me to be little remote from insanity, notwithstanding a man so borne down with infirmities he passed thro' a hard rain down to the Capitol on Sunday last . . . when we look at him so venerable is his appearance and with such unsullied dignity he behaves, he involuntarily . . . commands the low bow of respect, such is the man who notwithstanding his imperfections, yet seems to have gained the esteem of all his citizens."[4]

By this time Wythe's labors in his Court were not so arduous as they had been formerly, for in 1802, the Assembly had divided Virginia into three Chancery districts, and Wythe was given the Richmond district, the other two Chancellors being stationed at Williamsburg and Staunton. The pay for all his years of work was still not very much. Of course he lived simply, and it is well he did, for the other chancellors, newly-appointed, found that while the honor was great, the pay was small.

> "This honour of being a Chancellor is a very empty thing, stomachically speaking, that is, although a man be full of honour his stomach may be empty; or in other words, honour will not go to market and buy a peck of potatoes . . . It is possible that I may, like Mr. Wythe, grow old in judicial honours and Roman poverty. I may die beloved, reverenced almost to canonization by my country, and my wife and children, as they beg for bread, may have to boast that they were mine. . . ."[5]

Thus Chancellor Wirt to his friend Dabney Carr in 1803.

But poor or not, the old man was honored. For the city of Richmond was almost entirely Republican. And again, Wythe was chosen as a member of Virginia's Electoral College, and again he voted for Jefferson for President in the election of 1804. Some months earlier, there had been on 4 March of that year (which was the old time for the taking of the oath of office by an incoming United States President) a banquet at the Bell Tavern, which celebrated the fourth year of Jefferson's ascendancy, the jubilation lasting all the day long.

In the morning the cannon on Capitol Hill roared out their salute, and orations and declamations by politicians and school children followed. The affair had a sort of Fourth of July air, and truly that was to the Republicans a Fourth of July, for their hero had brought them into the political promised land and true democracy seemed assured. In the late afternoon, a most elegant dinner was held at the Washington Tavern, the most respectable inhabitants of the city being in attendance. These included the then Governor John Page (Wythe's old friend of Revolutionary Days), Judge Nelson, Dr. William Foushee, Wythe's neighbor, Major William Duval, and many another hero of democracy. And, of course, the celebration wasn't complete without Chancellor Wythe. The assembled company gave the first toast of the day to the day itself—"The 4th of March, The day on which the will of the people prevailed against the intrigues of party and schemes of ambition." (Just as though the Jeffersonian party didn't now have intrigues and schemes of ambition of its own, now that it was in office and the Federalists were out.) The feasting went on, however, with the toasts following one another, accompanied with three cheers and three salutes from the guns. And so on. The bands played, the politicians orated, and feasters drank toasts.

In the course of the festivities, Governor Page, old friend of both Jefferson and Wythe, and now governor of the State, proposed a toast to Wythe himself. And the assembled company gave nine cheers to Page's words:

> "George Wythe, distinguished alike for his wisdom and integrity as a magistrate, and his zeal and disinterestedness as a patriot."[6]

Nine cheers—as many as were given even for Thomas Jefferson himself.

But such celebrations were a rare thing in Wythe's life. Mostly he lived withdrawn from the world. Because of his age, and since he had no children of his own, he brought to live with him in his home in Richmond his grand-nephew, George Wythe Sweeney, a descendant of his sister. This boy, together with Lydia Broadnax, and Michael Brown, a colored child whom Wythe was educating, and a servant man, Benjamin, comprised his household in his later years.

So involved was Wythe with the law and with the Classics that they often became inextricably intermingled in his decisions. To the children born of a later generation, who had little in the way of the old style education, Wythe's decisions must have seemed insane indeed. His fellow citizens called him "the walking library," so replete with Homer, Cicero, Milton was he. In one of his decrees, he quoted on 18 September 1805 from the Institutes of Justinian, the Odyssey of Homer, Xenophon, and Euripides' Alcestis. And again, when in May, 1804, he decreed on the will of Patrick Henry, on what his daughter, Martha Henry Fontaine, was to receive from the estate, he alluded to the Parable of the laborers in the vineyard, from the Gospel according to St. Matthew, chapter 20, and from Milton, saying:

> the effusion of
> > 'a grateful mind
> > which owing owes not, but still pays,
> > At once indebted and discharged.'[7]

To this verse is given at the bottom of the page (all in Wythe's printed writing) the footnote:

Paraphrase by Milton of 'commode autem quicumque dicit:
"pecuniam qui habeat, non redidisse; qui reddiderit, non habere: gratiam autem et qui retulerit, habere; et qui habeat, retulisse." Cicero de officiis, liber 2, caput 20. One, whoever he

was, said well, "a debitor before paiment, may have the money due, and have it not after paiment, but he, who is grateful, both hath what he paieth, and paieth what he hath." The same sentiment occurs in this passage.

"Dissimilis est pecuniae debitio et gratiae, nam qui autem debet, aes retinet alienum, gratiam autem et qui refert habet; et qui habet, in eo ipso quod habet, refert." Cicero, pro Cnaeus Plancio, caput 19. And he gives credit where it is due: ". . . for which i was obliged to Mr. Warden."

Just what all this had to do with the law is far from being easily understood. Either the estate owed Mrs. Fontaine money, or it did not. But how wonderful that the Judges of Virginia should be so learned! Could our present-day judges, even of, let us say, the United States Supreme Court, do as much today?

But whatever the people of his time thought of Wythe's decisions, and however much they may have respected his learning or been puzzled by it, they venerated the old man himself. But there was one who did not. And that one was within his own household. The boy whom he had taken into his home proved to be a disgrace and a thief. He had from time to time stolen books from Wythe's library and peddled them about the city. He was gone from home early morning to sundown, roistering about with evil and dissolute companions. The old man was distressed at this development, and must doubtless have wondered what to do. Should he be sent home? Who then would be the companion of Wythe's old age? But how could he continue to keep this young thief, some seventeen years of age, in his home? The boy had no taste for learning—indeed, the colored child undoubtedly knew more, under Wythe's teaching, of Latin and Greek than did the white boy. What companionship could Sweeney give the old man, when their tases were so disparate?

It is out of this tangled and tragic situation that the final part of the story of George Wythe comes. It is a mystery even today, haunted by gossip and selfishness, and by the most shortsighted legalism and medical incompetence. In the course of his holiganism, it is evident that George Wythe Sweeney had gotten himself deeply in debt. He needed money, and there was only one way for him to get it, and he took that way.

We must go back some three years, to the 20th of April 1803 to discover the way Sweeney had in mind. On that day, his grand uncle wrote his will. The will cited here must be at least a second, for Henry Clay stated he wrote Wythe's will at the old man's dictation when he was the Chancellor's secretary. Since Clay went to Kentucky in 1797, the will he wrote then cannot be this one.

"Contemplating that event, which one in the second year of his sixteenth lustrum may suppose to be fast approaching, at this time, the twentieth day of April in the third year of the nineteenth centurie since the christian epoch, when such is my health of bodie that vivere amen, and yet such my disposition of mind that, convinced of this truth, what Supreme Wisdom destinateth is best, obeam libens, i, George Wythe, of the citie of Richmond, declare what is hereinafter written to be my testament, probablie the last: Appointing my friendlie neighbour William Duval executor, and desiring him to accept fifty pounds for his trouble in performing that office over a commission upon his disbursements and receipts inclusive, i

devise to him the houses and ground in Richmond, which i bought of William Nelson, and my stock in the funds, in trust, with the rents of one and interest of the other, to support my freed woman Lydia Broadnax, and freed man Benjamin, and freed boy Michael Brown, during the lives of the two former, and, after their deaths, in trust to the use of the said Michael Brown: and all the other estate to which i am and shall at the time of my death be intitled, i devise to George Wythe Sweeney the grandson of my sister.
GEORGE [L. S.] WYTHE"[8]

Thus the boy would have been 13 or 14 years old at the time the will was written.

It must be assumed from the will that if Sweeney had not already come to live with his grand uncle, he was about to do so. For the devising of his property was the inducement for the boy to come to Richmond to stay with the old man. At any rate, by this time Wythe had the arrangement well in mind, and the boy either at that time or later came to his home. From a letter written by the former Agnes Gamble, the daughter of one of Wythe's neighbors and now the wife of William H. Cabell, Governor of Virginia and another of Wythe's pupils, we learn that Wythe taught the white boy and the colored child:

"To test the theory that there was no natural inferiority of intellect in the negro, compared with the white man, he had one of his own servant boys and one of his nephews both educated exactly alike. I believe, however, that neither of them did much credit to their teacher."[9]

The last statement is, from other and rather more creditable accounts, simply not true. The colored child was, if George Wythe Munford's account is to be trusted, very skilled in Latin and Greek. "He taught one of his negro boys Latin and Greek, and the rudiments of science."
This latter child, of course, was the Michael Brown mentioned in the will.

How long Sweeney lived with George Wythe can't be discovered but three years after Wythe made the will quoted above, he discovered that the boy was swindling him and warned him to stop or he would revoke the provision for him in the will.

"The young villain [only about 16 or 17] had been in the habit of robbing his uncle with a false-key, had sold three trunks of his most valuable law-books . . ."[10]

Since the servant man, Benjamin, had meanwhile died, and since Wythe desired apparently to remember his old friend Thomas Jefferson, in some way, he added a codicil to his will.

"I, who have hereunder written my name, this nineteenth day of January, in the sixth year of the before mentioned centurie, revoke so much of the preceding devise to George Wythe Sweeney as is inconsistent with what followeth. The residuary estate devised to him is hereby charged with debts and demands. I give my books and small philosophical apparatus to Thomas Jefferson, president of the United States of America: a legacie, considered by my good will to him, the most valuable to him of anything which i have power to bestow. My stock in the funds before mentioned hath been changed into stock in the bank of Virginia. I devise the latter to the same uses, except as to Ben who is dead, as those to which the former was devoted. To the said Thomas Jefferson's patronage i recommend the freed boy Michael Brown in my testament named, for whose maintenance, education or other benefit, as the said Thomas Jefferson shall direct, i will the said bank stock, or the value thereof, if it be changed again, to be disponed. And now,

'Good Lord, most mercifull, let poenitence
Sincere to me restore lost innocence;
In wrath my grievous sins remember not;
My secret faults out of thy record blot;
That, after death's sleep, when i shall awake,
Of pure beatitude i may partake."

GEORGE WYTHE   ******
Seal[11]
******

In about three weeks, the venerable old man added a codicil to the above will—an addition which was to have sad consequences indeed.

"I will that Michael Brown have no more than one half my bank stock, and George Wythe Sweeney have the other immediatelie.
I give to my friend Thomas Jefferson my silver cups and gold headed cane, and to my friend William Duval my silver ladle and tablespoons.
If Michael die before his full age, i give what is devised to him to George Wythe Sweeney. I give to Lydia Broadnax my fuel. This is to be part of my will and as it were written of the parchment inclosed with my name in two places.

GEORGE WYTHE   seal[12]

24 of february 1806

The household lived in seeming content, save for the dissolute boy, who apparently continued his ways despite his grand uncle's admonitions to straighten himself out morally. This he certainly didn't do, for on Tuesday, 27 May, George Wythe Sweeney was charged at a Court of Hustings in Richmond with having forged his uncle's name to several checks which he presented for payment at the Bank of Virginia. One of the checks was for $500.; another was for $100.[13] The very clerk of Wythe's own High Court of Chancery had caught the boy in his swindling, and had carried the several checks to the old Chancellor who, according to Tinsley's testimony on June 2, 1806, had stated that he "hadn't drawn or signed more than one of them." The boy was accordingly put into jail on this charge of forgery. Sweeney asked that Wythe bail him out, but this the old gentleman refused to do. The reason for the refusal of this otherwise kindly and generous old man was apparent to all who knew the circumstances. For at that very moment when Sweeney was so charged, the 81-year old Chancellor lay on his sickbed, horribly tortured by arsenic—arsenic which was presumably given him by the very nephew who now asked to be bailed out of jail.

It is comparatively easy to trace the boy's movements before this date since the records of the court examination of the witnesses are still extant.[14] The examination at the Court of Hustings took place, this time for murder, first of

all on 18 June before Mayor Carrington and two other magistrates, and secondly the more formal presentment on 23 June. Here it is worthy to note that
only white persons were allowed to testify. The colored servants of Wythe's
household (who alone were privy to what had happened in the Wythe home)
were prevented from giving their testimony since the law forbade that colored
persons should give evidence against whites. In any case, one of the negroes
who could have testified was dead, presumably from the same dose of poison
that felled Wythe himself.

The first witness was Tarlton Webb who stated that some two or three weeks
prior to 27 May, that is, in the period from 7 May to 13 May, Sweeney had
approached him on the subject of ratsbane.[15] Webb's statement reveals that the
adolescent Sweeney was tortured by worry and fear, for Webb declared that
Sweeney had come to Webb on 26 May (the day before he was taken on the
charge of forgery) and had showed him a paper envelope or bag containing ratsbane. Sweeney told Webb that he (Sweeney) was going to kill himself. It is indi-
cative of Sweeney's state of mind that he offered to give Webb some too if the
latter wanted to commit suicide.

A further witness was one William Rose, the jailer of Richmond. Incredibly,
in view of what we know, but not incredibly in view of what the jailer at the
time didn't know, when Sweeney was taken to the jail (being at that time
charged only with forgery) he wasn't searched. But on 28 May, Rose's servant
girl, Pleasant, found in the garden a paper full of arsenic which had obviously
been—from its position—thrown over the jail wall. The moment this was
found, Rose recalled that he had touched the pockets of the accused and felt
therein a heavy packet of paper. Knowing nothing at all about the old Chancellor's sickness, Rose supposed that this was perhaps a few pieces of change
wrapped in paper. The rescued package containing the arsenic was then shown
to Webb who admitted that it and the substance which Sweeney had shown him
on 26 May were alike.

Yet another witness was brought forward by the Commonwealth, Samuel
McCraw, who declared that he had on 1 June gone to George Wythe's house to
attest to a new will that Wythe had had drawn up. While there, the old Chancellor asked him to search Sweeney's room. McCraw and the others present did
so, and found there a "quire of blotting paper" which was identical to that
paper in which the arsenic found in the garden was contained. Further, in the
same room were found a few strawberries over which arsenic had apparently
been sprinkled. Not only this, but also a glass was discovered which had contained a liquid, now dried, which was a compound of arsenic and sulphur.

And so it went. Witness after witness traced Sweeney's movements and
speech in the days prior to the arrest for forgery and his actions in the jail after
the arrest. (He had apparently been taken by the police officer in Wythe's house
where, at that moment his grand uncle lay tortured by the first beginnings of his
pain. Sweeney probably had gone home after disclosing his state of mind to

Webb, and must have been in a wild turmoil indeed, since he offered some of the arsenic to Webb '. . . if he wanted to die.')

But the witness who gave the most important (if hearsay) testimony was William Claiborne. For he told the Court what Wythe himself had said about the case. Claiborne had gone to the Wythe home on Wednesday, the day after Sweeney had been jailed on suspicion of forgery. Wythe then told Claiborne that he had been "as well as usual" in the early hours of the previous Sunday morning. Wythe, as we know from other sources, rose at daybreak, took his shower, dressed, rang for his breakfast and ate it. This was his invariable custom, and on that Sunday, it being Pentecost, there is no reason to believe that he changed his routine. The aged, after all, usually do not like to vary their habits. Wythe informed Claiborne that right after breakfast he came down with a sickness which he diagnosed as cholera morbus. This was accompanied with a powerful form of diarrhea ". . . a violent lax, went forty times that day, and had at least fifteen large evacuations . . ." Wythe further stated that he had eaten strawberries and milk the evening before. It is, of course, quite natural to assign the cause of a sickness to "something I ate." And this apparently was what Wythe was doing, since he had, at that time, with his trusting and unsuspecting nature, no reason to believe that he had been poisoned. But Wythe also stated that his servants had likewise been taken ill at that same time. This assertion is not true, for Lydia Broadnax, his housekeeper, was not taken ill until 26 May and Michael Brown not until 27 May. At least so said William Duval in a letter to Thomas Jefferson.

For on 4 June, 1806, William Duval, in great excitement informed Thomas Jefferson of what had happened. That gentleman was, of course, in the White House as President, and had much else to think about, what with the trouble with Britain and the Embargo he had put on the nation's shipping. Duval's letter gave him more to consider, for the letter went:

> "Worthy Sir: Geo. W. Sweeney who lived with Mr. Wythe was committed to gaol on the 27th of May last for forging six checks on the Bank of Virginia. Mr. Wythe was taken with a cholera morbus on the 25th and 27 all the rest of the family were seized with the same violent disorder on the 27 we had no idea that Sweeney had poisoned the whole Family—On Sunday Morning June the first inst. Michael the Mulatto Boy Died—Yellow Arsenic was found in Sweeney's Room and many other strong circumstances concurred to induce a believe he had poisoned the whole family . . . ."[16]

However, Claiborne's testimony went on, *he* at once began to suspect Sweeney of having poisoned the whole family. He, immediately, went to William Duval's house, which was next door, and told him what he suspected. Claiborne formed his opinion on the basis that Sweeney had been taken in forgery and knew that if he was guilty, Wythe would certainly disinherit him. Claiborne evidently knew the prisoner well, for he said that he had often told Sweeney that Wythe would make good provision for him if he would only behave himself. Only the death of Wythe could now prevent Sweeney's being disinherited. And according to Claiborne's deposition, Wythe on that Wednesday also had come to believe that he had been poisoned, for Wythe said that his executor should search Sweeney's trunk. All through the account, Wythe was apparently asking that Sweeney's room and effects be searched, but no one seems to have done so until McCraw performed this service on 1 June, exactly one week after Wythe was taken with the illness.

It should be noted that Duval wrote to Jefferson only on 4 June, or some eleven days *after* Wythe was taken ill. In his letter, Duval went on to tell Jefferson that on Sunday Evening of 25 May, he had gone to Wythe's home and found him ill. He wrote that Wythe had said ". . . he never suffered more in his life—" that in the morning he attended to his Official Duties, the Chancery Court being in Session, that he ate his Breakfast as usual, that about Nine O'Clock in the Morning he was attacked in the most violent manner." Unless Duval meant by 'Official Duties' the going over or studying of various Chancery Papers, then he was guilty of error, for the average person would take the expression 'Official Duties' to mean the actual attendance on the Chancery Court, which during the month of May was in session. And certainly it wouldn't have been in session on Sunday morning. In all the conflicting testimony, not one person has testified that Wythe was taken ill on any morning other than Sunday. And so it must have been. The point is that Duval could be mistaken in this fact of "Official Duties." And if in this, then in other facts as well. Including the time of the servants' falling ill. It is just possible that Wythe and consequently Claiborne was right—that the servants also fell ill on that Sunday morning.

In his letter to Jefferson Duval also stated that he called on Wythe in the *evening* of that day. That means that Wythe had been suffering—"more than he ever had before in his life"—from nine o'clock in the morning until the evening. Then, says Duval, "I had Doctors McClurg, Currie and McCaw to attend him—." By McCaw's testimony, the doctors came between 4 and 5 o'clock. It is difficult to believe that all three members of the Wythe Household could be so very ill without doctors being called before the evening. Even if Wythe himself could have stoically endured the pain without any remedy, is it sensible in the light of what we know of his character to believe that he would not have called in medical assistance for Lydia and Michael?

We must turn next to a source somewhat more romantic than that of a court of law—to a work entitled *The Two Parsons*. This was written many years after the event by George Wythe Munford, the son of William Munford. The two parsons were, of course, the ones we've met before: Buchanan and Blair.

"One morning" (the account by Munford doesn't say Sunday morning) Buchanan knocked on the door of Blair's house and told him that Chancellor Wythe ". . . is thought . . . poisoned."

"Poisoned!" said the good man. "I saw him but a day or two ago, and he was uncommonly well and cheerful. Who could have perpetrated such a deed?"

"I hear it was his own nephew, George Wythe Sweeney." (If this *was* on Sunday morning and not just on "one" morning, then the story is already demonstrably false, for no one on Sunday suspected that Sweeney had done any poisoning.) However the account continues: "Dr. Foushee called . . . The Doctor has been to see him twice already.—the last time in consultation with Dr. McCaw . . ." (If this took place on Monday morning, then Dr. Foushee had been called in during some time Sunday, as well as Sunday evening, even though Duval did not mention him. For Dr. McCaw with the other two who *were* mentioned, Drs. McClurg and Currie, went, (as Duval has pointed out) to visit Wythe on Sunday evening.) Buchanan then continued to recount ostensibly to Dr. Blair what Dr. Foushee had told him, including Lydia Broadnax' story. This was that "Mass George Sweeney came here yesterday, as he sometimes does when old master is at court, and went into his room, and finding his keys in the door of his private desk, he opened it, and when she went in, she found him reading a paper that her old master had told her was his will. It was tied with a blue ribbon. Mass George said his uncle had sent him to read that paper, and tell him what he thought of it. Then he went away, and, after the Chancellor had gone to bed, came back again late at night, and went to the room he always stays in when he sleeps here. In the morning, when breakfast was nearly ready, he came into the kitchen and said, 'Aunt Lydy, I want you to give me a cup of coffee and some bread, because I haven't time to stay to breakfast.' She said, 'Mass George, breakfast is nearly ready; I have only got to poach a few eggs, and make some toast for old master; so you had better stay and eat with him.' "No," he said, "I'll just take a cup of hot coffee now, and you can toast me a slice of bread."

"He went to the fire, and took the coffee-pot to the table, while I was toasting the bread. He poured out a cupful for himself and then set the pot down. I saw him throw a little white paper in the fire. He then drank the coffee he had poured out for himself, and ate the toast with some fresh butter. He told me good-bye and went about his business. I didn't think there was anything wrong then."

"In a little while I heard old master's bell. He always rings it when he is ready for his breakfast; so I carried it up to him. He poured out a cup of coffee for himself, took his toast and eggs, and ate and drank while he was reading the newspaper."

" 'Lyddy,' said he, 'did I leave my keys in my desk yesterday, for I found them there last night?' "

"I suppose so, master, for I saw Mass George at the desk reading that paper you gave me to put there, and which you said was your will. He said you had sent him to read it, and to tell you what he thought of it."

"Master said, 'I fear I am getting old, Lyddy, for I am becoming more and more forgetful every day. Take these things away, and give Michael his breakfast, and get your own, Lyddy.' "

"I gave Michael as much coffee as he wanted, and then I drank a cup myself. After that, with the hot water in the kettle I washed the plates, emptied the coffee-grounds out and scrubbed the coffee-pot bright, and by that time I became so sick I could hardly see, and had a violent cramp. Michael was sick, too; and old master was as sick as he could be. He told me to send for the doctor. All these things makes me think Mass George must have put something in the coffee-pot. I didn't see him, but it looks monstrous strange."

This is the story which has been called into question by other investigators of Wythe's death. The main reason for questioning its veracity is that 1: Lydia and Michael weren't taken sick the same day Wythe was. But we have seen that only Duval says they weren't, while Claiborne's testimony indicates they were. 2: Dr. Foushee wasn't called in on Sunday. It must be admitted that when Foushee testified in the court examination, he didn't say that he had been called in. He testified only that he was present when Wythe's autopsy was performed. But this doesn't mean he hadn't visited Wythe other times. Indeed, Wythe had told Lydia Broadnax, according to her testimony, to send for the doctor. And that doctor could have been Foushee.

It is true that other parts of the story as related by George Wythe Munford are not accurate. But however that may be, the fact remains that the testimony at the examination of George Wythe Sweeney points so very strongly to poisoning. It was all circumstantial, it is true. Some heard him talk about poison; others found poison in his room; others found a packet thrown over the garden wall of the jail. Others heard him talk of suicide, and so forth. Only one person said she *saw* "him throw a little white paper in the fire" immediately after being near the coffee pot. But strawberries covered with arsenic were found in the boy's room.

If we can trust the Munford chronicle, and while untrustworthy in some respects, its overall veracity has the strong sound of truth, the old man died with trust in God in his heart and forgiveness for his murderer on his lips, and with the sign of faith in the sight of his friends. When the two clergymen first came to him—presumably in the first stages of his illness—he told them that an old man could not continue to suffer so and still live. The doctor's medicines had been as yet of no relief. He must have already suspected that he was poisoned, for he told them he did not fear death. That would come in any case since he was now by the standards of the day a very old man. But that one of his name should have brought about his death would be a stigma on the Wythe family, and that he regretted. Typically, he mourned that his sister's grandchild would have brought such sorrow to the family.

The suspicion that George Wythe Sweeney had poisoned him deepened into strong belief, for the aged Chancellor sent for his old friend and comrade of the Revolution, Edmund Randolph, to write a last codicil to his will. This was accordingly done, and in it he disenherited the ingrate who had brought obloquy to his name, sorrow to his family, and an end to his life.

"In the name of God, Amen!

I George Wythe, of the city of Richmond, having heretofore made my last will on the 20th April, in the third year of the nineteenth century since the christian epoch, and a codicil hereto on the 19th day of January, the sixth year of the aforesaid century, and another codicil on the 24th day of February 1806, do ordain and constitute the following to be a third codicil to my said will; hereby revoking the said wills and codicils in all the devises and legacies in them or either of them contained, relating to, or in any manner concerning George Wythe Sweeney, the grandson of my sister; but I confirm the said will and codicils in all other parts, except as to the devise and bequest to Michael Brown, in the said will mentioned, who, I am told, died this morning, and therefore they are void. And I do hereby devise and bequeath all the estate, which I have therein devised or bequesthed in trust for, or to the use of the said Michael Brown, to the brothers and sisters of the said George Wythe Sweeney, the grand-children of my said sister, to be equally divided among them, share and share alike. In testi-

mony whereof I have hereunto subscribed my name and affixed my seal, this first day of
June, in the year 1806."

G. WYTHE

****
* Seal *
****

"Signed, sealed, published and declared by the said George Wythe the testator as and for his
last will and testament in our presence; and at his desire we have unto subscribed our names
and witnesses, in his presence and in the presence of each other.
(The interlineations of the words, 'and another codicil on the 24th of February 1806,' and of
the words 'will and codicils' and 'grand' being first made; and the whole being distinctly
read to the testator, before the execution of this codicil.)

Edm. Randolph,
Wm. Price,
Samuel Greenhow,
Sam'l McGraw"[18]

Upon the envelope in which the foregoing parchment was placed, the old man
apparently had still enough strength to write:

"To William Duval,
to be opened when G. Wythe shall
cease to breathe, unless by him required
before that event."

The city of Richmond waited from hour to hour and from day to day to learn
that the old patriot had gone to his death. But day after day he continued his
painful life. The health habits of exercise, temperance, and self-control of a lifetime kept his body, now racked with the most hideous pain, yet alive when
surely he must often have wished for the relief of death. The daily visitors were,
as ever, his two beloved friends, the Parsons Buchanan and Blair, who together
prayed with him for everlasting mercy. When he expressed his gratitude for
their presence, the one replied that there was

". . . a better Friend than either of us . . . He has gone before to prepare mansions for us in
a better home than this."

To which the other added

"He is the staff that will not break, nor pierce the hand that leans upon it."

And the man who had spent his life in Deism had also in these last moments
come around to his old faith, for he answered

"This is my consolation."

When finally they left, they told the dying patriarch:

"We hope to see you again. God be with you."

The answer came:

"Not in this world."
"And they passed out sorrowing."[19]

Finally, on the 8th day of June, came the moment for which the citizens had been fearfully waiting. The old man sank into merciful unconsciousness when his two friends came to visit, and shortly afterwards died. The bells of the city's churches rang out the sorrowful news, and the people of the little town were thus told that George Wythe, Signer and Chancellor, had gone.

The body of the dead man was at once cut open, as the Chancellor had requested. Samuel McCraw had testified that the old man, as he lay twisted with pain, had told the onlookers to cut him open—at first they had thought he meant they should cut off his clothing. But after, they interpreted his strangled mutterings to mean that he wanted his body examined after his death.[20] The old man could, by this time, give no coherent, understandable signs of exactly what he did want.

But so it was done. The physicians present were, however, equivocal in the matter. The affair demanded caution and they were accordingly most cautious. Dr. James McClurg, Wythe's old companion of the Constitutional Convention, was present and declared that the internal organs, being examined, were "uncommonly bloody." However, it was McClurg's opinion that if arsenic had been the cause of Wythe's death, the old man would have died much sooner than he did.

Dr. James McCaw also stated that he too was present, and thought that Wythe's death might have been caused by a ". . . great accumulation of bile." Dr. William Foushee, however, was willing to admit that arsenic ". . . or any other acrid matter" might have produced the effect they had found in his stomach and intestines.

But not one physician would declare that arsenic positively did destroy the life of George Wythe. Nonetheless, the evidence is too great to allow the fact to escape that George Wythe Sweeney did poison the family. Arsenic was found in copious quantities. And alone of the family, George Wythe Sweeney was undisturbed by any illness, although he too ate at the Wythe house and slept there. If the disease was truly cholera, how could he alone have escaped?

One of the fantastic aspects of this whole fantastic episode is that those responsible for the medical inquiry did not, as far as any evidence has survived, use even the proper methods of their own day to determine the presence of the poison in the remains of either the old Chancellor or the slain child, Michael Brown. True, the modern methods of chemical analysis were beyond them then. But it was possible even in that day to detect evidence of arsenic—even in minute quantities. Somehow the responsible people did not take even this precaution. If they had, the resultant trial would undoubtedly have taken a turn for justice.

Another strange fact is that the funeral of the slain patriot took place almost immediately. He died on 8 June, and on 9 June he was buried. True, the month was June, and no prolonged obsequies were possible in the heat which infests Virginia during that month. Nonetheless, the body could have been preserved for at least three days. But it wasn't. A most impressive funeral was arranged and it took place at once, William Munford being asked to deliver the oration—

> "Kings may require mausoleums to consecrate their memory; saints may claim the privileges of canonization; but the venerable GEORGE WYTHE needs no other monument than the services rendered to his country, and the universal sorrow which that country sheds over his grave."[21]

Wythe was given a state funeral, arranged by the Executive Council. The body lay in state in the Capitol where he had labored so long. As it lay in the Hall of the House of Delegates, Munford pronounced his funeral eulogy at four o'clock in the afternoon. The body was followed to the grave by the highest officials of the Commonwealth: the Governor and his Council, the Officers of the High Court of Chancery, the Judges and lawyers of the city, the Mayor and Common Council, and a great concourse of citizens. The procession wound its way down the ravines from the Capitol and up the side of the neighboring hill to the Church of St. John, in which so many years before Patrick Henry had given his "Give me Liberty" speech. And there—just a short way from the western wall of the Church—the patriot's grave received his body.

Although the statement was made that Wythe needed no monument, it is an historical fact that the Virginians of that day took the statement literally. And he who had done good all his life was not honored by even a tablet, so that today there is no certain knowledge of the exact location of his grave. Of this simple detail, not one of his numerous pupils took care to provide. Not Thomas Jefferson, not Henry Clay, not John Marshall. There is, it is true, a monument there now, but it was placed many years later. Truly, as St. George Tucker said in another context, Socrates himself could have walked abroad through Virginia and nobody would have paid any attention.[22] It is typical that Wythe himself would not have made any provision for a marker while still alive. Probably the thought never occurred to him. And if it occurred to those who had benefitted by his great goodness, they took care to stifle the thought. This was not a generous people.

As far as Wythe's temporal goods were concerned, it was left to his Executor, William Duval, to gather up the bits and pieces and arrange them in order. To Jefferson went, as Wythe had directed, his books and "philosophical apparatus," his silver cups and his gold-headed cane. No part of the apparatus has come down to us, it having been lost in the turmoil of the years. The silver cups are now at Monticello where they may be seen today. Some of the books have survived the years, but precious few. Jefferson incorporated many of them into his own library and some years later this was sold to the nation to found the Library of Congress. In the fires which have plagued the Congressional library since that time, many of Wythe's books have gone to oblivion, although some few still exist and may be seen there now.

The death of his old teacher called from Thomas Jefferson a pure and beautiful tribute:

> ". . . the horror of his falling by the hand of a parricide. Such an instance of depravity has been hitherto known to us only in the fables of the poets . . . . he was my antient master, my earliest & best friend; and to him I am indebted for first impressions which have had the most salutary influence on the course of my life."[23]

The news of Wythe's death did not reach Kentucky until the Fourth of July, where the national holiday was being celebrated at Maxwell's Spring. Henry Clay was the speaker on the occasion, but he could not bring himself, with the news of the death of his great benefactor in his heart, to produce the usual bombastic and perfervid oratory. Instead, he eulogized the Chancellor as "The Wise and Modest Wythe." The toast was made with sadness to the memory of the man—". . . a faithful laborer in the vineyard of the Republic."[24]

But a part of the business remained. For the murderer must be tried. George Wythe Sweeney had been examined and his examiners were convinced that he had committed murder on the body of his grand uncle. He was therefore continued in jail to await trial. The family of the accused boy applied to William Wirt, the lawyer who had some years before been Wythe's colleague as Chancellor and who had abandoned the office as not paying a sufficient salary. Wirt argued himself into taking the case, writing his wife that Judge Nelson, one of Wythe's own relatives, had pointed out to him that the Doctors in the autopsy had said the old man's death was caused "simply by bile and not by poison."[25] Of course, the accused had to be defended. That was Sweeney's simple right under the law, and so somebody had to do it. Wirt found his conscience perfectly clear in the matter, and so, apparently, did Edmund Randolph, the other defense lawyer.

That Wythe had been murdered by Sweeney was apparent to most people. And that justice was not done in this case only proves that in some cases the law is, as Dickens said it was, assinine. Since the only witnesses were negroes and these, by Virginia law, were not allowed to testify against a white man, the case went by default. Lydia Broadnax, for example, was not permitted to testify. Not because she was a slave. She was not, for she had been freed many years before. Rather because she was a negress. Since the medical people who had performed the autopsy would not definitely state that death was caused by arsenic, the accused was given the benefit of the doubt and was freed of the charge of murder. Philip Norborne Nicholas, a former pupil of Wythe, was Attorney General of Virginia then, and therefore the prosecuting attorney in the case. The trial took place on 2 September 1806. And when the various lawyers had finished their arguments, the jury retired and in a few minutes returned their verdict: "Not Guilty." Thus Virginia justice. The charge of murder in the case of Michael Brown brought forth the same verdict.

What arguments were used by the Defense counsel to produce this remarkable verdict will not be known until Judgement Day. The records of the Court were burned, probably, in the fires which flamed up in Richmond when the City was taken by the Union troops during the Civil War, and so we can only conjecture the state of mind which produced this result. Certainly nobody whose testimony was accepted in the law court could say he had *seen* Sweeney put arsenic in Wythe's food, nor would the doctors state unequivocally that arsenic brought about his death. And without these two pieces of evidence, all other evidence was circumstantial. And so George Wythe Sweeney, despite the belief in his guilt of everybody who has written or commented on the case, was free.

Even the earlier indictment of the forged checks was quashed. For his lawyers here argued that the Virginia laws against forgery, passed in 1789, could not punish forgery where a bank was concerned. For no banks existed in Virginia at the time when the law was passed. Therefore the law could not have applied to banks. Not only that, but the law was written as regards "private individuals," and no bank was a private individual. There was much else, a great deal of legal trickery, hocus pocus with a solemn judicial face. But the fact was that George Wythe Sweeney did not spend one hour in jail as punishment even for the forgery charge, being declared innocent even of that.

It is ironical that a man who spent his life serving and defending the cause not of legality, but of justice, as Chancellor George Wythe most certainly did, should not have received justice in his death, being beaten out by legality. But justice of a kind was meted out to his evil grand nephew. For while we do not for certain know what happened to him later, rumours bruited around over the years had it that he wandered out to the West, was caught at horse-stealing, was sent to the penitentiary, and disappeared from all sight.

And, sadly, George Wythe too, after his death, disappeared from not only the sight but also the memory of his fellow Americans. Of his splendid career and of his many works and deeds of patriotism, later generations knew little. Even scholars recalled him only as a name, vague and distant. But he deserves the honor and veneration of his fellow countrymen. For he was a patriot of sternest conviction. For he was again, a lawyer and judge of deepest honesty. And yet again, a scholar of profound learning and gentle humanity. In his country's infancy, all that he was he poured out upon his beloved state and nation, his dear college and honored profession. America has had few men who have served her better.

Notes to Chapter XII

1. David Caldwell to Thomas H. Ellis. No date. Richmond, in, Meade, *Old Churches*—. Vol. 1, p. 463.
2. Mays. *Edmund Pendleton*—. Vol. 2, p. 340 et sequor.
3. George Wythe Munford. *The Two Parsons*—. p. 416.

4. Manuscript Collection. University of Virginia Library.
5. William Wirt, 13 February 1803, Richmond, in, John P. Kennedy. *Memoirs of the Life of William Wirt*—. Vol. 1, p. 86.
6. Richmond Enquirer. 8 March 1805.
7. Virginia. High Court of Chancery. *Decisions*—. Minor Edition. p. xxv.
8. *Ibidem.* p. xxvi.
9. To Mrs. William Wirt, 13 July 1806, in, Kennedy. *Opus citatum,* Vol. 1, p. 141.
10. William Wirt to James Monroe, 10 June 1806. Manuscript Collection. Library of Congress.
11. George Wythe. Will of 19 January 1806, in, "Memoir of the Author," in, Virginia. High Court of Chancery. *Decisions*—. Minor Edition, p. xxxviii–xxxix.
12. George Wythe. Codicil of 24 February 1806, in, *Ibidem.*
13. George Wythe Munford. *Opus citatum,* p. 421.
14. William E. Hemphill. "Examinations of George Wythe Swinney for Forgery & Murder: A Documentary Essay," in Julian P. Boyd and Edwin Hemphill. *The Murder of George Wythe. Two Essays.* (Williamsburg, Institute of Early American History and Culture, 1955), p. 43.
15. *Ibidem.* p. 44.
16. Manuscript Collection. Library of Congress.
17. George Wythe Munford. *Opus citatum,* p. 422 et sequor.
18. George Wythe. Will of 1 June 1806, in, "Memoir of the Author," in, Virginia. High Court of Chancery. *Decisions*—. Minor Edition, p. xxxviii–xxxix.
19. George Wythe Munford. *Opus citatum,* p. 425 et sequor.
20. Hemphill. "Examinations—," p. 46 et sequor.
21. Richmond Enquirer. 10 June 1806.
22. To William Wirt, 4 April 1813, Williamsburg, in, Kennedy. *Opus citatum,* Vol. 1, p. 316.
23. To William Duvall, 14 June 1806, Washington. Manuscript Collection. Library of Congress.
24. Kentucky Gazette. 8 July and 11 August 1806.
25. Kennedy. *Opus citatum,* Vol. 1, p. 142.

Bibliography

Ambler, Charles H. *Sectionalism in Virginia from 1776 to 1851.* Chicago, University of Chicago Press, 1910).

Ambler, Charles H. *Thomas Ritchie: A Study in Virginia Politics.* (Richmond, Bell Book & Stationery Company, 1913).

American Archives: consisting of a collection of authentick records, state papers, debates, and letters and other notices of publick affairs, the whole forming a documentary history of the origin and progress of the North American colonies; of the causes and accomplishments of the American revolution, and of the constitution of government for the United States to the final ratification thereof in six series. Edited by Peter Force. (Washington, M. St. Clair Clarke & Peter Force, 1837–53).

Adams, John. *The Works of—, Second President of the United States: with a life of the author, notes and illustrations, by his grandson Charles Francis Adams.* 10 Vols. (Boston, Little, Brown & Co., 1859–).

Adams, John. *Adams-Jefferson Letters. The Complete Correspondence between Thomas Jefferson and Abigail and John Adams.* Edited by Lester J. Cappon. (Chapel Hill, University of North Carolina Press, 1959).

Adams, John. *Diary and Autobiography.* Series 1 of the Adams Papers. Edited by Lyman H. Butterfield. 4 Vols. (Cambridge, Harvard University Press, 1961).

Adams, John. *Family Correspondence.* Series 2 of The Adams Papers. Edited by Lyman H. Butterfield. 2 Vols. (Cambridge, Harvard University Press, 1963).

Alden, John Richard. *The First South.* (Baton Rouge, Louisiana State University Press, 1961).

Alden, John Richard. *The South in the Revolution, 1763–1789.* (Baton Rouge, Louisiana State University Press, 1957).

Anderson, Dice Robins. *William Branch Giles: A Study in the Politics of Virginia and the Nation from 1790 to 1830.* (Menasha, Wisc., George Banta Pub. Co., 1914).

Axelrad, Jacob. *Patrick Henry, the Voice of Freedom.* (New York, Random House, 1947).

Ballagh, James Curtis. *A History of Slavery in Virginia.* (Baltimore. Johns Hopkins Press, 1902).

Bancroft, George. *The History of the United States from the Discovery of the Continent.* 5th ed., 6 Vols. (New York, D. Appleton & Co., 1883–85).

Bates, Ralph S. *Scientific Societies in the United States.* (New York, J. Wiley & Sons, 1945).

Beveridge, Albert Jeremiah. *The Life of John Marshall.* 4 Vols. (Boston, Houghton Mifflin, 1916–19).

Blake, William. *Complete Writings, with all the variant readings.* Edited by Geoffrey Keynes. (New York, Random House, 1935).

Bodley, Temple. *George Rogers Clark, his life and public services.* (Boston, Houghton Mifflin, 1926).

Bowen, Catherine D. *John Adams and the American Revolution.* (Boston, Little Brown & Co., 1950).

Bowers, Claude Gernade. *The Young Jefferson, 1743–1789.* (Boston, Houghton Mifflin, 1945).

Boyd, Julian P. *The Murder of George Wythe, Two Essays.* (Williamsburg, Va., Institute of Early American History and Culture, 1955).

Brant, Irving. *James Madison.* (Indianapolis, Bobbs-Merrill, 1941).

Bridenbaugh, Carl & Jessica. *Rebels and Gentlemen. Philadelphia in the Age of Franklin.* (New York, Reynal and Hitchock, 1942).

Bridenbaugh, Carl. *Seat of Empire. The Political Role of Eighteenth Century Williamsburg.* (Colonial Williamsburg, Inc., 1958).

Brock, Robert Alonzo. *Virginia and Virginians, Eminent Virginians, executives of the colony of Virginia, from Sir Thomas Smyth to Lord Dunmore, Executives of the State of Virginia, from Patrick Henry to Fitzhugh Lee. Sketches of Generals Ambrose Powell Hill, Robert E. Lee, Thomas Jonathan Jackson, Commodore Maury.* By Dr. —, secretary of the Virginian Historical Society. History of Virginia from the Settlement of Jamestown to the close of the Civil War written by Prof. Virgil Lewis. (Richmond & Toledo, H. H. Hardisty, 1888).

Brock, Robert K. *Archibald Cary of Ampthill, Wheelhorse of the Revolution.* (Richmond, Garrett & Massie, 1937).

Brown, Alexander. *The Cabells & Their Kin. A Memorial Volume of History, Biography & Genealogy.* (Boston, Houghton Mifflin, 1895).

Bruce, William Cabell. *John Randolph of Roanoke, 1773–1833.* A Biography based largely on New Material. 2 Vols. (New York and London, G. P. Putnam's Sons, 1922).

Brydon, George Maclaren. *Virginia's Mother Church and the Political Conditions under which it grew. An Interpretation of the Records of the Colony of Virginia and of the Anglican Church of that Colony 1607–1727.* (Richmond, Virginia Historical Society, 1947).

Burk, John Daly. *History of Virginia from its First Settlement to the Present Day.* 4 Vols., (Petersburg, Va., Dickson & Pescud, 1804–16).

Burnaby, Andrew. *Travels Through the Middle Settlements in North America in the Years 1759 and 1760 with observations Upon the State of the Colonies.* 3rd ed. (London, T. Payne, 1798).

Burnett, Edmund Cody. *The Continental Congress.* (New York, Macmillan, 1941).

Burnett, Edmund Cody, editor. *Letters of the Members of the Continental Congress.* 8 Vols. (Washington, D. C., Carnegie Institution of Washington, 1921–36).

Campbell, John W. *History of Virginia to 1781 with Biographical Sketches of all the most distinguished Characters that occur in the Colonial, Revolutionary or Subsequent Period of our History.* (Petersburg, Va., J. W. Campbell, 1813).

Campbell, William W. *Annals of Tryon County.* (New York, Dodd, Mead & Co., 1831, reprinted 1924).

Chandler, Julian Albin Carroll and T. B. Thames. *Colonial Virginia.* (Richmond, Times-Dispatch, 1907).

Chastellux, Francois Jean, Marquis de. *Travels in North America, in the Years 1780, 1781, & 1782.* (New York, White, Gallaher & White, 1828).

Chastellux, Francois Jean, Marquis de. *Travels in North America, in the Years 1780, 1781, and 1782.* A Rev'd ed., with introduction and Notes by Howard C. Rice, Jr. 2 Vols. (Chapel Hill, University of North Carolina Press, 1963).

Chumbley, George Lewis. *Colonial Justice in Virginia. The Development of a Judicial System. Typical laws and Cases of the Period.* (Richmond, Dietz Press, 1938).

Closen, Ludwig, Baron von. *Revolutionary Journal, 1780–1783.* Trans. and Edited with an Introduction by Evelyn M. Acomb. (Chapel Hill, University of North Carolina Press, 1958).

Cobbett, William. *Porcupine's Works, containing various writings and selections, exhibiting a faithful picture of the United States of America, of their government, laws, politics, and resources; of the character of their presidents, governors, legislators, magistrates and military men and of their customs, manners, morals, religion, virtues, and vices of the people, comprising also a complete series of historical documents and remarks, from the end of the war in 1783 to the election of the President in March 1801.* 12 Vols. (London, Cobbett & Morgan, 1801).

Coleman, Mary Haldane. *St. George Tucker, Citizen of No Mean City.* (Richmond, Dietz Press, 1938).

Colonial Williamsburg, Inc. *Survey Report.* Colonial Williamsburg, Inc. Number 2396.

Colonial Williamsburg, Inc. *Wythe House Report.* No date.

Colton, Calvin. *Life, Correspondence and Speeches of Henry Clay.* 6 Vols. (New York, A. S. Barnes & Co., 1857).

Conway, Moncure Daniel. *Omitted Chapters of History, disclosed in the Life and Papers of Edmund Randolph.* (New York, G. P. Putnam's Sons, 1888).

Cunningham, Noble E., Jr. *The Jeffersonian Republicans. The Formation of Party Organization, 1789–1801.* (Chapel Hill, University of North Carolina Press, 1957).

Davis, Curtis Carroll. *The King's Chevalier. A Biography of Lewis Littlepage.* (Indianapolis & New York, Bobbs-Merrill, 1961).

Delaplaine, Edward Schley. *Life of Thomas Johnson, member of the Continental Congress, First Governor of the State of Maryland and Associate Justice of the United States Supreme Court.* (New York, F. H. Hitchcock, 1927).

De Puy, Henry W. *Ethan Allen and the Green-Mountain Heroes of '76 with a Sketch of the Early History of Vermont.* (Boston, Dayton & Wentworth, 1853).

Dictionary of American Biography. Edited by Allen Johnson. 20 Vols. (New York, Charles Scribner's Sons, 1928).

Dictionary of National Biography. Edited by Sir Leslie Stephen and Sir Sidney Lee. From the Earliest Times to 1900. 22 Vols. (New York, Oxford University Press, 1921–22).

Eaton, Clement. *Freedom of Thought in the Old South.* (Durham, Duke University Press, 1940).

Eaton, Clement. *Henry Clay and the Art of American Politics.* (Boston, Little, Brown & Co., 1957).

Eckenrode, Hamilton James. *The Revolution in Virginia.* (Boston, Houghton Mifflin, 1916).

Elliot, Jonathan, Editor. *The Debates in the Several State Conventions on the Adoption of the Federal Constitution, as Recommended by the General Convention at Philadelphia, in 1787.* 5 Vols. (Philadelphia, J. R. Lippincott, 1836–59).

Embry, Alvin T. *History of Fredericksburg, Virginia.* (Richmond, Old Dominion Press, 1937).

English, William H. *Earliest Virginia. Conquest of the Country Northwest of the River Ohio 1778–1783 and the Life of General George R. Clark.* (Indianapolis, Ind. and Kansas City, Mo., Bowen-Merrill, 1898).

Ezekiel, Herbert T. and Gaston Lichtenstein. *The History of the Jews of Richmond from 1769 to 1917.* (Richmond, Herbert T. Ezekiel, 1917).

Fiske, John. *The American Revolution.* (Boston, Houghton Mifflin, 1902).

Foote, Henry W. *The Religion of Thomas Jefferson.* (Boston, Beacon Press, 1947).

Franklin, Benjamin. *The Complete Works of—, including his private as well as his official and scientific correspondence, and numerous letters and documents now for the first time printed with many others not included in any former collection, also the unmutilated and correct version of his autobiography.* Compiled and Edited by John Bigelow. 10 Vols. (New York, G. P. Putnam's Sons, 1887–88).

Freeman, Douglas Southall. *George Washington. A Biography.* 7 Vols. (New York, Scribner, 1948).

Frothingham, Richard. *The Rise of the Republic of the United States.* 3rd ed. (Boston, Little Brown & Co., 1881).

Gilman, Daniel C. *James Monroe.* (Boston, Houghton Mifflin, 1898).

Goodwin, Edward Lewis. *The Colonial Church in Virginia, with Biographical Sketches of the First Six Bishops of the Diocese of Virginia and other Historical Papers, together with brief biographical sketches of the Colonial Clergy of Virginia.* (Milwaukee, Morehouse, 1927).

Goodwin, William Archer Rutherfoord. *Historical Sketch of Bruton Church, Williamsburg, Virginia.* (Petersburg, Va., Privately Published, 1903).

Goolrich, John T. *Fredericksburg and the Cavalier Country. America's Most Historical Section.* Its Homes, Its People, and Romances. (Richmond, Garrett & Massie, 1936).

Gordon, Thomas F. *History of New Jersey from its Discovery by Europeans, to the adoption of the Federal Constitution.* (Trenton, D. Fenton, 1834).

Great Britain. Board of Trade and Plantations. *Minutes, 1754.*

Great Britain. Public Record Office. *Loyalist Claims. Minutes.*

Griffith, Lucile. *The Virginian House of Burgesses 1750–1774.* (Northpore, Alabama, Colonial Press, 1963).

Grigsby, Hugh Blair. *Discourse on the Life and Character of the Honorable Littleton Waller Tazewell, Delivered in the Freemason Street Baptist Church, before the Bar of Norfolk, Virginia, and the Citizens, generally, on the 29th of June, 1860,* by—. (Norfolk, J. D. Ghiselin, Jr., 1904).

Grigsby, Hugh Blair. *The History of the Virginia Federal Convention of 1788, with some account of the eminent Virginians of that era who were members of the body.* 2 Vols. (Richmond, Virginia Historical Society, 1890–91).

Grigsby, Hugh Blair. *The Virginia Convention of 1776. A Discourse delivered before the Virginia Alpha of the Phi Beta Kappa Society, in the Chapel of William and Mary College in the City of Williamsburg on the Afternoon of July the 3rd, 1855.* (Richmond, J. W. Randolph, 1855).

Hamilton, Alexander. *The Works of—.* Edited by Henry Cabot Lodge. 12 Vols. (New York, G. P. Putnam's Sons, 1904).

Hamilton, Alexander. *The Works of—comprising his correspondence and his political and official Letters, exclusive of the Federalist, civil and military.* Edited by John C. Hamilton. 7 Vols. (New York, John F. Trow, 1851).

Hamilton, Stanislaus Murray, ed. *Letters to Washington, and Accompanying Papers.* 5 Vols. (Boston, Houghton Mifflin, 1898–1902).

Harrell, Isaac S. *Loyalism in Virginia.* (Durham, Duke University Press, 1926).

Hatch, Louis C. *The Administration of the American Revolutionary Army.* (New York, Longmans Green, 1904).

Hawthorne, Hildegard. *Williamsburg, Old And New.* (New York, D. Appleton Century, Inc., 1941).

Hayden, Horace Edwin. *Virginia Genealogies. A Genealogy of the Glassell Family of Scotland and Virginia, also of the families of Ball, Brown, Bryan, Conway, Daniel, Ewell, Holladay, Lewis, Littlepage, Moncure, Peyton, Robinson, Scott, Taylor, Wallace, and others of Virginia and Maryland.* (Wilkes-Barre, E. B. Yordy, 1891).

Haywood, Marshall D. *Lives of the Bishops of North Carolina.* (Raleigh, Alfred Williams & Co., 1910).

Hemphill, William Edwin. *Examinations of George Wythe Swinney for forgery and murder. A Documentary Essay in: The Murder of George Wythe, Two Essays.* (Williamsburg, Institute of Early American History and Culture, 1955).

Hemphill, William Edwin. *George Wythe the Colonial Briton: A Biographical Study of the Prerevolutionary Era in Virginia.* University of Virginia Thesis (Ph. D.), 1937.

Hendrick, Burton J. *The Lees of Virginia. Biography of a Family.* (Boston, Little Brown, 1935).

Henry, William Wirt. *Patrick Henry: Life, Correspondence and Speeches.* 3 Vols. (New York, Chas. Scribner's Sons, 1891).

Hildreth, Richard. *The History of the United States.* 6 Vols. (New York, Harper & Brothers, 1863).

Hill, Helen. *George Mason, Constitutionalist.* (Cambridge, Harvard University Press, 1938).

Hindle, Brooke. *Pursuit of Science in Revolutionary America, 1735–1789.* (Chapel Hill, University of North Carolina Press, 1956).

Holmes, Abdiel. *Annals of America from the Discovery by Columbus in the Year 1492 to the Year 1826.* 2d ed. 2 Vols. (Cambridge, Hilliard and Brown, 1829).

Hosmer, James Kendall. *Samuel Adams.* (Boston, Houghton Mifflin, 1885).

Hunter, George Marshall. *Report of Research on George Wythe submitted to Colonial Williams-burg, Inc.* 1961.

Jefferson, Thomas. *The Papers of—.* Edited by Julian P. Boyd. 17 Vols. (Princeton, Princeton University Press, 1950).

Jefferson, Thomas. *The Writings of—, Collected and Edited by Paul Leicester Ford.* 10 Vols. (New York, G. P. Putnam's Sons, 1895).

Jefferson, Thomas. *Memoir, Correspondence and Miscellanies from the Papers of—,* Edited by Thomas Jefferson Randolph. 4 Vols. (Boston, Gray & Brown, 1830).

Jefferson, Thomas. *Notes on the State of Virginia.* Edited by William Peden. (University of North Carolina Press, 1955).

Jefferson, Thomas. *Writings of—. Containing his autobiography, Notes on Virginia, Parliamentary Manual, official papers, Messages and Addresses, and other Writings, official and private.* Edited by Andrew A. Lipscomb. 20 Vols. (Washington, D. C., 1904–5).

Jefferson, Thomas. *Writings of—.* Edited by H. A. Washington, 9 Vols. (Washington, D.C., Taylor & Maury, 1854).

Jones, Hugh. *The Present State of Virginia. Giving a particular and short Account of the Indians, English and Negroe inhabitants of that Colony. Shewing their religion, manners, government, trade, way of living, &c., with a description of the country, from whence is inferred a short view of Maryland and North Carolina.* (London, Printed for J. Clarke, 1724).

Jones, Joseph. *Letters of—.* Edited by Worthington C. Ford. (Washington, D. C., United States Department of State, 1889).

Kane, Joseph Nathan. *The American Counties.* (New York, Scarecrow Press, 1960).

Keith, George. *A Journal of Travels from New-Hampshire to Caratuck, on the Continent of North America.* (London, Printed for B. Aylmer by J. Downing, 1706).

Kennedy, John Pendleton. *Memoirs of the Life of William Wirt, Attorney General of the United States.* 2 Vols. (Philadelphia, Lee & Blanchard, 1850).

Kimball, Marie. *Jefferson, War and Peace 1766 to 1784.* (New York, Coward McCann, 1947).

Kirby, Ethyn Williams. *George Keith, 1638–1716.* (New York, D. Appleton-Century Co., 1942).

Koontz, Louis K. *Robert Dinwiddie, His Career in American Colonial Government and Westward Expansion.* (Glendale, Calif., Arthur H. Clark Co., 1941).

Kuntzleman, Oliver C. *Joseph Galloway, Loyalist.* (Philadelphia, Temple University Thesis, 1941).

Leake, James Miller. *The Virginia Committee System and the American Revolution.* (Baltimore, Johns Hopkins University Press, 1917).

Lee, Richard Henry. *Letters of—.* Edited by James C. Ballagh. 4 Vols. (New York, Macmillan, 1911–14).

Lee, Richard Henry. *Memoir of Richard Henry Lee and his Correspondence with the most distinguished Men in America and Europe illustrative of their characters and of the Events of the American Revolution.* 2 Vols. in 1. (Philadelphia, Carey, 1825).

Lee, William. *Letters of—, Sheriff and Alderman of London.* Edited by Worthington C. Ford. (Brooklyn, Historical Printing Company, 1891).

Lewis, William Draper. *Great American Lawyers, the Lives and Influence of Judges and Lawyers who have acquired permanent National Reputation and have developed the jurisprudence of the United States. A History of the Legal Profession in America.* 8 Vols. (Philadelphia, Winston, 1907).

Link, Eugene P. *Democratic-Republican Societies, 1790–1800.* (New York, Columbia University Press, 1942).

Little, John P. *History of Richmond.* (Richmond, Dietz, 1933).

MacDonald, William, Editor. *Select Documents of United States History, 1776–1861.* (New York, Macmillan, 1898).

Madison, James. *The Papers of—, purchased by order of Congress being the correspondence and reports of debates during the Congress of the Confederation and his reports of debates in the Federal Convention, now published from the original manuscripts deposited in the Department of State, by direction of the Joint Library Committee of Congress under the Superintendence of Henry D. Gilpin.* 3 Vols. (Mobile, A. Mygatt, 1842).

Madison, James. *The Writings of—, comprising his public papers and private correspondence including numerous letters and documents now for the first time printed.* Edited by Gaillard Hunt. 9 Vols. (New York, G. P. Putnam's Sons, 1900–10).

Madison, James. *Papers.* Ed. by Wm. T. Hutchinson and Wm. M. E. Rachel. (Chicago, University of Chicago Press, 1962–).

Malone, Dumas. *Jefferson and His Time.* 2 Vols. (Boston, Little Brown, 1951).

Mapp, Alfred J., Jr. *The Virginia Experiment. The Old Dominion's Role in the Making of America, 1607–1781.* (Richmond, Dietz Press, 1957).

Mayo, Bernard. *Henry Clay.* (Boston, Houghton Mifflin, 1937).

Mays, David J. *Edmund Pendleton. A Biography, 1721–1803.* 2 Vols. (Cambridge, Harvard University Press, 1952).

Mazzei, Filippo. *Memoirs of the Life and Pregrinations of the Florentine, Philip Mazzei, 1730–1816.* (New York, Columbia University Press, 1942).

Meade, Robert D. *Patrick Henry. Patriot in the Making.* (Philadelphia, Lippincott, 1957).

Meade, William. *Old Churches, Ministers and Families of Virginia.* 2 Vols. (Philadelphia, Lippincott, 1861).

Miller, John C. *Samuel Adams: Pioneer in Propaganda.* (Boston, Little, Brown, 1943).

Miller, John C. *Origins of the American Revolution.* (Boston, Little, Brown, 1943).

Monroe, James. *Autobiography.* Edited by Stuart G. Brown, (Syracuse, Syracuse University Press, 1959).

Morais, Herbert M. *Deism in Eighteenth Century America.* (Russell and Russell, 1960).

Mordecai, Samuel. *Richmond in By-Gone Days, Being Reminiscences of An Old Citizen.* (Richmond, G. M. West, 1856).

Morton, Louis. *Robert Carter of Nomini Hall, A Virginia Tobacco Planter of the 18th Century.* (Williamsburg, Colonial Williamsburg, Inc., 1941).

Morton, Richard L. *Colonial Virginia.* 2 Vols. (Chapel Hill, University of North Carolina, 1960).

Munford, George Wythe. *The Two Parsons: Cupid's Sports, The Dream, and The Jewels of Virginia, with a Biographical Sketch of the Author.* (Richmond, J. D. K. Sleight, 1884).

Nevins, Allan. *The American States During and After the Revolution, 1775–1789.* (New York, Macmillan, 1927).

Nickerson, Hoffman. *The Turning Point of the Revolution or Burgoyne in America.* (Boston, Houghton Mifflin, 1928).

Norton, John. *John Norton and Sons Papers,* Colonial Williamsburg, Inc., Williamsburg, Virginia.

Norton, John N. *Life of Bishop Ravenscroft.* (New York, General Protestant Episcopal Sunday School Union and Church Book Society, 1858).

Pennington, Edgar L. *The Apostle to New Jersey, John Talbot.* (Philadelphia, Church Historical Society, 1938).

Perry, William S., ed. *Papers Relating to the History of the Church in Virginia, A.D., 1650–1776.* (Richmond, 1870).

Pitkin, Timothy. *A Political and Civil History of the United States of America from the year 1763 to the close of the Administration of President Washington, in March 1797: including a Summary View of the Political and Civil State of the North American Colonies, prior to the Period.* 2 Vols., (New Haven, H. Howe and Dueeie & Peck, 1828).

Porter, Albert O. *County Government in Virginia, A Legislative History 1706–1904.* New York, 1947).

Randolph Macon College, Department of History. *John P. Branch Historical Papers*. 5 Vols. (Richmond, 1901–1918).

Randolph, Edmund. *Manuscript History of Virginia*. Library, Virginia Historical Society. (Richmond, Virginia).

Randolph, Sarah H. *Domestic Life of Thomas Jefferson*. (New York, Harper & Brothers, 1871).

Rives, William C. *History of the Life and Times of James Madison*. 3 Vols. (Boston, Little Brown, 1859–68).

Rowland, Kate Mason. *Life of Charles Carroll of Carrollton*. 2 Vols. (New York, G. P. Putnam's Sons, 1898).

Rowland, Kate Mason. *Life of George Mason 1725–1792*. 2 Vols. (New York, G. P. Putnam's Sons, 1892).

Rush. Benjamin. *The Autobiography of—, His "Travels Through Life" together with his Commonplace Book*. ed. by G. W. Corner. (Princeton, Princeton University Press, 1948).

Russell, John H. *The Free Negro in Virginia, 1619–1865*. (Baltimore, John Hopkins University Press, 1913).

Rutland, Robert A. *George Mason, Reluctant Statesman*. (Williamsburg, Colonial Williamsburg, Inc., 1961).

Sanderson, John. *Biography of the Signers to The Declaration of Independence*. 9 Vols. (Philadelphia, Pomeroy, 1823–27).

Schachner, Nathan. *Thomas Jefferson, A Biography*. (New York, Yoseloff, 1957).

Schouler, James. *Americans of 1776*. (New York, Dodd Mead, 1906).

Schurz, Carl. *Life of Henry Clay*. 2 Vols. (Boston, Houghton Mifflin, 1892).

Shepperson, Archibald B. *John Paradise & Lucy Ludwell of London and Williamsburg*. (Richmond, Dietz, 1942).

Shewmake, Oscar L. *The Honorable George Wythe, Teacher and Lawyer, Jurist, Statesman. An Address delivered before the Wythe Law Club of the College of William and Mary in Williamsburg, Virginia*. December 18, 1921.

Simpkins, Francis B. *A History of the South*. (New York, Knopf, 1953).

Smith, Edgar F. *Priestley in America 1794–1804*. (Philadelphia, Blakiston's Sons, 1920).

Smith, Justin H. *Our Struggle for the 14th Colony*. Canada and The American Revolution. 2 Vols. (New York, Putnam's Sons, 1907).

Smith, Margaret P. *Old Yorktown and its History* (Richmond, 1920).

Smyth, John Ferdinand Dalziel. *A Tour in The United States of America*. 2 Vols. (London, 1784).

Sparks, Jared. *Life of Gouverneur Morris*. 3 Vols. (Boston, G. Gray, Bowen, 1832).

Starkey, Marion L. *The First Plantation, A History of Hampton and Elizabeth City County, Virginia, 1607–1887*. (Hampton, 1936).

Sydnor, Charles. *Gentlemen Freeholders. Political Practices in Washington's Virginia*. (Chapel Hill, University of North Carolina Press, 1952).

Tazewell, Littleton Waller. *An Account and History of the Tazewell Family*. Typescript. Library, William and Mary College.

Thomson, Charles. *The Thomson Papers*. Collections of the New York Historical Society for the Year 1878. (New York, The Society, 1879).

Trumbull, John. *Autobiography, Reminiscences and Letters of—from 1756 to 1841*. (New York, Wiley and Putnam, 1841).

Tyler, Lyon G. *The College of William and Mary: Its History and Work, 1693–1907*. (Richmond, Whittet & Shepperson, 1907).

Tyler, Lyon G. *Encyclopedia of Virginia Biography*. 5 Vols. (New York, Lewis Historical Pub. Col., 1915).

Tyler, Lyon G. *History of Hampton and Elizabeth City County*. (Board of Supervisors of Elizabeth City Count, 1922).

Tyler, Lyon G. *Letters and Times of the Tylers*. 3 Vols. (Richmond, Whittet & Shepperson, 1884–96).

Tyler, Moses Coit. *Patrick Henry.* (Boston, Houghton, 1899).

United States. Second Continental Congress. *Journals, 1774–1789.* 34 Vols. (Washington, D. C., 1904–37).

Van Deusen, Glyndon. *The Life of Henry Clay.* (Boston, Little, Brown, 1937).

Virginia (Colony). Council. *Executive Journals Council of Colonial Virginia.* Ed. by H. R. McIlwaine. (Richmond, D. Bottom, 1925–).

Virginia (Colony). General Assembly. *Journals of the House of Burgesses of Virginia.* Ed. by H. R. McIlwaine. (Richmond, 1909).

Virginia (Colony). Lt-Gov. Alexander Spotswood. *Official Letters of—.* Ed. by R. A. Brock, Virginia Historical Society Collections, New Series., (Richmond, The Society, 1882–85).

Virginia (Colony). Lt-Gov. Robert Dinwiddie. *Official Records of.—.* Ed. by R. A. Brock, 2 Vols. Virginia Historical Society Collections, New Series. (Richmond, The Society, 1883–84).

Virginia. *Calendar of Virginia State Papers and Other Manuscripts Preserved in the Capitol at Richmond.* Ed. by W. P. Palmer, (Richmond, 1875–93).

Virginia. Council of State. *Journals of the Council of the State of Virginia.* Ed. by H. R. McIlwaine. 5 Vols. (Richmond, 1931).

Virginia. Governor. *Official Letters of the Governors of the State of Virginia.* (Richmond, 1926).

Virginia. High Court of Chancery. *Decisions of Cases in Virginia by the—with remarks upon decrees by the Court of Appeals reversing some of those decisions.* by George Wythe. 2d and only complete edition. Ed. by R. B. Minor (Richmond, J. W. Randolph, 1852).

Virginia. Laws, Statutes, etc. *The Statutes at Large, being a collection of all the laws of Virginia from the 1st session of the legislature in the year 1916.* 13 Vols. Edited by William Waller Hening. (Richmond, Samuel Pleasants, 1810–1823).

Virginia. State Library. *Bulletin. Jan-April-July, 1916. Virginia Counties, Those resulting from Virginia Legislation.* by Morgan P. Robinson, (Richmond, Supt. of Public Printing, 1916).

Virginia. Supreme Court of Appeals. *Reports of Cases Argued and Adjudged in the Court of Appeals of Virginia,* edited by Daniel Call. (Richmond, P. Cottom, 1824).

Walpole, Horace. The Letters of—. Edited by Mrs. Paget Toynbee. 16 Vols. (Oxford, Clarendon Press, 1903–5).

Washington, George. *The Diaries of—, 1748–99,* Edited by John C. Fitzpatrick. 4 Vols., (Boston, Houghton Mifflin Co., 1925).

Washington, George. *The Writings of—, Collected and edited by* Worthington C. Ford, 14 Vols. (New York, Putnam's Sons, 1889).

Washington, George, *The Writings of—from the Original Manuscript Sources, 1745–1799.* Edited by John C. Fitzpatrick. 39 Vols. (Washington, 1931–44).

Weddell, Alexander W. ed. *A Memorial Volume of Virginia Historical Portraiture 1585–1830.* (Richmond, William Byrd Press, 1930).

Weld, Isaac. *Travels Through the States of North America and the Provinces of Upper and Lower Canada during the Years 1795, 1796, 1797.* 2 Vols. (London, J. Stockdale, 1800).

Wells, William V. *The Life and Public Services of Samuel Adams.* 3 Vols. (Boston, Little, Brown, 1865).

Whiffen, Marcus. *Eighteenth Century Houses of Williamsburg, A Study of Architecture and Building in the Colonial Capital* of Virginia. (Colonial Williamsburg, Inc., 1960).

Whiffen, Marcus. *Public Buildings of Williamsburg.* (Williamsburg, Colonial Williamsburg, Inc., 1958).

Wilbur, Earl M. *A History of Unitarianism in Transylvania, England and America.* (Cambridge, Harvard, 1952).

Wirt, William. *Sketches of the Life and Character of Patrick Henry.* (Philadelphia, Thomas Cowperthwait and Co., 1845).

Manuscript Collections:

New York Public Library.

Alderman Library, University of Virginia.

Library of Congress
Library, Maine Historical Society
Library, New York Historical Society.
Library, Yale University.
J. P. Morgan Library.
American Philosophical Society Library, Philadelphia.
Huntington Library, California.
Duke University Library.
Massachusetts Historical Society Library.
New York State Library at Albany.
Haverford College Library
Historical Society of Pennsylvania.
Wisconsin Historical Society
William and Mary College Library
Virginia State Library.
Virginia: Augusta County Order Books
            Elizabeth City County. Order Book 1731–1747.
            Warwick County Court. Minutes 1748–1762.
            Prince Edward County. Will Book of 1797.
            York County Court. Judgements and Orders. Order Book, 1752–1754.
Virginia Gazette
Virginia Gazette and General Advertiser
Virginia Independent Chronicle
Richmond Enquirer
Kentucky Gazette
Massachusetts Gazette
Pennsylvania Magazine of History and Biography
Virginia Magazine of History and Biography
William and Mary College Historical Quarterly (Three Series)
American Historical Review
Magazine of American History
Tyler's Quarterly and Genealogical Magazine.
Southern Literary Messenger.

Index